I0039635

# Where's the Blood?

## 25 Creative Writing Exercises
### with Motivational Anthology

Copyright © 2013 David Fairchild

ISBN 978-0-9826355-3-7

All rights reserved. No part of this publication may be reproduced, stored in a retrieval system, or transmitted in any form or by any means, electronic, mechanical, recording or otherwise, without the prior written permission of the author.

All literary titles contributing to anthology support may be found in the public domain.

Editing by Montressa Thompson

Four Doors Publishing
Provo, UT 84601

Printed in the United States of America.

# Where's the Blood?

## 25 Creative Writing Exercises
### with Motivational Anthology

**David Fairchild**

# Table of Contents

# Introduction

You are the only master of your voice. Your uniqueness is shared by none other. It can be quite troubling to pick up a book that's supposed to help you learn to write, only to discover that it's telling you how to write like the author who crafted the book in the first place. You don't want to write like someone else! You want to write like yourself.

The only way to learn to master your voice and find confidence in your writing approaches is to have opportunity to practice. Many authors want to tell you how to write, but there's an even greater poison out there for authors.

Lets take a little quiz. Answer honestly.

**Have you ever been told that you don't need to take classes to write?**

**Has anyone ever told you that you don't need to read books on writing to become a better writer?**

**Do you find yourself writing by yourself and waiting until you are finished before you show anyone your work, if, that is, you show anyone at all?**

If you answered yes to any of these, get ready for a reality check. The single-most damaging piece of counsel any writer can buy into is to think that he or she doesn't need practice, feedback, and instruction or mentorship.

As with any skill, there are good and bad ways to practice. The bad way is to practice alone. Writers who practice alone create stubborn learning barriers, and their skills eventually stagnate. A writer who practices with others will always be the stronger and better writer. The best writers continually seek opportunities to work with experienced teachers, mentors and peers with similar goals. These people understand what sells; what others want to read; how difficult the road is; and can help you understand that you are not alone.

Be warned, there are devils disguised as wise old men and women who want to tell you that taking classes, reading books or putting yourself in situations where you have to work or learn from others will only teach you bad habits. They're ignorant—all of them—and should not be trusted because they are not teally writers, but we'll talk more about these destructive demons later.

The key to successful writing is all about practice, and this book is designed to help you do just that.

Here, you will find exercises devoted to helping you understand your own voices: how they work; their weaknesses; their potential strengths; and how to allow them to grow. You will find experiments that may open up your understanding of words, focus, sensory and humanity.

Each exercise grants you the freedom to explore these practices, yourself and your own boundaries. This is not a book of "dos" or "do nots." This is a book of discovering yourself, your skills and your talents. Through making these exercises your own, you can find joy in your new untapped potential.

And you're not going to be working alone. For each exercise included in this book is an example of someone else's writing. You will be able to see how the approach of each writing exercise may appear in someone else's practice. These stories and poems should already be familiar and they should inspire you. The best writers aren't those who write all the time. The best writers are those who read. If you feel that you can't seem to get the creative juices working on a particular exercise, read the story or poem that follows. It may remind you of a word you might want to use; a type of story you might want to try your hand at; or maybe it might just refresh your mind in some personal way. Reading others' works often has an ability to bring clarity to your own voice.

Following each sample work and exercise, you will find a set of questions designed to help you discover what the author may or may not have done to give their story or poem intrigue. Yes, we all know that these text book approaches are boring, so ignore the questions if you'd like (no one's grading you here), but if you really want to discover connections between the exercise, the author and your own free potential, the questions may just open your eyes to more growth. You may discover a specific place on the page where you can literally point your finger and say, "That's what this can look like," or "that's something I want to try myself."

So give the questions a try (or not). Just remember, the more you discover about practice, the stronger your potential will become in mastering your voice and sharing it with others.

Some of the exercises in this book may require you to step outside of your office and explore the world and some of the people around you. Feel free to plan time to allow you to do some of these exercises—they may be a little out of your way, but the power that these exercises will help you find in your own voice may greatly surprise you.

Let's try one out for practice now.

# Stone or Clay

Let's begin by defining why we care about writing. It's a fact that people who write down goals or "to-do" lists are more likely to realize their outcomes than people who don't. So let's start there.

We all have our strengths and our weaknesses. How many times have you had someone look at what you can do and tell you, "I sure wish I could do that?" How often did you think your talent was no big deal?

What about you? How many times have you watched someone share a talent and made a similar statement to that person? Did you think that person's talent was a big deal?

For this exercise, make a list of writing talents you wish you were better at. Do you wish you were a poet? Or that you could finish a novel? Do you wish you were better at writing dialogue or creating characters? Or is there something else you desire to be stronger at?

Choose the one item on your list you wish you could do the most.

Write down ten details about this item that explain why you wish you were better at it. Is it because you have something to say? Is it because you want to be part of the crowd who can do it? Is it because it appears to be fun?

Now, write down ten reasons why that item is even attractive to you. Why do you care about it? Is it because of how it sounds? How it smells, looks or feels? Is it because of a nostalgic matter? Is it because of what it could mean to another person whom you care about? Is it because you think it's just pretty? Is it because someone who used to do it the best is now gone and no one else seems to know how to do it right anymore?

Based on these details, write a paragraph or two showing why this item is so important to humanity. It can be a story. It can be a personal essay. It can be any statement that you want to make. Once you've written it, write down what that statement is and use it for your title of your work.

# Anne of Green Gables
By L. M. Montgomery
(1874-1942)

## CHAPTER XXV.
## Matthew Insists on Puffed Sleeves

Matthew was having a bad ten minutes of it. He had come into the kitchen, in the twilight of a cold, gray December evening, and had sat down in the woodbox corner to take off his heavy boots, unconscious of the fact that Anne and a bevy of her schoolmates were having a practice of "The Fairy Queen" in the sitting room. Presently they came trooping through the hall and out into the kitchen, laughing and chattering gaily. They did not see Matthew, who shrank bashfully back into the shadows beyond the woodbox with a boot in one hand and a bootjack in the other, and he watched them shyly for the aforesaid ten minutes as they put on caps and jackets and talked about the dialogue and the concert. Anne stood among them, bright eyed and animated as they; but Matthew suddenly became conscious that there was something about her different from her mates. And what worried Matthew was that the difference impressed him as being something that should not exist. Anne had a brighter face, and bigger, starrier eyes, and more delicate features than the other; even shy, unobservant Matthew had learned to take note of these things; but the difference that disturbed him did not consist in any of these respects. Then in what did it consist?

Matthew was haunted by this question long after the girls had gone, arm in arm, down the long, hard-frozen lane and Anne had betaken herself to her books. He could not refer it to Marilla, who, he felt, would be quite sure to sniff scornfully and remark that the only difference she saw between Anne and the other girls was that they sometimes kept their tongues quiet while Anne never did. This, Matthew felt, would be no great help.

He had recourse to his pipe that evening to help him study it out, much to Marilla's disgust. After two hours of smoking and hard reflection Matthew arrived at a solution of his problem. Anne was not dressed like the other girls!

The more Matthew thought about the matter the more he was convinced that Anne never had been dressed like the other girls—never since she had come to Green Gables. Marilla kept her clothed in plain, dark dresses, all made after the same unvarying pattern. If Matthew knew there was such a thing as fashion in dress it was as much as he did; but he was quite sure that Anne's sleeves did not look at all like the sleeves the other girls wore. He recalled the cluster of little girls he had seen around her that evening—all gay in waists of red and blue and pink and white—and he wondered why Marilla always kept her so plainly and soberly gowned.

Of course, it must be all right. Marilla knew best and Marilla was bringing her up. Probably some wise, inscrutable motive was to be served thereby. But surely it would do no harm to let the child have one pretty dress—something like Diana Barry always wore. Matthew decided that he would give her one; that surely could not be objected to as an unwarranted putting in of his oar. Christmas was only a fortnight off. A nice new dress would be the very thing for a present. Matthew, with a sigh of satisfaction, put away his pipe and went to bed, while Marilla opened all the doors and aired the house.

The very next evening Matthew betook himself to Carmody to buy the dress, determined to get the worst over and have done with it. It would be, he felt assured, no trifling ordeal. There were some things Matthew could buy and prove himself no mean bargainer; but he knew he would be at the mercy of shopkeepers when it came to buying a girl's dress.

After much cogitation Matthew resolved to go to Samuel Lawson's store instead of William Blair's. To be sure, the Cuthberts always had gone to William Blair's; it was almost as much a matter of conscience with them as to attend the Presbyterian church and vote Conservative. But William Blair's two daughters frequently waited on customers there and Matthew held them in absolute dread. He could contrive to deal with them when he knew exactly what he wanted and could point it out; but in such a matter as this, requiring explanation and consultation, Matthew felt that he must be sure of a man behind the counter. So he would go to Lawson's, where Samuel or his son would wait on him.

Alas! Matthew did not know that Samuel, in the recent expansion of his business, had set up a lady clerk also; she was a niece of his wife's and a very dashing young person indeed, with a huge, drooping pompadour, big, rolling brown eyes, and a most extensive and bewildering smile. She was dressed with exceeding smartness and wore several bangle bracelets that glittered and rattled and tinkled with every movement of her hands. Matthew was covered with confusion at finding her there at all; and those bangles completely wrecked his wits at one fell swoop.

"What can I do for you this evening, Mr. Cuthbert?" Miss Lucilla Harris inquired, briskly and ingratiatingly, tapping the counter with both hands.

"Have you any—any—any—well now, say any garden rakes?" stammered Matthew.

Miss Harris looked somewhat surprised, as well she might, to hear a man inquiring for garden rakes in the middle of December.

"I believe we have one or two left over," she said, "but they're upstairs in the lumber room. I'll go and see." During her absence Matthew collected his scattered senses for another effort.

When Miss Harris returned with the rake and cheerfully inquired: "Anything else tonight, Mr. Cuthbert?" Matthew took his courage in both hands and replied: "Well now, since you suggest it, I might as well—take—that is—look at—buy some—some hayseed."

Miss Harris had heard Matthew Cuthbert called odd. She now concluded that he was entirely crazy.

"We only keep hayseed in the spring," she explained loftily. "We've none on hand just now."

"Oh, certainly—certainly—just as you say," stammered unhappy Matthew, seizing the rake and making for the door. At the threshold he recollected that he had not paid for it and he turned miserably back. While Miss Harris was counting out his change he rallied his powers for a final desperate attempt.

"Well now—if it isn't too much trouble—I might as well—that is—I'd like to look at—at—some sugar."

"White or brown?" queried Miss Harris patiently.

"Oh—well now—brown," said Matthew feebly.

"There's a barrel of it over there," said Miss Harris, shaking her bangles at it. "It's the only kind we have."

"I'll—I'll take twenty pounds of it," said Matthew, with beads of perspiration standing on his forehead.

Matthew had driven halfway home before he was his own man again. It had been a gruesome experience, but it served him right, he thought, for committing the heresy of going to a strange store. When he reached home he hid the rake in the tool house, but the sugar he carried in to Marilla.

"Brown sugar!" exclaimed Marilla. "Whatever possessed you to get so much? You know I never use it except for the hired man's porridge or black fruit cake. Jerry's gone and I've made my cake long ago. It's not good sugar, either—it's coarse and dark—William Blair doesn't usually keep sugar like that."

"I—I thought it might come in handy sometime," said Matthew, making good his escape.

When Matthew came to think the matter over he decided that a woman was required to cope with the situation. Marilla was out of the question. Matthew felt sure she would throw cold water on his project at once. Remained only Mrs. Lynde; for of no other woman in Avonlea would Matthew have dared to ask advice. To Mrs. Lynde he went accordingly, and that good lady promptly took the matter out of the harassed man's hands.

"Pick out a dress for you to give Anne? To be sure I will. I'm going to Carmody tomorrow and I'll attend to it. Have you something particular in mind? No? Well, I'll just go by my own judgment then. I believe a nice rich brown would just suit Anne, and William Blair has some new gloria in that's real pretty. Perhaps you'd like me to make it up for her, too, seeing that if Marilla was to make it Anne would probably get wind of it before the time and spoil the surprise? Well, I'll do it. No, it isn't a mite of trouble. I like sewing. I'll make it to fit my niece, Jenny Gillis, for she and Anne are as like as two peas as far as figure goes."

"Well now, I'm much obliged," said Matthew, "and—and—I dunno—but I'd like—I think they make the sleeves different nowadays to what they used to be. If it wouldn't be asking too much I—I'd like them made in the new way."

"Puffs? Of course. You needn't worry a speck more about it, Matthew. I'll make it up in the very latest fashion," said Mrs. Lynde. To herself she added when Matthew had gone:

"It'll be a real satisfaction to see that poor child wearing something decent for once. The way Marilla dresses her is positively ridiculous, that's what, and I've ached to tell her so plainly a dozen times. I've held my tongue though, for I can see Marilla doesn't want advice and she thinks she knows more about bringing children up than I do for all she's an old maid. But that's always the way. Folks that has brought up children know that there's no hard and fast method in the world that'll suit every child. But them as never have think it's all as plain and easy as Rule of Three—just set your three terms down so fashion, and the sum'll work out correct. But flesh and blood don't come under the head of arithmetic and that's where Marilla Cuthbert makes her mistake. I suppose she's trying to cultivate a spirit of humility in Anne by dressing her as she does; but it's more likely to cultivate envy and discontent. I'm sure the child must feel the difference between her clothes and the other girls'. But to think of Matthew taking notice of it! That man is waking up after being asleep for over sixty years."

Marilla knew all the following fortnight that Matthew had something on his mind, but what it was she could not guess, until Christmas Eve, when Mrs. Lynde brought up the new dress. Marilla behaved pretty well on the whole, although it is very likely she distrusted Mrs. Lynde's diplomatic explanation that she had made the dress because Matthew was afraid Anne would find out about it too soon if Marilla made it.

"So this is what Matthew has been looking so mysterious over and grinning about to himself for two weeks, is it?" she said a little stiffly but tolerantly. "I knew he was up to some foolishness. Well, I must say I don't think Anne needed any more dresses. I made her three good, warm, serviceable ones this fall, and anything more is sheer extravagance. There's enough material in those sleeves alone to make a waist, I declare there is. You'll just pamper Anne's vanity, Matthew, and she's as vain as a peacock now. Well, I hope she'll be satisfied at last, for I know she's been hankering after those silly sleeves ever since they came in, although she never said a word after the first. The puffs have been getting bigger and more ridiculous right along; they're as big as balloons now. Next year anybody who wears them will have to go through a door sideways."

Christmas morning broke on a beautiful white world. It had been a very mild December and people had looked forward to a green Christmas; but just enough snow fell softly in the night to transfigure Avonlea. Anne peeped out from her frosted gable window with delighted eyes. The firs in the Haunted Wood were all feathery and wonderful; the birches and wild cherry trees were outlined in pearl; the plowed fields were stretches of snowy dimples; and there was a crisp tang in the air that was glorious. Anne ran downstairs singing until her voice reechoed through Green Gables.

"Merry Christmas, Marilla! Merry Christmas, Matthew! Isn't it a lovely Christmas? I'm so glad it's white. Any other kind of Christmas doesn't seem real, does it? I don't like green Christmases. They're not green—they're just nasty faded browns and grays. What makes people call them green? Why—why—Matthew, is that for me? Oh, Matthew!"

Matthew had sheepishly unfolded the dress from its paper swathings and held it out with a deprecatory glance at Marilla, who feigned to be contemptuously filling the teapot, but nevertheless watched the scene out of the corner of her eye with a rather interested air.

Anne took the dress and looked at it in reverent silence. Oh, how pretty it was—a lovely soft brown gloria with all the gloss of silk; a skirt with dainty frills and shirrings; a waist elaborately pintucked in the most fashionable way, with a little ruffle of filmy lace at the neck. But the sleeves—they were the crowning glory! Long elbow cuffs, and above them two beautiful puffs divided by rows of shirring and bows of brown-silk ribbon.

"That's a Christmas present for you, Anne," said Matthew shyly. "Why—why—Anne, don't you like it? Well now—well now."

For Anne's eyes had suddenly filled with tears.

"Like it! Oh, Matthew!" Anne laid the dress over a chair and clasped her hands. "Matthew, it's perfectly exquisite. Oh, I can never thank you enough. Look at those sleeves! Oh, it seems to me this must be a happy dream."

"Well, well, let us have breakfast," interrupted Marilla. "I must say, Anne, I don't think you needed the dress; but since Matthew has got it for you, see that you take good care of it. There's a hair ribbon Mrs. Lynde left for you. It's brown, to match the dress. Come now, sit in."

"I don't see how I'm going to eat breakfast," said Anne rapturously. "Breakfast seems so commonplace at such an exciting moment. I'd rather feast my eyes on that dress. I'm so glad that puffed sleeves are still fashionable. It did seem to me that I'd never get over it if they went out before I had a dress with them. I'd never have felt quite satisfied, you see. It was lovely of Mrs. Lynde to give me the ribbon too. I feel that I ought to be a very good girl indeed. It's at times like this I'm sorry I'm not a model little girl; and I always resolve that I will be in future. But somehow it's hard to carry out your resolutions when irresistible temptations come. Still, I really will make an extra effort after this."

When the commonplace breakfast was over Diana appeared, crossing the white log bridge in the hollow, a gay little figure in her crimson ulster. Anne flew down the slope to meet her.

"Merry Christmas, Diana! And oh, it's a wonderful Christmas. I've something splendid to show you. Matthew has given me the loveliest dress, with SUCH sleeves. I couldn't even imagine any nicer."

"I've got something more for you," said Diana breathlessly. "Here—this box. Aunt Josephine sent us out a big box with ever so many things in it—and this is for you. I'd have brought it over last night, but it didn't come until after dark, and I never feel very comfortable coming through the Haunted Wood in the dark now."

Anne opened the box and peeped in. First a card with "For the Anne-girl and Merry Christmas," written on it; and then, a pair of the daintiest little kid slippers, with beaded toes and satin bows and glistening buckles.

"Oh," said Anne, "Diana, this is too much. I must be dreaming."

"I call it providential," said Diana. "You won't have to borrow Ruby's slippers now, and that's a blessing, for they're two sizes too big for you, and it would be awful to hear a fairy shuffling. Josie Pye would be delighted. Mind you, Rob Wright went home with Gertie Pye from the practice night before last. Did you ever hear anything equal to that?"

All the Avonlea scholars were in a fever of excitement that day, for the hall had to be decorated and a last grand rehearsal held.

The concert came off in the evening and was a pronounced success. The little hall was crowded; all the performers did excellently well, but Anne was the bright particular star of the occasion, as even envy, in the shape of Josie Pye, dared not deny.

"Oh, hasn't it been a brilliant evening?" sighed Anne, when it was all over and she and Diana were walking home together under a dark, starry sky.

"Everything went off very well," said Diana practically. "I guess we must have made as much as ten dollars. Mind you, Mr. Allan is going to send an account of it to the Charlottetown papers."

"Oh, Diana, will we really see our names in print? It makes me thrill to think of it. Your solo was perfectly elegant, Diana. I felt prouder than you did when it was encored. I just said to myself, 'It is my dear bosom friend who is so honored.'"

"Well, your recitations just brought down the house, Anne. That sad one was simply splendid."

"Oh, I was so nervous, Diana. When Mr. Allan called out my name I really cannot tell how I ever got up on that platform. I felt as if a million eyes were looking at me and through me, and for one dreadful moment I was sure I couldn't begin at all. Then I thought of my lovely puffed sleeves and took courage. I knew that I must live up to those sleeves, Diana. So I started in, and my voice seemed to be coming from ever so far away. I just felt like a parrot. It's providential that I practiced those recitations so often up in the garret, or I'd never have been able to get through. Did I groan all right?"

"Yes, indeed, you groaned lovely," assured Diana.

"I saw old Mrs. Sloane wiping away tears when I sat down. It was splendid to think I had touched somebody's heart. It's so romantic to take part in a concert, isn't it? Oh, it's been a very memorable occasion indeed."

"Wasn't the boys' dialogue fine?" said Diana. "Gilbert Blythe was just splendid. Anne, I do think it's awful mean the way you treat Gil. Wait till I tell you. When you ran off the platform after the fairy dialogue one of your roses fell out of your hair. I saw Gil pick it up and put it in his breast pocket. There now. You're so romantic that I'm sure you ought to be pleased at that."

"It's nothing to me what that person does," said Anne loftily. "I simply never waste a thought on him, Diana."

That night Marilla and Matthew, who had been out to a concert for the first time in twenty years, sat for a while by the kitchen fire after Anne had gone to bed.

"Well now, I guess our Anne did as well as any of them," said Matthew proudly.

"Yes, she did," admitted Marilla. "She's a bright child, Matthew. And she looked real nice too. I've been kind of opposed to this concert scheme, but I suppose there's no real harm in it after all. Anyhow, I was proud of Anne tonight, although I'm not going to tell her so."

"Well now, I was proud of her and I did tell her so 'fore she went upstairs," said Matthew. "We must see what we can do for her some of these days, Marilla. I guess she'll need something more than Avonlea school by and by."

"There's time enough to think of that," said Marilla. "She's only thirteen in March. Though tonight it struck me she was growing quite a big girl. Mrs. Lynde made that dress a mite too long, and it makes Anne look so tall. She's quick to learn and I guess the best thing we can do for her will be to send her to Queen's after a spell. But nothing need be said about that for a year or two yet."

"Well now, it'll do no harm to be thinking it over off and on," said Matthew. "Things like that are all the better for lots of thinking over."

# A Deeper Look:

1.  In this story, what specific event does the author find necessary to share with the reader that ultimately sends Matthew on a journey?

2.  Do you think this story was about Anne getting something she wanted or Matthew getting something he wanted? What did Anne/Matthew want? And why do you think the author chose puffed sleeves to show what this person wanted?

3.  What kind of writer do you want to be? Do you want to be a poet? A successful novelist? An investigative journalist? Do you just want to keep a strong journal for your generations that follow? Or is there some other goal you have in mind?

# Wordplay:

## Exercises to help think about the words you use

# 1

# What's the Difference

No writer should be without a dictionary or a thesaurus. A good one! Not all dictionaries are created equal, no matter how recognized their names are.

For this exercise, let's practice learning some new words and understanding the differences in similar words. This exercise can help you learn how to find the right word when you really need it.

Step one: Crack open your dictionary and find ten words that you are not familiar with. The only rule is that no two words can start with the same letter.

Step two: Time for the thesaurus. For each word, use a thesaurus to identify at least five alternative words or terms. You can pick any of the five terms that appear in the thesaurus. If fewer than five words appear, you must use all of the alternative suggestions. If no alternative words appear or your original word does not appear in the thesaurus at all, write down the definition to the original. If none of your words appear in the thesaurus, you must find ten new unfamiliar words and repeat the process.

Step three: Once you have used the thesaurus to identify alternative words. On a new piece of paper or in a new document, List one group of these words (up to six words total: your original and the five you found in the thesaurus).

Step four: Look up the definition for each of these words, but do not write them down.

Step five: Without using definitions provided by the dictionary, explain what makes the five words you found in the thesaurus different from each other and from your original word. If there is no difference between some of the words, explain why they are the same and explain why you might choose to use one word over the other in writing or speaking.

Why might learning new words be important? Because just the right word can carry power, lyricism and definition.

# A Nightmare

### By Sir W. S. Gilbert
### (1836-1911)

When you're lying awake with a dismal headache, and repose is
    taboo'd by anxiety,
I conceive you may use any language you choose to indulge in without
    impropriety;
For your brain is on fire—the bedclothes conspire of usual slumber to
    plunder you:
First your counterpane goes and uncovers your toes, and your sheet
    slips demurely from under you;
Then the blanketing tickles—you feel like mixed pickles, so terribly
    sharp is the pricking,
And you're hot, and you're cross, and you tumble and toss till there's
    nothing 'twixt you and the ticking.
Then the bedclothes all creep to the ground in a heap, and you pick
    'em all up in a tangle;
Next your pillow resigns and politely declines to remain at its usual
    angle!
Well, you get some repose in the form of a doze, with hot eyeballs and
    head ever aching,
But your slumbering teems with such horrible dreams that you'd very
    much better be waking;
For you dream you are crossing the Channel, and tossing about in a
    steamer from Harwich,
Which is something between a large bathing-machine and a very small
    second-class carriage;
And you're giving a treat (penny ice and cold meat) to a party of
    friends and relations -
They're a ravenous horde - and they all came on board at Sloane Square
    and South Kensington Stations.
And bound on that journey you find your attorney (who started that
    morning from Devon);
He's a bit undersized, and you don't feel surprised when he tells you
    he's only eleven.
Well, you're driving like mad with this singular lad (by the bye the
    ship's now a four-wheeler),
And you're playing round games, and he calls you bad names when you
    tell him that "ties pay the dealer";
But this you can't stand, so you throw up your hand, and you find
    you're as cold as an icicle,
In your shirt and your socks (the black silk with gold clocks), crossing
    Salisbury Plain on a bicycle:
And he and the crew are on bicycles too - which they've somehow or
    other invested in—
And he's telling the tars all the particulars of a company he's inter-
    ested in—
It's a scheme of devices, to get at low prices, all goods from cough
    mixtures to cables
(Which tickled the sailors) by treating retailers, as though they were all
    vege*ta*bles—

You get a good spadesman to plant a small tradesman (first take off his
    boots with a boot—tree),

And his legs will take root, and his fingers will shoot, and they'll
    blossom and bud like a fruit-tree—

From the greengrocer tree you get grapes and green pea, cauliflower,
    pineapple, and cranberries,

While the pastry-cook plant cherry-brandy will grant—apple puffs, and
    three-corners, and banberries—

The shares are a penny, and ever so many are taken by ROTHSCHILD
    and BARING,

And just as a few are allotted to you, you awake with a shudder
    despairing—

You're a regular wreck, with a crick in your neck, and no wonder you
    snore, for your head's on the floor, and you've needles and pins
    from your soles to your shins, and your flesh is a-creep, for your
    left leg's asleep, and you've cramp in your toes, and a fly on your
    nose, and some fluff in your lung, and a feverish tongue, and a
    thirst that's intense, and a general sense that you haven't been
    sleeping in clover;

But the darkness has passed, and it's daylight at last, and the night has
    been long - ditto, ditto my song - and thank goodness they're both
    of them over!

# A Deeper Look:

---

1.        What kind of sound does this poem seem to have to it? Does it sound happy? Morose? Lyrical? Redundant?

2.        At a glance, is there a word anywhere in this essay that seems out of place? A word that had the same meaning as another word on this page?

3.        What are some ways you could find to help you discover new words and their meanings? What are some steps you think you might be able to take to practice using them in your own writing?

# What Scares You?

Words have power. One word can sometimes have more power than an entire page of words. There are words we like the sound of, words we like the meaning of and words we absolutely hate (whether because of what it means; how it sounds; or the memories it draws forth). Writers can pass their personal connections with words onto their readers.

For this exercise, list one word that scares you. It can be how it sounds. It can be the meaning or a memory. It can even be a word that describes an object, idea or person that scares you. Write that word down and briefly explain why that word frightens you. Does it sum up a bad memory? Does it represent something dark and sinister? Does it represent a phobia? Is it a word that can seal a deal in a negative way?

What is your word?

Why is it scary?

Now, choose four other words that might help describe the detail of this one word.

Using all of the words that you have chosen, write a couple paragraphs that demonstrate this word's ability to frighten you or someone else. You can share a part of a terrifying scene or you can spend a paragraph (or stanza) taking some other approach defining why this word is scary.

# The Open Window

By Saki (H.H. Munro)

(1870-1916)

"My aunt will be down presently, Mr. Nuttel," said a very self-possessed young lady of fifteen; "in the meantime you must try and put up with me."

Framton Nuttel endeavoured to say the correct something which should duly flatter the niece of the moment without unduly discounting the aunt that was to come.  Privately he doubted more than ever whether these formal visits on a succession of total strangers would do much towards helping the nerve cure which he was supposed to be undergoing.

"I know how it will be," his sister had said when he was preparing to migrate to this rural retreat; "you will bury yourself down there and not speak to a living soul, and your nerves will be worse than ever from moping.  I shall just give you letters of introduction to all the people I know there.  Some of them, as far as I can remember, were quite nice."

Framton wondered whether Mrs. Sappleton, the lady to whom he was presenting one of the letters of introduction, came into the nice division.

"Do you know many of the people round here?" asked the niece, when she judged that they had had sufficient silent communion.

"Hardly a soul," said Framton.  "My sister was staying here, at the rectory, you know, some four years ago, and she gave me letters of introduction to some of the people here."

He made the last statement in a tone of distinct regret.

"Then you know practically nothing about my aunt?" pursued the self-possessed young lady.

"Only her name and address," admitted the caller.  He was wondering whether Mrs. Sappleton was in the married or widowed state.  An undefinable something about the room seemed to suggest masculine habitation.

"Her great tragedy happened just three years ago," said the child; "that would be since your sister's time."

"Her tragedy?" asked Framton; somehow in this restful country spot tragedies seemed out of place.

"You may wonder why we keep that window wide open on an October afternoon," said the niece, indicating a large French window that opened on to a lawn.

"It is quite warm for the time of the year," said Framton; "but has that window got anything to do with the tragedy?"

"Out through that window, three years ago to a day, her husband and her two young brothers went off for their day's shooting.  They never came back.  In crossing the moor to their favourite snipe-shooting ground they were all three engulfed in a treacherous piece of bog.  It had been that dreadful wet summer, you know, and places that were safe in other years gave way suddenly without warning.  Their bodies were never recovered.  That was the dreadful part of it."  Here the child's voice lost its self-possessed note and became falteringly human.  "Poor aunt always thinks that they will come back some day, they and the little brown spaniel that was lost with them, and walk in at that window just as they used to do.  That is why the window is kept open every evening till it is quite dusk.  Poor dear aunt, she has often told me how they went out, her husband with his white waterproof coat over his arm, and Ronnie, her youngest brother, singing 'Bertie, why do you bound?' as he always did to tease her, because she said it got on her nerves.  Do you know, sometimes on still, quiet evenings like this, I almost get a creepy feeling that they will all walk in through that window—"

She broke off with a little shudder.  It was a relief to Framton when the aunt bustled into the room with a whirl of apologies for being late in making her appearance.

"I hope Vera has been amusing you?" she said.

"She has been very interesting," said Framton.

"I hope you don't mind the open window," said Mrs. Sappleton briskly; "my husband and brothers will be home directly from shooting, and they always come in this way. They've been out for snipe in the marshes to-day, so they'll make a fine mess over my poor carpets. So like you men-folk, isn't it?"

She rattled on cheerfully about the shooting and the scarcity of birds, and the prospects for duck in the winter. To Framton it was all purely horrible. He made a desperate but only partially successful effort to turn the talk on to a less ghastly topic; he was conscious that his hostess was giving him only a fragment of her attention, and her eyes were constantly straying past him to the open window and the lawn beyond. It was certainly an unfortunate coincidence that he should have paid his visit on this tragic anniversary.

"The doctors agree in ordering me complete rest, an absence of mental excitement, and avoidance of anything in the nature of violent physical exercise," announced Framton, who laboured under the tolerably widespread delusion that total strangers and chance acquaintances are hungry for the least detail of one's ailments and infirmities, their cause and cure. "On the matter of diet they are not so much in agreement," he continued.

"No?" said Mrs. Sappleton, in a voice which only replaced a yawn at the last moment. Then she suddenly brightened into alert attention—but not to what Framton was saying.

"Here they are at last!" she cried. "Just in time for tea, and don't they look as if they were muddy up to the eyes!"

Framton shivered slightly and turned towards the niece with a look intended to convey sympathetic comprehension. The child was staring out through the open window with dazed horror in her eyes. In a chill shock of nameless fear Framton swung round in his seat and looked in the same direction.

In the deepening twilight three figures were walking across the lawn towards the window; they all carried guns under their arms, and one of them was additionally burdened with a white coat hung over his shoulders. A tired brown spaniel kept close at their heels. Noiselessly they neared the house, and then a hoarse young voice chanted out of the dusk: "I said, Bertie, why do you bound?"

Framton grabbed wildly at his stick and hat; the hall-door, the gravel-drive, and the front gate were dimly-noted stages in his headlong retreat. A cyclist coming along the road had to run into the hedge to avoid an imminent collision.

"Here we are, my dear," said the bearer of the white mackintosh, coming in through the window; "fairly muddy, but most of it's dry. Who was that who bolted out as we came up?"

"A most extraordinary man, a Mr. Nuttel," said Mrs. Sappleton; "could only talk about his illnesses, and dashed off without a word of good-bye or apology when you arrived. One would think he had seen a ghost."

"I expect it was the spaniel," said the niece calmly; "he told me he had a horror of dogs. He was once hunted into a cemetery somewhere on the banks of the Ganges by a pack of pariah dogs, and had to spend the night in a newly dug grave with the creatures snarling and grinning and foaming just above him. Enough to make anyone lose their nerve."

Romance at short notice was her speciality.

# A Deeper Look:

---

1.        What specific word does this author use to stir fear in this story?

2.        How does the author make this word scary for the story?

3.        Looking back on what you wrote for this exercise, do you feel that you have a word that you could center a scary story upon? Could you make it scarier than this story was? Or would you keep it less scary? How would you do it? What would your story be about?

# Setting Boundaries

Focus is perhaps one of the most difficult habits to master in writing. It can be tempting to stray from the path and write content that sounds good, but does not belong in your manuscript. While experienced writers will remove this content, newer writers frequently refuse to believe that anything they wrote could possibly be flawed. Losing your own focus causes readers to get lost in the writing. It becomes a disservice to aspiring writers.

Establishing boundaries, as you write, is one way to help your message stay on track. Some of these boundaries may be general—such as saying, "I am not going to write about religion in this book." Other boundaries may be more specific: "For artistic reasons, I want every chapter to start with the same word that the previous chapter ended with."

Some boundaries help you communicate more clearly with your audience, while others may be intended to help you personally grow as a writer. Despite your intent, these parameters help you learn to focus control over your writing while, at the same time, expanding your talent.

Let's practice setting a simple boundary and following it.

Start a document. On the first line, write down one word with only one letter in it. On the second line, write a word with two letters. The third line grows into three letters; the fourth, four letters; and continues in this manner until you can't think of a word with the appropriate number of letters you need for that line. Make sure that the words string together a cohesive thought. It doesn't have to sound perfectly intelligent, it just has to be a clear thought that any reader could follow.

Feel free to use the dictionary and thesaurus all you want. Cheat all you want by asking friends, searching the Internet or using other tools to get as far as you can. In the real world, creativity isn't a closed-book test.

When you come to a halt because you can't identify any more words, start the exercise again with a one-letter word and progress once more by adding an extra letter for every line you progress. If you run out of one-letter words, start your next string of words with a two letter word.If you run out of two letter words, begin with three the next round.

The final rule: you cannot start the process more than once with the same word. In fact, you can't repeat any of your words at all. Once you use a word, it's out of play. However, you may continue to use other variations of the word, provided they haven't been used before.

What's your longest streak? How many strings were you able to create?

# A Song About Myself

By John Keats
(1795-1821)

**I.**

There was a naughty boy,
A naughty boy was he,
He would not stop at home,
He could not quiet be-
He took
In his knapsack
A book
Full of vowels
And a shirt
With some towels,
A slight cap
For night cap,
A hair brush,
Comb ditto,
New stockings
For old ones
Would split O!
This knapsack
Tight at's back
He rivetted close
And followed his nose
To the north,
To the north,
And follow'd his nose
To the north.

**II.**

There was a naughty boy
And a naughty boy was he,
For nothing would he do
But scribble poetry-
He took
An ink stand
In his hand
And a pen
Big as ten
In the other,
And away
In a pother
He ran
To the mountains
And fountains
And ghostes

And postes
And witches
And ditches
And wrote
In his coat
When the weather
Was cool,
Fear of gout,
And without
When the weather
Was warm-
Och the charm
When we choose
To follow one's nose
To the north,
To the north,
To follow one's nose
To the north!

### III.

There was a naughty boy
And a naughty boy was he,
He kept little fishes
In washing tubs three
In spite
Of the might
Of the maid
Nor afraid
Of his Granny-good-
He often would
Hurly burly
Get up early
And go
By hook or crook
To the brook
And bring home
Miller's thumb,
Tittlebat
Not over fat,
Minnows small
As the stall
Of a glove,
Not above
The size
Of a nice
Little baby's
Little fingers-
O he made

'Twas his trade
Of fish a pretty kettle
A kettle-
A kettle
Of fish a pretty kettle
A kettle!

**IV.**

There was a naughty boy,
And a naughty boy was he,
He ran away to Scotland
The people for to see-
There he found
That the ground
Was as hard,
That a yard
Was as long,
That a song
Was as merry,
That a cherry
Was as red,
That lead
Was as weighty,
That fourscore
Was as eighty,
That a door
Was as wooden
As in England-
So he stood in his shoes
And he wonder'd,
He wonder'd,
He stood in his
Shoes and he wonder'd.

# A Deeper Look:

1.      What kind of boundaries do you think this author set for
        himself?

2.      What kind of unique quality do you think these
        boundaries brought to this poem?

3.      What kind of boundaries have you tried in some of your
        own writing? Why did you try them?

# Sensory:

## Exercises to help recognize detail

# 2

# Onomatopoeia

Did you know that there are real sounds and there are fake sounds? A real sound comes from a source that we can readily identify, and we know what that sound is like just from naming that source. However, we don't always know where fake or undefined sounds come from. These fake sounds have a fun and unique name, *onomatopoeia*. We commonly say it's a "sounds like" sound, such as "it sounds like the engine's knocking," or we say it's a type of sound, such as "it was a booming sound" or a "thumping noise."

Real sounds have a distinct identifying source and definition. Thunder, for instance, is a real sound from a unique and real source: collision of warm and cold air. Applause is also a real sound that defines numerous repetitive handclaps. However, if we say *thunderous applause*, then we are using an onomatopoeia because we are saying the applause was like thunder. It wasn't thunder. And it wasn't distinct applause. It was applause that had characteristics like another sound, thunder.

For this exercise list ten words that define sound that are not onomatopoeia in nature.

**STOP! Complete this first step before reading further.**

Got your list?

Let's see how you did.

Do any of your sounds refer to an event? Throw those words out. For instance, a finger snap is a unique sound created by fingers snapping past each other. Snapping fingers is an event where one or many finger snaps take place. It refers to the event of the sound, not to the actual sound. Snapping fingers, for instance is onomatopoeia. Finger snap is a distinct sound.

Do any of your sounds refer to stereotypic sounds that animals make? Throw these words out. For instance, a "MOO" is the sound that it seems like a cow is making. *Low* defines the actual sound that a cow makes. Cows in the pasture lowing refers to the event of one or many cows actually creating a low or many lows. Not every animal has a specific word for the sounds they make. Some of this is because we have become a society that has accepted onomatopoeia as defining words for sound, when they really don't. A dog bark, a snake hiss, a person's yell are all onomatopoeias. Some animals have specific sounds: mewl instead of meow; whinny instead of neigh. Incidentally, yell and whisper are also onomatopoeia.

How many of your ten words are left? Any?

OK, how about a second chance to create a list, and you can use any words that you got correct in your first list, but this time, list 30 words that define a definitive sound instead of just ten.

Now, pick one item on this list and write a paragraph or two describing an event where this specific sound transpires.

# The Hunchback of Notre Dame

By Victor Hugo
(1802-1885)

## Vol 2, Book 7, Chapter III
## The Bells

After the morning in the pillory, the neighbors of Notre-Dame thought they noticed that Quasimodo's ardor for ringing had grown cool. Formerly, there had been peals for every occasion, long morning serenades, which lasted from prime to compline; peals from the belfry for a high mass, rich scales drawn over the smaller bells for a wedding, for a christening, and mingling in the air like a rich embroidery of all sorts of charming sounds. The old church, all vibrating and sonorous, was in a perpetual joy of bells. One was constantly conscious of the presence of a spirit of noise and caprice, who sang through all those mouths of brass. Now that spirit seemed to have departed; the cathedral seemed gloomy, and gladly remained silent; festivals and funerals had the simple peal, dry and bare, demanded by the ritual, nothing more. Of the double noise which constitutes a church, the organ within, the bell without, the organ alone remained. One would have said that there was no longer a musician in the belfry. Quasimodo was always there, nevertheless; what, then, had happened to him? Was it that the shame and despair of the pillory still lingered in the bottom of his heart, that the lashes of his tormentor's whip reverberated unendingly in his soul, and that the sadness of such treatment had wholly extinguished in him even his passion for the bells? or was it that Marie had a rival in the heart of the bellringer of Notre-Dame, and that the great bell and her fourteen sisters were neglected for something more amiable and more beautiful?

It chanced that, in the year of grace 1482, Annunciation Day fell on Tuesday, the twenty-fifth of March. That day the air was so pure and light that Quasimodo felt some returning affection for his bells. He therefore ascended the northern tower while the beadle below was opening wide the doors of the church, which were then enormous panels of stout wood, covered with leather, bordered with nails of gilded iron, and framed in carvings "very artistically elaborated."

On arriving in the lofty bell chamber, Quasimodo gazed for some time at the six bells and shook his head sadly, as though groaning over some foreign element which had interposed itself in his heart between them and him. But when he had set them to swinging, when he felt that cluster of bells moving under his hand, when he saw, for he did not hear it, the palpitating octave ascend and descend that sonorous scale, like a bird hopping from branch to branch; when the demon Music, that demon who shakes a sparkling bundle of strette, trills and arpeggios, had taken possession of the poor deaf man, he became happy once more, he forgot everything, and his heart expanding, made his face beam.

He went and came, he beat his hands together, he ran from rope to rope, he animated the six singers with voice and gesture, like the leader of an orchestra who is urging on intelligent musicians.

"Go on," said he, "go on, go on, Gabrielle, pour out all thy noise into the Place, 'tis a festival to-day. No laziness, Thibauld; thou art relaxing; go on, go on, then, art thou rusted, thou sluggard? That is well! quick! quick! let not thy clapper be seen! Make them all deaf like me. That's it, Thibauld, bravely done! Guillaume! Guillaume! thou art the largest, and Pasquier is the smallest, and Pasquier does best. Let us wager that those who hear him will understand him better than they understand thee. Good! good! my Gabrielle, stoutly, more stoutly! Eli! what are you doing up aloft there, you two Moineaux (sparrows)? I do not see you making the least little shred of noise. What is the meaning of those beaks of copper which seem to be gaping when they should sing? Come, work now, 'tis the Feast of the Annunciation. The sun is fine, the chime must be fine also. Poor Guillaume! thou art all out of breath, my big fellow!"

He was wholly absorbed in spurring on his bells, all six of which vied with each other in leaping and shaking their shining haunches, like a noisy team of Spanish mules, pricked on here and there by the apostrophes of the muleteer.

All at once, on letting his glance fall between the large slate scales which cover the perpendicular wall of the bell tower at a certain height, he beheld on the square a young girl, fantastically dressed, stop, spread out on the ground a carpet, on which a small goat took up its post, and a group of spectators collect around her. This sight suddenly changed the course of his ideas, and congealed his enthusiasm as a breath of air congeals melted rosin. He halted, turned his back to the bells, and crouched down behind the projecting roof of slate, fixing upon the dancer that dreamy, sweet, and tender look which had already astonished the archdeacon on one occasion. Meanwhile, the forgotten bells died away abruptly and all together, to the great disappointment of the lovers of bell ringing, who were listening in good faith to the peal from above the Pont du Change, and who went away dumbfounded, like a dog who has been offered a bone and given a stone.

# A Deeper Look:

1.       What kinds of onomatopoeia appear in this story? Are there any?

2.       What kind of sound does this story conjure up, and what words does the author use to share them with the reader?

3.       What words might you use to demonstrate the sound of ringing bells? Why would you use those words?

# A Piece of Paper

Our fingertips can feel many sensations. The palm side of our fingers, including the tips have more nerves than most other places in the human body. Because we use these nerves so much, it can become easy to take the details of touch sensory for granted.

For this exercise, you will need a piece of paper of some sort. It can be any kind of paper with any kind of texture, one you can handle without causing yourself injury. Don't do anything to prepare it. Although you can use a new sheet of plain paper, you may notice this exercise is more interesting when you use older paper.

Go ahead and get yourself a piece of paper. It doesn't have to be a plain sheet. It can be anything made out of paper: an envelope, the side of a paper (cardboard) box, a square of tissue paper, etc.

Now, place the paper on a flat surface and close your eyes. Place your fingertips on the paper and quickly drag them down the face of it.

How does the surface feel? Write down as many words as you can to describe any detail that you noticed. Repeat this quick action as many times as you want and see if any other details jump out at you. How do your fingers themselves feel? How does the paper feel? What kind of details do you notice about the texture?

Once you have recorded these details, move on to the next part of this exercise.

Close your eyes again and place your fingertips on the paper once more. This time, drag them very slowly down the paper.

Do you notice any differences? What are they? Does the texture seem different? Do your fingertips feel differently? Does anything different happen during the process of moving your hand slowly as opposed to going fast?

# The Yellow Wallpaper

By Charlotte Perkins Stetson
(a.k.a. Charlotte Perkins Gilman)
(1860-1935)

It is very seldom that mere ordinary people like John and myself secure ancestral halls for the summer.

A colonial mansion, a hereditary estate, I would say a haunted house, and reach the height of romantic felicity—but that would be asking too much of fate!

Still I will proudly declare that there is something queer about it.

Else, why should it be let so cheaply? And why have stood so long untenanted?

John laughs at me, of course, but one expects that in marriage.

John is practical in the extreme. He has no patience with faith, an intense horror of superstition, and he scoffs openly at any talk of things not to be felt and seen and put down in figures.

John is a physician, and PERHAPS—(I would not say it to a living soul, of course, but this is dead paper and a great relief to my mind)—PERHAPS that is one reason I do not get well faster.

You see he does not believe I am sick!

And what can one do?

If a physician of high standing, and one's own husband, assures friends and relatives that there is really nothing the matter with one but temporary nervous depression—a slight hysterical tendency—what is one to do?

My brother is also a physician, and also of high standing, and he says the same thing.

So I take phosphates or phosphites—whichever it is, and tonics, and journeys, and air, and exercise, and am absolutely forbidden to "work" until I am well again.

Personally, I disagree with their ideas.

Personally, I believe that congenial work, with excitement and change, would do me good.

But what is one to do?

I did write for a while in spite of them; but it DOES exhaust me a good deal—having to be so sly about it, or else meet with heavy opposition.

I sometimes fancy that in my condition if I had less opposition and more society and stimulus—but John says the very worst thing I can do is to think about my condition, and I confess it always makes me feel bad.

So I will let it alone and talk about the house.

The most beautiful place! It is quite alone, standing well back from the road, quite three miles from the village. It makes me think of English places that you read about, for there are hedges and walls and gates that lock, and lots of separate little houses for the gardeners and people.

There is a DELICIOUS garden! I never saw such a garden—large and shady, full of box-bordered paths, and lined with long grape-covered arbors with seats under them.

There were greenhouses, too, but they are all broken now.

There was some legal trouble, I believe, something about the heirs and coheirs; anyhow, the place has been empty for years.

That spoils my ghostliness, I am afraid, but I don't care—there is something strange about the house—I can feel it.

I even said so to John one moonlight evening, but he said what I felt was a DRAUGHT, and shut the window.

I get unreasonably angry with John sometimes. I'm sure I never used to be so sensitive. I think it is due to this nervous condition.

But John says if I feel so, I shall neglect proper self-control; so I take pains to control myself—before him, at least, and that makes me very tired.

I don't like our room a bit. I wanted one downstairs that opened on the piazza and had roses all over the window, and such pretty old-fashioned chintz hangings! but John would not hear of it.

He said there was only one window and not room for two beds, and no near room for him if he took another.

He is very careful and loving, and hardly lets me stir without special direction.

I have a schedule prescription for each hour in the day; he takes all care from me, and so I feel basely ungrateful not to value it more.

He said we came here solely on my account, that I was to have perfect rest and all the air I could get. "Your exercise depends on your strength, my dear," said he, "and your food somewhat on your appetite; but air you can absorb all the time." So we took the nursery at the top of the house.

It is a big, airy room, the whole floor nearly, with windows that look all ways, and air and sunshine galore. It was nursery first and then playroom and gymnasium, I should judge; for the windows are barred for little children, and there are rings and things in the walls.

The paint and paper look as if a boys' school had used it. It is stripped off—the paper— in great patches all around the head of my bed, about as far as I can reach, and in a great place on the other side of the room low down. I never saw a worse paper in my life.

One of those sprawling flamboyant patterns committing every artistic sin.

It is dull enough to confuse the eye in following, pronounced enough to constantly irritate and provoke study, and when you follow the lame uncertain curves for a little distance they suddenly commit suicide—plunge off at outrageous angles, destroy themselves in unheard of contradictions.

The color is repellent, almost revolting; a smouldering unclean yellow, strangely faded by the slow-turning sunlight.

It is a dull yet lurid orange in some places, a sickly sulphur tint in others.

No wonder the children hated it! I should hate it myself if I had to live in this room long.

There comes John, and I must put this away,—he hates to have me write a word.

We have been here two weeks, and I haven't felt like writing before, since that first day.

I am sitting by the window now, up in this atrocious nursery, and there is nothing to hinder my writing as much as I please, save lack of strength.

John is away all day, and even some nights when his cases are serious.

I am glad my case is not serious!

But these nervous troubles are dreadfully depressing.

John does not know how much I really suffer. He knows there is no REASON to suffer, and that satisfies him.

Of course it is only nervousness. It does weigh on me so not to do my duty in any way!

I meant to be such a help to John, such a real rest and comfort, and here I am a comparative burden already!

Nobody would believe what an effort it is to do what little I am able,—to dress and entertain, and order things.

It is fortunate Mary is so good with the baby. Such a dear baby!

And yet I CANNOT be with him, it makes me so nervous.

I suppose John never was nervous in his life. He laughs at me so about this wall-paper!

At first he meant to repaper the room, but afterwards he said that I was letting it get the better of me, and that nothing was worse for a nervous patient than to give way to such fancies.

He said that after the wall-paper was changed it would be the heavy bedstead, and then the barred windows, and then that gate at the head of the stairs, and so on.

"You know the place is doing you good," he said, "and really, dear, I don't care to renovate the house just for a three months' rental."

"Then do let us go downstairs," I said, "there are such pretty rooms there."

Then he took me in his arms and called me a blessed little goose, and said he would go down to the cellar, if I wished, and have it whitewashed into the bargain.

But he is right enough about the beds and windows and things.

It is an airy and comfortable room as any one need wish, and, of course, I would not be so silly as to make him uncomfortable just for a whim.

I'm really getting quite fond of the big room, all but that horrid paper.

Out of one window I can see the garden, those mysterious deepshaded arbors, the riotous old-fashioned flowers, and bushes and gnarly trees.

Out of another I get a lovely view of the bay and a little private wharf belonging to the estate. There is a beautiful shaded lane that runs down there from the house. I always fancy I see people walking in these numerous paths and arbors, but John has cautioned me not to give way to fancy in the least. He says that with my imaginative power and habit of story-making, a nervous weakness like mine is sure to lead to all manner of excited fancies, and that I ought to use my will and good sense to check the tendency. So I try.

I think sometimes that if I were only well enough to write a little it would relieve the press of ideas and rest me.

But I find I get pretty tired when I try.

It is so discouraging not to have any advice and companionship about my work. When I get really well, John says we will ask Cousin Henry and Julia down for a long visit; but he says he would as soon put fireworks in my pillow-case as to let me have those stimulating people about now.

I wish I could get well faster.

But I must not think about that. This paper looks to me as if it KNEW what a vicious influence it had!

There is a recurrent spot where the pattern lolls like a broken neck and two bulbous eyes stare at you upside down.

I get positively angry with the impertinence of it and the everlastingness. Up and down and sideways they crawl, and those absurd, unblinking eyes are everywhere. There is one place where two breadths didn't match, and the eyes go all up and down the line, one a little higher than the other.

I never saw so much expression in an inanimate thing before, and we all know how much expression they have! I used to lie awake as a child and get more entertainment and terror out of blank walls and plain furniture than most children could find in a toy store.

I remember what a kindly wink the knobs of our big, old bureau used to have, and there was one chair that always seemed like a strong friend.

I used to feel that if any of the other things looked too fierce I could always hop into that chair and be safe.

The furniture in this room is no worse than inharmonious, however, for we had to bring it all from downstairs. I suppose when this was used as a playroom they had to take the nursery things out, and no wonder! I never saw such ravages as the children have made here.

The wall-paper, as I said before, is torn off in spots, and it sticketh closer than a brother—they must have had perseverance as well as hatred.

Then the floor is scratched and gouged and splintered, the plaster itself is dug out here and there, and this great heavy bed which is all we found in the room, looks as if it had been through the wars.

But I don't mind it a bit—only the paper.

There comes John's sister. Such a dear girl as she is, and so careful of me! I must not let her find me writing.

She is a perfect and enthusiastic housekeeper, and hopes for no better profession. I verily believe she thinks it is the writing which made me sick!

But I can write when she is out, and see her a long way off from these windows.

There is one that commands the road, a lovely shaded winding road, and one that just looks off over the country. A lovely country, too, full of great elms and velvet meadows.

This wall-paper has a kind of sub-pattern in a different shade, a particularly irritating one, for you can only see it in certain lights, and not clearly then.

But in the places where it isn't faded and where the sun is just so—I can see a strange, provoking, formless sort of figure, that seems to skulk about behind that silly and conspicuous front design.

There's sister on the stairs!

Well, the Fourth of July is over! The people are gone and I am tired out. John thought it might do me good to see a little company, so we just had mother and Nellie and the children down for a week.

Of course I didn't do a thing. Jennie sees to everything now.

But it tired me all the same.

John says if I don't pick up faster he shall send me to Weir Mitchell in the fall.

But I don't want to go there at all. I had a friend who was in his hands once, and she says he is just like John and my brother, only more so!

Besides, it is such an undertaking to go so far.

I don't feel as if it was worth while to turn my hand over for anything, and I'm getting dreadfully fretful and querulous.

I cry at nothing, and cry most of the time.

Of course I don't when John is here, or anybody else, but when I am alone.

And I am alone a good deal just now. John is kept in town very often by serious cases, and Jennie is good and lets me alone when I want her to.

So I walk a little in the garden or down that lovely lane, sit on the porch under the roses, and lie down up here a good deal.

I'm getting really fond of the room in spite of the wall-paper. Perhaps BECAUSE of the wall-paper.

It dwells in my mind so!

I lie here on this great immovable bed—it is nailed down, I believe—and follow that pattern about by the hour. It is as good as gymnastics, I assure you. I start, we'll say, at the bottom, down in the corner over there where it has not been touched, and I determine for the thousandth time that I WILL follow that pointless pattern to some sort of a conclusion.

I know a little of the principle of design, and I know this thing was not arranged on any laws of radiation, or alternation, or repetition, or symmetry, or anything else that I ever heard of.

It is repeated, of course, by the breadths, but not otherwise.

Looked at in one way each breadth stands alone, the bloated curves and flourishes—a kind of "debased Romanesque" with delirium tremens—go waddling up and down in isolated columns of fatuity.

But, on the other hand, they connect diagonally, and the sprawling outlines run off in great slanting waves of optic horror, like a lot of wallowing seaweeds in full chase.

The whole thing goes horizontally, too, at least it seems so, and I exhaust myself in trying to distinguish the order of its going in that direction.

They have used a horizontal breadth for a frieze, and that adds wonderfully to the confusion.

There is one end of the room where it is almost intact, and there, when the crosslights fade and the low sun shines directly upon it, I can almost fancy radiation after all,—the interminable grotesques seem to form around a common centre and rush off in headlong plunges of equal distraction.

It makes me tired to follow it. I will take a nap I guess.

I don't know why I should write this.

I don't want to.

I don't feel able.

And I know John would think it absurd. But I MUST say what I feel and think in some way—it is such a relief!

But the effort is getting to be greater than the relief.

Half the time now I am awfully lazy, and lie down ever so much.

John says I musn't lose my strength, and has me take cod liver oil and lots of tonics and things, to say nothing of ale and wine and rare meat.

Dear John! He loves me very dearly, and hates to have me sick. I tried to have a real earnest reasonable talk with him the other day, and tell him how I wish he would let me go and make a visit to Cousin Henry and Julia.

But he said I wasn't able to go, nor able to stand it after I got there; and I did not make out a very good case for myself, for I was crying before I had finished.

It is getting to be a great effort for me to think straight. Just this nervous weakness I suppose.

And dear John gathered me up in his arms, and just carried me upstairs and laid me on the bed, and sat by me and read to me till it tired my head.

He said I was his darling and his comfort and all he had, and that I must take care of myself for his sake, and keep well.

He says no one but myself can help me out of it, that I must use my will and self-control and not let any silly fancies run away with me.

There's one comfort, the baby is well and happy, and does not have to occupy this nursery with the horrid wall-paper.

If we had not used it, that blessed child would have! What a fortunate escape! Why, I wouldn't have a child of mine, an impressionable little thing, live in such a room for worlds.

I never thought of it before, but it is lucky that John kept me here after all, I can stand it so much easier than a baby, you see.

Of course I never mention it to them any more—I am too wise,—but I keep watch of it all the same.

There are things in that paper that nobody knows but me, or ever will.

Behind that outside pattern the dim shapes get clearer every day.

It is always the same shape, only very numerous.

And it is like a woman stooping down and creeping about behind that pattern. I don't like it a bit. I wonder—I begin to think—I wish John would take me away from here!

It is so hard to talk with John about my case, because he is so wise, and because he loves me so.

But I tried it last night.

It was moonlight. The moon shines in all around just as the sun does.

I hate to see it sometimes, it creeps so slowly, and always comes in by one window or another.

John was asleep and I hated to waken him, so I kept still and watched the moonlight on that undulating wall-paper till I felt creepy.

The faint figure behind seemed to shake the pattern, just as if she wanted to get out.

I got up softly and went to feel and see if the paper DID move, and when I came back John was awake.

"What is it, little girl?" he said. "Don't go walking about like that—you'll get cold."

I though it was a good time to talk, so I told him that I really was not gaining here, and that I wished he would take me away.

"Why darling!" said he, "our lease will be up in three weeks, and I can't see how to leave before.

"The repairs are not done at home, and I cannot possibly leave town just now. Of course if you were in any danger, I could and would, but you really are better, dear, whether you can see it or not. I am a doctor, dear, and I know. You are gaining flesh and color, your appetite is better, I feel really much easier about you."

"I don't weigh a bit more," said I, "nor as much; and my appetite may be better in the evening when you are here, but it is worse in the morning when you are away!"

"Bless her little heart!" said he with a big hug, "she shall be as sick as she pleases! But now let's improve the shining hours by going to sleep, and talk about it in the morning!"

"And you won't go away?" I asked gloomily.

"Why, how can I, dear? It is only three weeks more and then we will take a nice little trip of a few days while Jennie is getting the house ready. Really dear you are better!"

"Better in body perhaps—" I began, and stopped short, for he sat up straight and looked at me with such a stern, reproachful look that I could not say another word.

"My darling," said he, "I beg of you, for my sake and for our child's sake, as well as for your own, that you will never for one instant let that idea enter your mind! There is nothing so dangerous, so fascinating, to a temperament like yours. It is a false and foolish fancy. Can you not trust me as a physician when I tell you so?"

So of course I said no more on that score, and we went to sleep before long. He thought I was asleep first, but I wasn't, and lay there for hours trying to decide whether that front pattern and the back pattern really did move together or separately.

On a pattern like this, by daylight, there is a lack of sequence, a defiance of law, that is a constant irritant to a normal mind.

The color is hideous enough, and unreliable enough, and infuriating enough, but the pattern is torturing.

You think you have mastered it, but just as you get well underway in following, it turns a back-somersault and there you are. It slaps you in the face, knocks you down, and tramples upon you. It is like a bad dream.

The outside pattern is a florid arabesque, reminding one of a fungus. If you can imagine a toadstool in joints, an interminable string of toadstools, budding and sprouting in endless convolutions—why, that is something like it.

That is, sometimes!

There is one marked peculiarity about this paper, a thing nobody seems to notice but myself, and that is that it changes as the light changes.

When the sun shoots in through the east window—I always watch for that first long, straight ray—it changes so quickly that I never can quite believe it.

That is why I watch it always.

By moonlight—the moon shines in all night when there is a moon—I wouldn't know it was the same paper.

At night in any kind of light, in twilight, candle light, lamplight, and worst of all by moonlight, it becomes bars! The outside pattern I mean, and the woman behind it is as plain as can be.

I didn't realize for a long time what the thing was that showed behind, that dim sub-pattern, but now I am quite sure it is a woman.

By daylight she is subdued, quiet. I fancy it is the pattern that keeps her so still. It is so puzzling. It keeps me quiet by the hour.

I lie down ever so much now. John says it is good for me, and to sleep all I can.

Indeed he started the habit by making me lie down for an hour after each meal.

It is a very bad habit I am convinced, for you see I don't sleep.

And that cultivates deceit, for I don't tell them I'm awake—O no!

The fact is I am getting a little afraid of John.

He seems very queer sometimes, and even Jennie has an inexplicable look.

It strikes me occasionally, just as a scientific hypothesis,—that perhaps it is the paper!

I have watched John when he did not know I was looking, and come into the room suddenly on the most innocent excuses, and I've caught him several times LOOKING AT THE PAPER! And Jennie too. I caught Jennie with her hand on it once.

She didn't know I was in the room, and when I asked her in a quiet, a very quiet voice, with the most restrained manner possible, what she was doing with the paper—she turned around as if she had been caught stealing, and looked quite angry—asked me why I should frighten her so!

Then she said that the paper stained everything it touched, that she had found yellow smooches on all my clothes and John's, and she wished we would be more careful!

Did not that sound innocent? But I know she was studying that pattern, and I am determined that nobody shall find it out but myself!

Life is very much more exciting now than it used to be. You see I have something more to expect, to look forward to, to watch. I really do eat better, and am more quiet than I was.

John is so pleased to see me improve! He laughed a little the other day, and said I seemed to be flourishing in spite of my wall-paper.

I turned it off with a laugh. I had no intention of telling him it was BECAUSE of the wall-paper—he would make fun of me. He might even want to take me away.

I don't want to leave now until I have found it out. There is a week more, and I think that will be enough.

I'm feeling ever so much better! I don't sleep much at night, for it is so interesting to watch developments; but I sleep a good deal in the daytime.

In the daytime it is tiresome and perplexing.

There are always new shoots on the fungus, and new shades of yellow all over it. I cannot keep count of them, though I have tried conscientiously.

It is the strangest yellow, that wall-paper! It makes me think of all the yellow things I ever saw—not beautiful ones like buttercups, but old foul, bad yellow things.

But there is something else about that paper—the smell! I noticed it the moment we came into the room, but with so much air and sun it was not bad. Now we have had a week of fog and rain, and whether the windows are open or not, the smell is here.

It creeps all over the house.

I find it hovering in the dining-room, skulking in the parlor, hiding in the hall, lying in wait for me on the stairs.

It gets into my hair.

Even when I go to ride, if I turn my head suddenly and surprise it—there is that smell!

Such a peculiar odor, too! I have spent hours in trying to analyze it, to find what it smelled like.

It is not bad—at first, and very gentle, but quite the subtlest, most enduring odor I ever met.

In this damp weather it is awful, I wake up in the night and find it hanging over me.

It used to disturb me at first. I thought seriously of burning the house—to reach the smell.

But now I am used to it. The only thing I can think of that it is like is the COLOR of the paper! A yellow smell.

There is a very funny mark on this wall, low down, near the mopboard. A streak that runs round the room. It goes behind every piece of furniture, except the bed, a long, straight, even SMOOCH, as if it had been rubbed over and over.

I wonder how it was done and who did it, and what they did it for. Round and round and round—round and round and round—it makes me dizzy!

I really have discovered something at last.

Through watching so much at night, when it changes so, I have finally found out.

The front pattern DOES move—and no wonder! The woman behind shakes it!

Sometimes I think there are a great many women behind, and sometimes only one, and she crawls around fast, and her crawling shakes it all over.

Then in the very bright spots she keeps still, and in the very shady spots she just takes hold of the bars and shakes them hard.

And she is all the time trying to climb through. But nobody could climb through that pattern—it strangles so; I think that is why it has so many heads.

They get through, and then the pattern strangles them off and turns them upside down, and makes their eyes white!

If those heads were covered or taken off it would not be half so bad.

I think that woman gets out in the daytime!

And I'll tell you why—privately—I've seen her!

I can see her out of every one of my windows!

It is the same woman, I know, for she is always creeping, and most women do not creep by daylight.

I see her on that long road under the trees, creeping along, and when a carriage comes she hides under the blackberry vines.

I don't blame her a bit. It must be very humiliating to be caught creeping by daylight!

I always lock the door when I creep by daylight. I can't do it at night, for I know John would suspect something at once.

And John is so queer now, that I don't want to irritate him. I wish he would take another room! Besides, I don't want anybody to get that woman out at night but myself.

I often wonder if I could see her out of all the windows at once.

But, turn as fast as I can, I can only see out of one at one time.

And though I always see her, she MAY be able to creep faster than I can turn!

I have watched her sometimes away off in the open country, creeping as fast as a cloud shadow in a high wind.

If only that top pattern could be gotten off from the under one! I mean to try it, little by little.

I have found out another funny thing, but I shan't tell it this time! It does not do to trust people too much.

There are only two more days to get this paper off, and I believe John is beginning to notice. I don't like the look in his eyes.

And I heard him ask Jennie a lot of professional questions about me. She had a very good report to give.

She said I slept a good deal in the daytime.

John knows I don't sleep very well at night, for all I'm so quiet!

He asked me all sorts of questions, too, and pretended to be very loving and kind.

As if I couldn't see through him!

Still, I don't wonder he acts so, sleeping under this paper for three months.

It only interests me, but I feel sure John and Jennie are secretly affected by it.

Hurrah! This is the last day, but it is enough. John is to stay in town over night, and won't be out until this evening.

Jennie wanted to sleep with me—the sly thing! but I told her I should undoubtedly rest better for a night all alone.

That was clever, for really I wasn't alone a bit! As soon as it was moonlight and that poor thing began to crawl and shake the pattern, I got up and ran to help her.

I pulled and she shook, I shook and she pulled, and before morning we had peeled off yards of that paper.

A strip about as high as my head and half around the room.

And then when the sun came and that awful pattern began to laugh at me, I declared I would finish it to-day!

We go away to-morrow, and they are moving all my furniture down again to leave things as they were before.

Jennie looked at the wall in amazement, but I told her merrily that I did it out of pure spite at the vicious thing.

She laughed and said she wouldn't mind doing it herself, but I must not get tired.

How she betrayed herself that time!

But I am here, and no person touches this paper but me—not ALIVE!

She tried to get me out of the room—it was too patent! But I said it was so quiet and empty and clean now that I believed I would lie down again and sleep all I could; and not to wake me even for dinner—I would call when I woke.

So now she is gone, and the servants are gone, and the things are gone, and there is nothing left but that great bedstead nailed down, with the canvas mattress we found on it.

We shall sleep downstairs to-night, and take the boat home to-morrow.

I quite enjoy the room, now it is bare again.

How those children did tear about here!

This bedstead is fairly gnawed!

But I must get to work.

I have locked the door and thrown the key down into the front path.

I don't want to go out, and I don't want to have anybody come in, till John comes.

I want to astonish him.

I've got a rope up here that even Jennie did not find. If that woman does get out, and tries to get away, I can tie her!

But I forgot I could not reach far without anything to stand on!

This bed will NOT move!

I tried to lift and push it until I was lame, and then I got so angry I bit off a little piece at one corner—but it hurt my teeth.

Then I peeled off all the paper I could reach standing on the floor. It sticks horribly and the pattern just enjoys it! All those strangled heads and bulbous eyes and waddling fungus growths just shriek with derision!

I am getting angry enough to do something desperate. To jump out of the window would be admirable exercise, but the bars are too strong even to try.

Besides I wouldn't do it. Of course not. I know well enough that a step like that is improper and might be misconstrued.

I don't like to LOOK out of the windows even—there are so many of those creeping women, and they creep so fast.

I wonder if they all come out of that wall-paper as I did?

But I am securely fastened now by my well-hidden rope—you don't get ME out in the road there!

I suppose I shall have to get back behind the pattern when it comes night, and that is hard!

It is so pleasant to be out in this great room and creep around as I please!

I don't want to go outside. I won't, even if Jennie asks me to.

For outside you have to creep on the ground, and everything is green instead of yellow.

But here I can creep smoothly on the floor, and my shoulder just fits in that long smooch around the wall, so I cannot lose my way.

Why there's John at the door!

It is no use, young man, you can't open it!

How he does call and pound!

Now he's crying for an axe.

It would be a shame to break down that beautiful door!

"John dear!" said I in the gentlest voice, "the key is down by the front steps, under a plantain leaf!"

That silenced him for a few moments.

Then he said—very quietly indeed, "Open the door, my darling!"

"I can't," said I. "The key is down by the front door under a plantain leaf!"

And then I said it again, several times, very gently and slowly, and said it so often that he had to go and see, and he got it of course, and came in. He stopped short by the door.

"What is the matter?" he cried. "For God's sake, what are you doing!"

I kept on creeping just the same, but I looked at him over my shoulder.

"I've got out at last," said I, "in spite of you and Jane. And I've pulled off most of the paper, so you can't put me back!"

Now why should that man have fainted? But he did, and right across my path by the wall, so that I had to creep over him every time!

# A Deeper Look:

1.       What kind of detail does the author use to describe the paper in this story?

2.       How does the detail change over the course of this story? What do you think is the cause for this change?

3.       How could simply touching something help you show it better to your readers in your own writing?

# Colors

How well do you know your colors? If I say, "Hand me a red crayon," do you trust your ability to hand me a red crayon? Can you find it based on shade? Or do you have to rely on reading the text printed on the crayon's paper wrapper? Or can you find it at all? Is the concept of colors even a topic that you can comprehend? That's OK, if you can't, it's not required for this exercise.

Part one: What is your favorite color? Write that color down. Or if you can't, write down a color that you think could be your favorite.

Why is this (or world this be) your favorite color? Write down your reasons next to where you wrote your favorite color. Use real reasons, reasons that can justify why it's your favorite. Don't say, "I don't know, it's just my favorite is all." Give specific reasons.

How many reasons did you come up with? Ten? Five? Three? Were you able to come up with even one? If you couldn't come up with any, write down any reasons that explain how you can be sure it's your favorite color?

Part two: What's your least favorite color? Write that down.

Why is this your least favorite color? Write down your reasons?

Was one color easier to come up with reasons for than the other?

Do you feel comfortable that you know these colors well enough to say they are your favorite and least favorite? You should. We tend to create strong associations with items we like the most and with items we dislike the most. So it's only reasonable that we should be able to justify why we like or dislike a color.

So let's test this.

Part Three: Imagine at this very moment, that a woman approaches you and asks you to explain what your favorite and least favorite colors are like.

OH!

And her vision is completely gone. She probably has never seen any color before so she has nothing to compare it to. But she has all of her other senses.

Without using visual references, list ten ways that you can define your favorite color and ten ways to define your least favorite color. You can use any of your other senses to define or describe your colors.

# Moby Dick
By Herman Melville
(1819-1891)

## Chapter XLII
## THE WHITENESS OF THE WHALE

What the White Whale was to Ahab, has been hinted; what, at times, he was to me, as yet remains unsaid.

Aside from those more obvious considerations touching Moby Dick, which could not but occasionally awaken in any man's soul some alarm, there was another thought, or rather vague, nameless horror concerning him, which at times by its intensity completely overpowered all the rest; and yet so mystical and well nigh ineffable was it, that I almost despair of putting it in a comprehensible form. It was the whiteness of the whale that above all things appalled me. But how can I hope to explain myself here; and yet, in some dim, random way, explain myself I must, else all these chapters might be naught.

Though in many natural objects, whiteness refiningly enhances beauty, as if imparting some special virtue of its own, as in marbles, japonicas, and pearls; and though various nations have in some way recognised a certain royal pre-eminence in this hue; even the barbaric, grand old kings of Pegu placing the title 'Lord of the White Elephants' above all their other magniloquent ascriptions of dominion; and the modern kings of Siam unfurling the same snow-white quadruped in the royal standard; and the Hanoverian flag bearing the one figure of a snow-white charger; and the great Austrian Empire, Caesarian, heir to overlording Rome, having for the imperial color the same imperial hue; and though this pre-eminence in it applies to the human race itself, giving the white man ideal mastership over every dusky tribe; and though, besides all this, whiteness has been even made significant of gladness, for among the Romans a white stone marked a joyful day; and though in other mortal sympathies and symbolizings, this same hue is made the emblem of many touching, noble things -- the innocence of brides, the benignity of age; though among the Red Men of America the giving of the white belt of wampum was the deepest pledge of honor; though in many climes, whiteness typifies the majesty of Justice in the ermine of the Judge, and contributes to the daily state of kings and queens drawn by milk-white steeds; though even in the higher mysteries of the most august religions it has been made the symbol of the divine spotlessness and power; by the Persian fire worshippers, the white forked flame being held the holiest on the altar; and in the Greek mythologies, Great Jove himself made incarnate in a snow-white bull; and though to the noble Iroquois, the midwinter sacrifice of the sacred White Dog was by far the holiest festival of their theology, that spotless, faithful creature being held the purest envoy they could send to the Great Spirit with the annual tidings of their own fidelity; and though directly from the Latin word for white, all Christian priests derive the name of one part of their sacred vesture, the alb or tunic, worn beneath the cassock; and though among the holy pomps of the Romish faith, white is specially employed in the celebration of the Passion of our Lord; though in the Vision of St. John, white robes are given to the redeemed, and the four- and-twenty elders stand clothed in white before the great white throne, and the Holy One that sitteth there white like wool; yet for all these accumulated associations, with whatever is sweet, and honorable, and sublime, there yet lurks an elusive something in the innermost idea of this hue, which strikes more of panic to the soul than that redness which affrights in blood.

This elusive quality it is, which causes the thought of whiteness, when divorced from more kindly associations, and coupled with any object terrible in itself, to heighten that terror to the furthest bounds. Witness the white bear of the poles, and the white shark of the tropics; what but their smooth, flaky whiteness makes them the transcendent horrors they are? That ghastly whiteness it is which imparts such an abhorrent mildness, even more loathsome than terrific, to the dumb gloating of their aspect. So that not the fierce-fanged tiger in his heraldic coat can so stagger courage as the white-shrouded bear or shark.[1]

Bethink thee of the albatross, whence come those clouds of spiritual wonderment and pale dread, in which that white phantom sails in all imaginations? Not Coleridge first threw that spell; but God's great, unflattering laureate, Nature.[2]

Most famous in our Western annals and Indian traditions is that of the White Steed of the Prairies; a magnificent milk-white charger, large-eyed, small-headed, bluff-chested, and with the dignity of a thousand monarchs in his lofty, overscorning carriage. He was the elected Xerxes of vast herds of wild horses, whose pastures in those days were only fenced by the Rocky Mountains and the Alleghanies. At their flaming head he westward trooped it like that chosen star which every evening leads on the hosts of light. The flashing cascade of his mane, the curving comet of his tail, invested him with housings more resplendent than gold and silver-beaters could have furnished him. A most imperial and archangelical apparition of that unfallen, western world, which to the eyes of the old trappers and hunters revived the glories of those primeval times when Adam walked majestic as a god, bluff-bowed and fearless as this mighty steed. Whether marching amid his aides and marshals in the van of countless cohorts that endlessly streamed it over the plains, like an Ohio; or whether with his circumambient subjects browsing all around at the horizon, the White Steed gallopingly reviewed them with warm nostrils reddening through his cool milkiness; in whatever aspect

1. With reference to the Polar bear, it may possibly be urged by him who would fain go still deeper into this matter, that it is not the whiteness, separately regarded, which heightens the intolerable hideousness of that brute; for, analysed, that heightened hideousness, it might be said, only arises from the circumstance, that the irresponsible ferociousness of the creature stands invested in the fleece of celestial innocence and love; and hence, by bringing together two such opposite emotions in our minds, the Polar bear frightens us with so unnatural a contrast. But even assuming all this to be true; yet, were it not for the whiteness, you would not have that intensified terror.

As for the white shark, the white gliding ghostliness of repose in that creature, when beheld in his ordinary moods, strangely tallies with the same quality in the Polar quadruped. This peculiarity is most vividly hit by the French in the name they bestow upon that fish. The Romish mass for the dead begins with Requiem eternam (eternal rest), whence Requiem denominating the mass itself, and any other funeral music. Now, in allusion to the white, silent stillness of death in this shark, and the mild deadliness of his habits, the French call him Requin.
2. I remember the first albatross I ever saw. It was during a prolonged gale, in waters hard upon the Antarctic seas. From my forenoon watch below, I ascended to the overclouded deck; and there, dashed upon the main hatches, I saw a regal, feathery thing of unspotted whiteness, and with a hooked, Roman bill sublime. At intervals, it arched forth its vast archangel wings, as if to embrace some holy ark. Wondrous flutterings and throbbings shook it. Though bodily unharmed, it uttered cries, as some king's ghost in supernatural distress. Through its inexpressible, strange eyes, methought I

peeped to secrets which took hold of God. As Abraham before the angels, I bowed myself; the white thing was so white, its wings so wide, and in those for ever exiled waters, I had lost the miserable warping memories of traditions and of towns. Long I gazed at that prodigy of plumage. I cannot tell, can only hint, the things that darted through me then. But at last I awoke; and turning, asked a sailor what bird was this. A goney, he replied. Goney! I never had heard that name before; is it conceivable that this glorious thing is utterly unknown to men ashore! never! But some time after, I learned that goney was some seaman's name for albatross. So that by no possibility could Coleridge's wild Rhyme have had aught to do with those mystical impressions which were mine, when I saw that bird upon our deck. For neither had I then read the Rhyme, nor knew the bird to be an albatross. Yet, in saying this, I do but indirectly burnish a little brighter the noble merit of the poem and the poet.

I assert, then, that in the wondrous bodily whiteness of the bird chiefly lurks the secret of the spell; a truth the more evinced in this, that by a solecism of terms there are birds called grey albatrosses; and these I have frequently seen, but never with such emotions as when I beheld the Antarctic fowl.

But how had the mystic thing been caught? Whisper it not, and I will tell; with a treacherous hook and line, as the fowl floated on the sea. At last the Captain made a postman of it; tying a lettered, leathern tally round its neck, with the ship's time and place; and then letting it escape. But I doubt not, that leathern tally, meant for man, was taken off in Heaven, when the white fowl flew to join the wing-folding, the invoking, and adoring cherubim! [Melville's notes] he presented himself, always to the bravest Indians he was the object of trembling reverence and awe. Nor can it be questioned from what stands on legendary record of this noble horse, that it was his spiritual whiteness chiefly, which so clothed him with divineness; and that this divineness had that in it which, though commanding worship, at the same time enforced a certain nameless terror.

But there are other instances where this whiteness loses all that accessory and strange glory which invests it in the White Steed and Albatross.

What is it that in the Albino man so peculiarly repels and often shocks the eye, as that sometimes he is loathed by his own kith and kin! It is that whiteness which invests him, a thing expressed by the name he bears. The Albino is as well made as other men -- has no substantive deformity -- and yet this mere aspect of all-pervading whiteness makes him more strangely hideous than the ugliest abortion. Why should this be so?

Nor, in quite other aspects, does Nature in her least palpable but not the less malicious agencies, fail to enlist among her forces this crowning attribute of the terrible. From its snowy aspect, the gauntleted ghost of the Southern Seas has been denominated the White Squall. Nor, in some historic instances, has the art of human malice omitted so potent an auxiliary. How wildly it heightens the effect of that passage in Froissart, when, masked in the snowy symbol of their faction, the desperate White Hoods of Ghent murder their bailiff in the market- place!

Nor, in some things, does the common, hereditary experience of all mankind fail to bear witness to the supernaturalism of this hue. It cannot well be doubted, that the one visible quality in the aspect of the dead which most appals the gazer, is the marble pallor lingering there; as if indeed that pallor were as much like the badge of consternation in the other world, as of mortal trepidation here. And from that pallor of the dead, we borrow the expressive hue of the shroud in which we wrap them. Nor even in our superstitions do we fail to throw the same snowy mantle round our phantoms; all ghosts rising in a milk-white fog -- Yea, while these terrors seize us, let us add, that even the king of terrors, when personified by the evangelist, rides on his pallid horse.

Therefore, in his other moods, symbolize whatever grand or gracious thing he will by whiteness, no man can deny that in its profoundest idealized significance it calls up a peculiar apparition to the soul.

But though without dissent this point be fixed, how is mortal man to account for it? To analyse it, would seem impossible. Can we, then, by the citation of some of those instances wherein this thing of whiteness -- though for the time either wholly or in great part stripped of all direct associations calculated to impart to it aught fearful, but, nevertheless, is found to exert over us the same sorcery, however modified; -- can we thus hope to light upon some chance clue to conduct us to the hidden cause we seek?

Let us try. But in a matter like this, subtlety appeals to subtlety, and without imagination no man can follow another into these halls. And though, doubtless, some at least of the imaginative impressions about to be presented may have been shared by most men, yet few perhaps were entirely conscious of them at the time, and therefore may not be able to recall them now.

Why to the man of untutored ideality, who happens to be but loosely acquainted with the peculiar character of the day, does the bare mention of Whitsuntide marshal in the fancy such long, dreary, speechless processions of slow-pacing pilgrims, downcast and hooded with new-fallen snow? Or, to the unread, unsophisticated Protestant of the Middle American States, why does the passing mention of a White Friar or a White Nun, evoke such an eyeless statue in the soul?

Or what is there apart from the traditions of dungeoned warriors and kings (which will not wholly account for it) that makes the White Tower of London tell so much more strongly on the imagination of an untravelled American, than those other storied structures, its neighbors -- the Byward Tower, or even the Bloody? And those sublimer towers, the White Mountains of New Hampshire, whence, in peculiar moods, comes that gigantic ghostliness over the soul at the bare mention of that name, while the thought of Virginia's Blue Ridge is full of a soft, dewy, distant dreaminess? Or why, irrespective of all latitudes and longitudes, does the name of the White Sea exert such a spectralness over the fancy, while that of the Yellow Sea lulls us with mortal thoughts of long lacquered mild afternoons on the waves, followed by the gaudiest and yet sleepiest of sunsets? Or, to choose a wholly unsubstantial instance, purely addressed to the fancy, why, in reading the old fairy tales of Central Europe, does 'the tall pale man' of the Hartz forests, whose changeless pallor unrestingly glides through the green of the groves -- why is this phantom more terrible than all the whooping imps of the Blocksburg?

Nor is it, altogether, the remembrance of her cathedral-toppling earthquakes; nor the stampedoes of her frantic seas: nor the tearlessness of arid skies that never rain; nor the sight of her wide field of leaning spires, wrenched cope- stones, and crosses all adroop (like canted yards of anchored fleets); and her suburban avenues of house-walls lying over upon each other, as a tossed pack of cards; -- it is not these things alone which make tearless Lima, the strangest, saddest city thou can'st see. For Lima has taken the white veil; and there is a higher horror in this whiteness of her woe. Old as Pizarro, this whiteness keeps her ruins for ever new; admits not the cheerful greenness of complete decay; spreads over her broken ramparts the rigid pallor of an apoplexy that fixes its own distortions.

I know that, to the common apprehension, this phenomenon of whiteness is not confessed to be the prime agent in exaggerating the terror of objects otherwise terrible; nor to the unimaginative mind is there aught of terror in those appearances whose awfulness to another mind almost solely consists in this one phenomenon, especially when exhibited under any form at all approaching to muteness or universality. What I mean by these two statements may perhaps be respectively elucidated by the following examples.

First: The mariner, when drawing nigh the coasts of foreign lands, if by night he hear the roar of breakers, starts to vigilance, and feels just enough of trepidation to sharpen all his faculties; but under precisely similar circumstances, let him be called from his hammock to view his ship sailing through a midnight sea of milky whiteness -- as if from encircling headlands shoals of combed white bears were swimming round him, then he feels a silent, superstitious dread; the shrouded phantom of the whitened waters is horrible to him as a real ghost; in vain the lead assures him he is still off soundings; heart and helm they both go down; he never rests till blue water is under him again. Yet where is the mariner who will tell thee, 'Sir, it was not so much the fear of striking hidden rocks, as the fear of that hideous whiteness that so stirred me?'

Second: To the native Indian of Peru, the continual sight of the snow-howdahed Andes conveys naught of dread, except, perhaps, in the mere fancying of the eternal frosted desolateness reigning at such vast altitudes, and the natural conceit of what a fearfulness it would be to lose oneself in such inhuman solitudes. Much the same is it with the backwoodsman of the West, who with comparative indifference views an unbounded prairie sheeted with driven snow, no shadow of tree or twig to break the fixed trance of whiteness. Not so the sailor, beholding the scenery of the Antarctic seas; where at times, by some infernal trick of legerdemain in the powers of frost and air, he, shivering and half shipwrecked, instead of rainbows speaking hope and solace to his misery, views what seems a boundless church-yard grinning upon him with its lean ice monuments and splintered crosses.

But thou sayest, methinks this white-lead chapter about whiteness is but a white flag hung out from a craven soul; thou surrenderest to a hypo, Ishmael.

Tell me, why this strong young colt, foaled in some peaceful valley of Vermont, far removed from all beasts of prey -- why is it that upon the sunniest day, if you but shake a fresh buffalo robe behind him, so that he cannot even see it, but only smells its wild animal muskiness -- why will he start, snort, and with bursting eyes paw the ground in phrensies of affright? There is no remembrance in him of any gorings of wild creatures in his green northern home, so that the strange muskiness he smells cannot recall to him anything associated with the experience of former perils; for what knows he, this New England colt, of the black bisons of distant Oregon?

No: but here thou beholdest even in a dumb brute, the instinct of the knowledge of the demonism in the world. Though thousands of miles from Oregon, still when he smells that savage musk, the rending, goring bison herds are as present as to the deserted wild foal of the prairies, which this instant they may be trampling into dust.

Thus, then, the muffled rollings of a milky sea; the bleak rustlings of the festooned frosts of mountains; the desolate shiftings of the windrowed snows of prairies; all these, to Ishmael, are as the shaking of that buffalo robe to the frightened colt!

Though neither knows where lie the nameless things of which the mystic sign gives forth such hints; yet with me, as with the colt, somewhere those things must exist. Though in many of its aspects this visible world seems formed in love, the invisible spheres were formed in fright.

But not yet have we solved the incantation of this whiteness, and learned why it appeals with such power to the soul; and more strange and far more portentous -- why, as we have seen, it is at once the most meaning symbol of spiritual things, nay, the very veil of the Christian's Deity; and yet should be as it is, the intensifying agent in things the most appalling to mankind.

Is it that by its indefiniteness it shadows forth the heartless voids and immensities of the universe, and thus stabs us from behind with the thought of annihilation, when beholding the white depths of the milky way? Or is it, that as in essence whiteness is not so much a color as the visible absence of color, and at the same time the concrete of all colors; is it for these reasons that there is such a dumb blankness, full of meaning, in a wide landscape of snows -- a colorless, all- color of atheism from which we shrink? And when we consider that other theory of the natural philosophers, that all other earthly hues -- every stately or lovely emblazoning -- the sweet tinges of sunset skies and woods; yea, and the gilded velvets of butterflies, and the butterfly cheeks of young girls; all these are but subtile deceits, not actually inherent in substances, but only laid on from without; so that all deified Nature absolutely paints like the harlot, whose allurements cover nothing but the charnel-house within; and when we proceed further, and consider that the mystical cosmetic which produces every one of her hues, the great principle of light, for ever remains white or colorless in itself, and if operating without medium upon matter, would touch all objects, even tulips and roses, with its own blank tinge -- pondering all this, the palsied universe lies before us a leper; and like wilful travellers in Lapland, who refuse to wear colored and coloring glasses upon their eyes, so the wretched infidel gazes himself blind at the monumental white shroud that wraps all the prospect around him. And of all these things the Albino Whale was the symbol. Wonder ye then at the fiery hunt?

# A Deeper Look:

1.      How does the author of this piece of writing show the color of animals?

2.      What kind of characteristics does the author associate with the color white?

3.      When might it be appropriate to simply mention a color in your own writing as a means to describe the color of an object? When might you find it appropriate to use other words to describe the color itself?

# Environment:

## Exercises to help set the scene

# 3

# In Your Shoes

Many people believe that shoes say a lot about who you are. That simply isn't true. No other piece of clothing is more deceiving than a pair of shoes. They act as a mask for what we may be trying to pretend to be to lure a specific respect from people who seem to be more interested in shoes than human nature.

Although shoes can be quite the little liars, their stories are often deep and hidden. How well do you know your own shoes? If they could talk what would they say about you?

For this exercise you will need a shoe. If you're wearing shoes, take them off. If you're not wearing shoes, get a pair that you often wear. Shoes are never perfect. Take a moment and inspect your shoes. Make a list of any unique marks left on the shoe. Are there any abrasions? Tears? Scuffs? Cut marks? Is there any wear in a specific place? Loose pieces of sole? Splitting in any areas? Are there scuffs hidden beneath polish that you wouldn't notice if you weren't looking for them?

List as many scars as you want. Then list where those marks came from. If you don't know, write down what you think could have caused the mark.

After you've inspected your shoe and recalled as much memory as you could, choose a mark on your list and in a page or two of writing, share a story about how that scar on your shoe came to be.

Shoes don't say anything about who you are, but they do keep a pretty good record of where you've been, how you got there and why you even went in the first place.

Where have your shoes taken you? Share one of their stories.

# The Little Match Girl

By Hans Christian Andersen

(1805-1875)

Most terribly cold it was; it snowed, and was nearly quite dark, and evening-- the last evening of the year. In this cold and darkness there went along the street a poor little girl, bareheaded, and with naked feet. When she left home she had slippers on, it is true; but what was the good of that? They were very large slippers, which her mother had hitherto worn; so large were they; and the poor little thing lost them as she scuffled away across the street, because of two carriages that rolled by dreadfully fast.

One slipper was nowhere to be found; the other had been laid hold of by an urchin, and off he ran with it; he thought it would do capitally for a cradle when he some day or other should have children himself. So the little maiden walked on with her tiny naked feet, that were quite red and blue from cold. She carried a quantity of matches in an old apron, and she held a bundle of them in her hand. Nobody had bought anything of her the whole livelong day; no one had given her a single farthing.

She crept along trembling with cold and hunger--a very picture of sorrow, the poor little thing!

The flakes of snow covered her long fair hair, which fell in beautiful curls around her neck; but of that, of course, she never once now thought. From all the windows the candles were gleaming, and it smelt so deliciously of roast goose, for you know it was New Year's Eve; yes, of that she thought.

In a corner formed by two houses, of which one advanced more than the other, she seated herself down and cowered together. Her little feet she had drawn close up to her, but she grew colder and colder, and to go home she did not venture, for she had not sold any matches and could not bring a farthing of money: from her father she would certainly get blows, and at home it was cold too, for above her she had only the roof, through which the wind whistled, even though the largest cracks were stopped up with straw and rags.

Her little hands were almost numbed with cold. Oh! a match might afford her a world of comfort, if she only dared take a single one out of the bundle, draw it against the wall, and warm her fingers by it. She drew one out. "Rischt!" how it blazed, how it burnt! It was a warm, bright flame, like a candle, as she held her hands over it: it was a wonderful light. It seemed really to the little maiden as though she were sitting before a large iron stove, with burnished brass feet and a brass ornament at top. The fire burned with such blessed influence; it warmed so delightfully. The little girl had already stretched out her feet to warm them too; but--the small flame went out, the stove vanished: she had only the remains of the burnt-out match in her hand.

She rubbed another against the wall: it burned brightly, and where the light fell on the wall, there the wall became transparent like a veil, so that she could see into the room. On the table was spread a snow-white tablecloth; upon it was a splendid porcelain service, and the roast goose was steaming famously with its stuffing of apple and dried plums. And what was still more capital to behold was, the goose hopped down from the dish, reeled about on the floor with knife and fork in its breast, till it came up to the poor little girl; when--the match went out and nothing but the thick, cold, damp wall was left behind. She lighted another match. Now there she was sitting under the most magnificent Christmas tree: it was still larger, and more decorated than the one which she had seen through the glass door in the rich merchant's house.

Thousands of lights were burning on the green branches, and gaily-colored pictures, such as she had seen in the shop-windows, looked down upon her. The little maiden stretched out her hands towards them when--the match went out. The lights of the Christmas tree rose higher and higher, she saw them now as stars in heaven; one fell down and formed a long trail of fire.

"Someone is just dead!" said the little girl; for her old grandmother, the only person who had loved her, and who was now no more, had told her, that when a star falls, a soul ascends to God.

She drew another match against the wall: it was again light, and in the lustre there stood the old grandmother, so bright and radiant, so mild, and with such an expression of love.

"Grandmother!" cried the little one. "Oh, take me with you! You go away when the match burns out; you vanish like the warm stove, like the delicious roast goose, and like the magnificent Christmas tree!" And she rubbed the whole bundle of matches quickly against the wall, for she wanted to be quite sure of keeping her grandmother near her. And the matches gave such a brilliant light that it was brighter than at noon-day: never formerly had the grandmother been so beautiful and so tall. She took the little maiden, on her arm, and both flew in brightness and in joy so high, so very high, and then above was neither cold, nor hunger, nor anxiety--they were with God.

But in the corner, at the cold hour of dawn, sat the poor girl, with rosy cheeks and with a smiling mouth, leaning against the wall--frozen to death on the last evening of the old year. Stiff and stark sat the child there with her matches, of which one bundle had been burnt. "She wanted to warm herself," people said. No one had the slightest suspicion of what beautiful things she had seen; no one even dreamed of the splendor in which, with her grandmother she had entered on the joys of a new year.

# A Deeper Look:

1.        What kind of role did shoes play in this short story?

2.        What kind of scars appeared on the little matchgirl's shoes? What did they show?

3.        What do you find more interesting to write about? Stories that show scars? Or stories that show none? Why?

# Windows

One of the world's greatest literary artists was Ernest Hemingway. Readers love his work while other readers hate it. However you feel about Hemingway, he shook literary circles by suggesting that a story is like an iceberg: only a small portion of ice appears above the water and a much larger portion hides beneath the surface. Like the iceberg, the reader sees only the text of a story. The real story can be what the reader doesn't see directly within the words on the page.

As writers, we encounter the common misconception that we need to spell out every little detail for a stupid audience, but audiences aren't stupid and if they are, it's only because too many artists and entertainers have trained them to be. We might think we have to show the happy ending rather than trust that the reader can see the resolution coming. We might even become repetitive trying to spell out everything.

For this exercise, we are going to look for a story we don't see in the text. I won't throw a Hemingway story at you. Instead we'll try a simpler approach. For this exercise, find a window or a doorway near a place where you can sit down with your pad of paper and pencil (or use your laptop). Don't be afraid to get out of the house for this exercise (In fact, it might even make the experience better for you). Sit as long as you like and watch out the window or doorway.

As you see action take place in the frame of the window or doorway, quickly jot it down. Without getting up and without trying to see beyond what you can already see, write a list of ten possibilities of why that action might be happening.

For instance, if you choose to stare out a doorway and you see a woman rush past holding a folder. Ask yourself about what you don't see. Where is she headed? Why is she headed that way? How is she pacing herself? Why might she be pacing herself this way?

Create a list of 20 questions (more if you like) about what you just witnessed through the window. Ask about behavior; facial expressions; sounds that you can't see; if there are sounds, does the person or object you observe seem to move towards or away from these sounds?

Once you have your list of 20 questions. Think of three possible answers to each question. Write them down.

Now study the answers that you have come up with. Do any of the answers relate to each other? Is there a common theme among some of your answers? If you have any that seem related to each other, circle them.

Now, let's write. Using only a view through a doorway or a window, write a short, one to three page story that alludes to something more epic than that doorway or window allow you to actually see. Use what you can view in this doorway to suggest a bigger story beyond the sight of its frame. In other words, create a scenario that's interesting enough to make your reader want to stand up from his or her chair and look through that opening at the bigger event.

Use the questions and answers you created to show little hints of the bigger story.

# The Adventures of Huckleberry Finn
By Mark Twain
(1835-1910)

## Chapter One

YOU don't know about me without you have read a book by the name of The Adventures of Tom Sawyer; but that ain't no matter. That book was made by Mr. Mark Twain, and he told the truth, mainly. There was things which he stretched, but mainly he told the truth. That is nothing. I never seen anybody but lied one time or another, without it was Aunt Polly, or the widow, or maybe Mary. Aunt Polly -- Tom's Aunt Polly, she is -- and Mary, and the Widow Douglas is all told about in that book, which is mostly a true book, with some stretchers, as I said before.

Now the way that the book winds up is this: Tom and me found the money that the robbers hid in the cave, and it made us rich. We got six thousand dollars apiece -- all gold. It was an awful sight of money when it was piled up. Well, Judge Thatcher he took it and put it out at interest, and it fetched us a dollar a day apiece all the year round -- more than a body could tell what to do with. The Widow Douglas she took me for her son, and allowed she would sivilize me; but it was rough living in the house all the time, considering how dismal regular and decent the widow was in all her ways; and so when I couldn't stand it no longer I lit out. I got into my old rags and my sugar-hogshead again, and was free and satisfied. But Tom Sawyer he hunted me up and said he was going to start a band of robbers, and I might join if I would go back to the widow and be respectable. So I went back.

The widow she cried over me, and called me a poor lost lamb, and she called me a lot of other names, too, but she never meant no harm by it. She put me in them new clothes again, and I couldn't do nothing but sweat and sweat, and feel all cramped up. Well, then, the old thing commenced again. The widow rung a bell for supper, and you had to come to time. When you got to the table you couldn't go right to eating, but you had to wait for the widow to tuck down her head and grumble a little over the victuals, though there warn't really anything the matter with them, -- that is, nothing only everything was cooked by itself. In a barrel of odds and ends it is different; things get mixed up, and the juice kind of swaps around, and the things go better.

After supper she got out her book and learned me about Moses and the Bulrushers, and I was in a sweat to find out all about him; but by and by she let it out that Moses had been dead a considerable long time; so then I didn't care no more about him, because I don't take no stock in dead people.

Pretty soon I wanted to smoke, and asked the widow to let me. But she wouldn't. She said it was a mean practice and wasn't clean, and I must try to not do it any more. That is just the way with some people. They get down on a thing when they don't know nothing about it. Here she was a-bothering about Moses, which was no kin to her, and no use to anybody, being gone, you see, yet finding a power of fault with me for doing a thing that had some good in it. And she took snuff, too; of course that was all right, because she done it herself.

Her sister, Miss Watson, a tolerable slim old maid, with goggles on, had just come to live with her, and took a set at me now with a spelling-book. She worked me middling hard for about an hour, and then the widow made her ease up. I couldn't stood it much longer. Then for an hour it was deadly dull, and I was fidgety. Miss Watson would say, "Don't put your feet up there, Huckleberry;" and "Don't scrunch up like that, Huckleberry -- set up straight;" and pretty soon she would say, "Don't gap and stretch like that, Huckleberry -- why don't you try to behave?" Then she told me all about the bad place, and I said I wished I was there. She got mad then, but I didn't mean no harm. All I wanted was to go somewheres; all I wanted was a change, I warn't particular. She said it was wicked to say what I said; said she wouldn't say it for the whole world; she was going to live so as to go to the good place. Well, I couldn't see no advantage in going where she was going, so I made up my mind I wouldn't try for it. But I never said so, because it would only make trouble, and wouldn't do no good.

Now she had got a start, and she went on and told me all about the good place. She said all a body would have to do there was to go around all day long with a harp and sing, forever and ever. So I didn't think much of it. But I never said so. I asked her if she reckoned Tom Sawyer would go there, and she said not by a considerable sight. I was glad about that, because I wanted him and me to be together.

Miss Watson she kept pecking at me, and it got tiresome and lonesome. By and by they fetched the niggers in and had prayers, and then everybody was off to bed. I went up to my room with a piece of candle, and put it on the table. Then I set down in a chair by the window and tried to think of something cheerful, but it warn't no use. I felt so lonesome I most wished I was dead. The stars were shining, and the leaves rustled in the woods ever so mournful; and I heard an owl, away off, who-whooing about somebody that was dead, and a whippowill and a dog crying about somebody that was going to die; and the wind was trying to whisper something to me, and I couldn't make out what it was, and so it made the cold shivers run over me. Then away out in the woods I heard that kind of a sound that a ghost makes when it wants to tell about something that's on its mind and can't make itself understood, and so can't rest easy in its grave, and has to go about that way every night grieving. I got so down-hearted and scared I did wish I had some company. Pretty soon a spider went crawling up my shoulder, and I flipped it off and it lit in the candle; and before I could budge it was all shriveled up. I didn't need anybody to tell me that that was an awful bad sign and would fetch me some bad luck, so I was scared and most shook the clothes off of me. I got up and turned around in my tracks three times and crossed my breast every time; and then I tied up a little lock of my hair with a thread to keep witches away. But I hadn't no confidence. You do that when you've lost a horseshoe that you've found, instead of nailing it up over the door, but I hadn't ever heard anybody say it was any way to keep off bad luck when you'd killed a spider.

I set down again, a-shaking all over, and got out my pipe for a smoke; for the house was all as still as death now, and so the widow wouldn't know. Well, after a long time I heard the clock away off in the town go boom -- boom -- boom -- twelve licks; and all still again -- stiller than ever. Pretty soon I heard a twig snap down in the dark amongst the trees -- something was a stirring. I set still and listened. Directly I could just barely hear a "me-yow! me-yow!" down there. That was good! Says I, "me-yow! me-yow!" as soft as I could, and then I put out the light and scrambled out of the window on to the shed. Then I slipped down to the ground and crawled in among the trees, and, sure enough, there was Tom Sawyer waiting for me.

# A Deeper Look:

1. In this story, where does there seem to be more life? Inside the room where the main character is? Or outside?

2. In what ways is Huck Finn drawn to be outside?

3. Think about your own observations during your own exercise. Did any of these events make you want to look outside? How might you convey this interest to readers through your writing?

# Life Goes On

For this exercise, you will need a pad of paper, a pen and a public place where you can watch other people freely. Pick a person and watch him or her. What is this person doing? How is she walking? Is she stopping, then walking with someone else? Does she have a unique way that she looks at items, how she steps, greets people, or keeps to herself? How does she sound when she speaks? Write this information all down.

If the person you're watching interacts with another, begin observing the new subject instead and continue to do so until he or she interacts with someone else. If a person interacts with you, you must pick an entirely new person and start the process over. Use your time to pick up on all the detail about how any of these people behave.

Spend 15 to 30 minutes sitting and watching. When you're done, go through your notes. Choose three common activities that may have been shared by several people.

What were these actions? Did several people pick up a book? Read a sign? Ask someone else for directions?

Now, choose two or more people who performed each activity and make one comment about one detail about that activity that each person performed differently from one another.

Once you've done this for three different activities, choose one example of the people you just watched and answer these following questions:

Who is this person?

Why do you think this person is in this place today?

Is this person confident or shy? What did this person do to make you think this?

What do you imagine this person does for a living?

Do you think this person is good at it?

If you walked up to this person and started talking to him or her, what would you say to start the conversation?

If you walked up to this person and started talking, how do you imagine they would respond to you?

# The Sign of Four

By Sir Arthur Conan Doyle

(1859-1930)

## Chapter I The Science of Deduction

Sherlock Holmes took his bottle from the corner of the mantel-piece and his hypodermic syringe from its neat morocco case. With his long, white, nervous fingers he adjusted the delicate needle, and rolled back his left shirt-cuff. For some little time his eyes rested thoughtfully upon the sinewy forearm and wrist all dotted and scarred with innumerable puncture-marks. Finally he thrust the sharp point home, pressed down the tiny piston, and sank back into the velvet-lined arm-chair with a long sigh of satisfaction.

Three times a day for many months I had witnessed this performance, but custom had not reconciled my mind to it. On the contrary, from day to day I had become more irritable at the sight, and my conscience swelled nightly within me at the thought that I had lacked the courage to protest. Again and again I had registered a vow that I should deliver my soul upon the subject, but there was that in the cool, nonchalant air of my companion which made him the last man with whom one would care to take anything approaching to a liberty. His great powers, his masterly manner, and the experience which I had had of his many extraordinary qualities, all made me diffident and backward in crossing him.

Yet upon that afternoon, whether it was the Beaune which I had taken with my lunch, or the additional exasperation produced by the extreme deliberation of his manner, I suddenly felt that I could hold out no longer.

"Which is it to-day?" I asked,—"morphine or cocaine?"

He raised his eyes languidly from the old black-letter volume which he had opened. "It is cocaine," he said,—"a seven-per-cent. solution. Would you care to try it?"

"No, indeed," I answered, brusquely. "My constitution has not got over the Afghan campaign yet. I cannot afford to throw any extra strain upon it."

He smiled at my vehemence. "Perhaps you are right, Watson," he said. "I suppose that its influence is physically a bad one. I find it, however, so transcendently stimulating and clarifying to the mind that its secondary action is a matter of small moment."

"But consider!" I said, earnestly. "Count the cost! Your brain may, as you say, be roused and excited, but it is a pathological and morbid process, which involves increased tissue-change and may at last leave a permanent weakness. You know, too, what a black reaction comes upon you. Surely the game is hardly worth the candle. Why should you, for a mere passing pleasure, risk the loss of those great powers with which you have been endowed? Remember that I speak not only as one comrade to another, but as a medical man to one for whose constitution he is to some extent answerable."

He did not seem offended. On the contrary, he put his finger-tips together and leaned his elbows on the arms of his chair, like one who has a relish for conversation.

"My mind," he said, "rebels at stagnation. Give me problems, give me work, give me the most abstruse cryptogram or the most intricate analysis, and I am in my own proper atmosphere. I can dispense then with artificial stimulants. But I abhor the dull routine of existence. I crave for mental exaltation. That is why I have chosen my own particular profession,—or rather created it, for I am the only one in the world."

"The only unofficial detective?" I said, raising my eyebrows.

"The only unofficial consulting detective," he answered. "I am the last and highest court of appeal in detection. When Gregson or Lestrade or Athelney Jones are out of their depths—which, by the way, is their normal state—the matter is laid before me. I examine the data, as an expert, and pronounce a specialist's opinion. I claim no credit in such cases. My name figures in no newspaper. The work itself, the pleasure of finding a field for my peculiar powers, is my highest reward. But you have yourself had some experience of my methods of work in the Jefferson Hope case."

"Yes, indeed," said I, cordially. "I was never so struck by anything in my life. I even embodied it in a small brochure with the somewhat fantastic title of 'A Study in Scarlet.'"

He shook his head sadly. "I glanced over it," said he. "Honestly, I cannot congratulate you upon it. Detection is, or ought to be, an exact science, and should be treated in the same cold and unemotional manner. You have attempted to tinge it with romanticism, which produces much the same effect as if you worked a love-story or an elopement into the fifth proposition of Euclid."

"But the romance was there," I remonstrated. "I could not tamper with the facts."

"Some facts should be suppressed, or at least a just sense of proportion should be observed in treating them. The only point in the case which deserved mention was the curious analytical reasoning from effects to causes by which I succeeded in unraveling it."

I was annoyed at this criticism of a work which had been specially designed to please him. I confess, too, that I was irritated by the egotism which seemed to demand that every line of my pamphlet should be devoted to his own special doings. More than once during the years that I had lived with him in Baker Street I had observed that a small vanity underlay my companion's quiet and didactic manner. I made no remark, however, but sat nursing my wounded leg. I had a Jezail bullet through it some time before, and, though it did not prevent me from walking, it ached wearily at every change of the weather.

"My practice has extended recently to the Continent," said Holmes, after a while, filling up his old brier-root pipe. "I was consulted last week by Francois Le Villard, who, as you probably know, has come rather to the front lately in the French detective service. He has all the Celtic power of quick intuition, but he is deficient in the wide range of exact knowledge which is essential to the higher developments of his art. The case was concerned with a will, and possessed some features of interest. I was able to refer him to two parallel cases, the one at Riga in 1857, and the other at St. Louis in 1871, which have suggested to him the true solution. Here is the letter which I had this morning acknowledging my assistance." He tossed over, as he spoke, a crumpled sheet of foreign notepaper. I glanced my eyes down it, catching a profusion of notes of admiration, with stray "magnifiques," "coup-de-maitres," and "tours-de-force," all testifying to the ardent admiration of the Frenchman.

"He speaks as a pupil to his master," said I.

"Oh, he rates my assistance too highly," said Sherlock Holmes, lightly. "He has considerable gifts himself. He possesses two out of the three qualities necessary for the ideal detective. He has the power of observation and that of deduction. He is only wanting in knowledge; and that may come in time. He is now translating my small works into French."

"Your works?"

"Oh, didn't you know?" he cried, laughing. "Yes, I have been guilty of several monographs. They are all upon technical subjects. Here, for example, is one 'Upon the Distinction between the Ashes of the Various Tobaccoes.' In it I enumerate a hundred and forty forms of cigar-, cigarette-, and pipe-tobacco, with colored plates illustrating the difference in the ash. It is a point which is continually turning up in criminal trials, and which is sometimes of supreme importance as a clue. If you can say definitely, for example, that some murder has been done by a man who was smoking an Indian lunkah, it obviously narrows your field of search. To the trained eye there is as much difference between the black ash of a Trichinopoly and the white fluff of bird's-eye as there is between a cabbage and a potato."

"You have an extraordinary genius for minutiae," I remarked.

"I appreciate their importance. Here is my monograph upon the tracing of footsteps, with some remarks upon the uses of plaster of Paris as a preserver of impresses. Here, too, is a curious little work upon the influence of a trade upon the form of the hand, with lithotypes of the hands of slaters, sailors, corkcutters, compositors, weavers, and diamond-polishers. That is a matter of great practical interest to the scientific detective,—especially in cases of unclaimed bodies, or in discovering the antecedents of criminals. But I weary you with my hobby."

"Not at all," I answered, earnestly. "It is of the greatest interest to me, especially since I have had the opportunity of observing your practical application of it. But you spoke just now of observation and deduction. Surely the one to some extent implies the other."

"Why, hardly," he answered, leaning back luxuriously in his arm-chair, and sending up thick blue wreaths from his pipe. "For example, observation shows me that you have been to the Wigmore Street Post-Office this morning, but deduction lets me know that when there you dispatched a telegram."

"Right!" said I. "Right on both points! But I confess that I don't see how you arrived at it. It was a sudden impulse upon my part, and I have mentioned it to no one."

"It is simplicity itself," he remarked, chuckling at my surprise,—"so absurdly simple that an explanation is superfluous; and yet it may serve to define the limits of observation and of deduction. Observation tells me that you have a little reddish mould adhering to your instep. Just opposite the Seymour Street Office they have taken up the pavement and thrown up some earth which lies in such a way that it is difficult to avoid treading in it in entering. The earth is of this peculiar reddish tint which is found, as far as I know, nowhere else in the neighborhood. So much is observation. The rest is deduction."

"How, then, did you deduce the telegram?"

"Why, of course I knew that you had not written a letter, since I sat opposite to you all morning. I see also in your open desk there that you have a sheet of stamps and a thick bundle of post-cards. What could you go into the post-office for, then, but to send a wire? Eliminate all other factors, and the one which remains must be the truth."

"In this case it certainly is so," I replied, after a little thought. "The thing, however, is, as you say, of the simplest. Would you think me impertinent if I were to put your theories to a more severe test?"

"On the contrary," he answered, "it would prevent me from taking a second dose of cocaine. I should be delighted to look into any problem which you might submit to me."

"I have heard you say that it is difficult for a man to have any object in daily use without leaving the impress of his individuality upon it in such a way that a trained observer might read it. Now, I have here a watch which has recently come into my possession. Would you have the kindness to let me have an opinion upon the character or habits of the late owner?"

I handed him over the watch with some slight feeling of amusement in my heart, for the test was, as I thought, an impossible one, and I intended it as a lesson against the somewhat dogmatic tone which he occasionally assumed. He balanced the watch in his hand, gazed hard at the dial, opened the back, and examined the works, first with his naked eyes and then with a powerful convex lens. I could hardly keep from smiling at his crestfallen face when he finally snapped the case to and handed it back.

"There are hardly any data," he remarked. "The watch has been recently cleaned, which robs me of my most suggestive facts."

"You are right," I answered. "It was cleaned before being sent to me." In my heart I accused my companion of putting forward a most lame and impotent excuse to cover his failure. What data could he expect from an uncleaned watch?

"Though unsatisfactory, my research has not been entirely barren," he observed, staring up at the ceiling with dreamy, lack-lustre eyes. "Subject to your correction, I should judge that the watch belonged to your elder brother, who inherited it from your father."

"That you gather, no doubt, from the H. W. upon the back?"

"Quite so. The W. suggests your own name. The date of the watch is nearly fifty years back, and the initials are as old as the watch: so it was made for the last generation. Jewelry usually descends to the eldest son, and he is most likely to have the same name as the father. Your father has, if I remember right, been dead many years. It has, therefore, been in the hands of your eldest brother."

"Right, so far," said I. "Anything else?"

"He was a man of untidy habits,—very untidy and careless. He was left with good prospects, but he threw away his chances, lived for some time in poverty with occasional short intervals of prosperity, and finally, taking to drink, he died. That is all I can gather."

I sprang from my chair and limped impatiently about the room with considerable bitterness in my heart.

"This is unworthy of you, Holmes," I said. "I could not have believed that you would have descended to this. You have made inquires into the history of my unhappy brother, and you now pretend to deduce this knowledge in some fanciful way. You cannot expect me to believe that you have read all this from his old watch! It is unkind, and, to speak plainly, has a touch of charlatanism in it."

"My dear doctor," said he, kindly, "pray accept my apologies. Viewing the matter as an abstract problem, I had forgotten how personal and painful a thing it might be to you. I assure you, however, that I never even knew that you had a brother until you handed me the watch."

"Then how in the name of all that is wonderful did you get these facts? They are absolutely correct in every particular."

"Ah, that is good luck. I could only say what was the balance of probability. I did not at all expect to be so accurate."

"But it was not mere guess-work?"

"No, no: I never guess. It is a shocking habit,—destructive to the logical faculty. What seems strange to you is only so because you do not follow my train of thought or observe the small facts upon which large inferences may depend. For example, I began by stating that your brother was careless. When you observe the lower part of that watch-case you notice that it is not only dinted in two places, but it is cut and marked all over from the habit of keeping other hard objects, such as coins or keys, in the same pocket. Surely it is no great feat to assume that a man who treats a fifty-guinea watch so cavalierly must be a careless man. Neither is it a very far-fetched inference that a man who inherits one article of such value is pretty well provided for in other respects."

I nodded, to show that I followed his reasoning.

"It is very customary for pawnbrokers in England, when they take a watch, to scratch the number of the ticket with a pin-point upon the inside of the case. It is more handy than a label, as there is no risk of the number being lost or transposed. There are no less than four such numbers visible to my lens on the inside of this case. Inference,—that your brother was often at low water. Secondary inference,—that he had occasional bursts of prosperity, or he could not have redeemed the pledge. Finally, I ask you to look at the inner plate, which contains the key-hole. Look at the thousands of scratches all round the hole,—marks where the key has slipped. What sober man's key could have scored those grooves? But you will never see a drunkard's watch without them. He winds it at night, and he leaves these traces of his unsteady hand. Where is the mystery in all this?"

"It is as clear as daylight," I answered. "I regret the injustice which I did you. I should have had more faith in your marvellous faculty. May I ask whether you have any professional inquiry on foot at present?"

"None. Hence the cocaine. I cannot live without brain-work. What else is there to live for? Stand at the window here. Was ever such a dreary, dismal, unprofitable world? See how the yellow fog swirls down the street and drifts across the dun-colored houses. What could be more hopelessly prosaic and material? What is the use of having powers, doctor, when one has no field upon which to exert them? Crime is commonplace, existence is commonplace, and no qualities save those which are commonplace have any function upon earth."

I had opened my mouth to reply to this tirade, when with a crisp knock our landlady entered, bearing a card upon the brass salver.

"A young lady for you, sir," she said, addressing my companion.

"Miss Mary Morstan," he read. "Hum! I have no recollection of the name. Ask the young lady to step up, Mrs. Hudson. Don't go, doctor. I should prefer that you remain."

# A Deeper Look:

1.          What kind of person is Holmes? What about Watson,
            what kind of person is he?

2.          Is there anything in the way these two speak to each
            other that gives away what kind of person each of these
            individuals is? Something they say? Something they don't
            say?

3.          Think about your own exercise and the people you
            observed. What kind of remark might he or she make
            that might suggest the type of person you analyzed him
            or her to be? Do you think that remark would be enough
            to convey that to your reader? What else might be needed
            to show one of these people to your reader?

# Wrapping Presents

Detail can be easy to write about—that is, the detail we like can be easy to write about. But what about the detail writer's don't like? The details we find boring? It's easy to skip those parts. Even the most boring detail can be entertaining to readers, if the author takes time to show it well.

Remember Christmas or your birthday, when you got presents? As a child, maybe even as a teen, you cared mostly about what someone had hidden rather than the useless wrapping paper and decoration. You tore off the paper and any ornament to get at the exciting center. As you grew older, maybe you stopped caring so much about the ritual wrapping and were simply content with someone handing you a gift in a plastic shopping bag and saying "here you go." As we get elderly, maybe fixed income and shaky hands make it difficult to wrap presents for all the would-be excited grandchildren and great-grandchildren. Maybe people who notice these difficulties might pay attention to all the work that mom or grandma put into wrapping a present before diving into the gift itself. We might hear their own children saying "that's beautiful paper, Dad."

For this exercise, we're going to practice presenting detail that might not interest you.

We're going to wrap a present.

First, pick someone you would like to give the perfect present to. Maybe it's something you wish you could afford. Maybe it's something you're saving up to purchase. Maybe it's a rare item. Write down what you would like to give a particular someone if you could.

Write down what that item is. Write down the name of the person you want to give this gift to. Even if the present seems unwrappable, every item has something about it that can be wrapped. For instance, if you said you'd like to give someone a trip around the world, plane tickets or tourist guides can be wrapped. Write down what the actual object is that you could give to your someone to represent your gift, either the gift itself or an item associated with the gift. Do not write down any detail of this object just identify what it is and write it down.

For what event would you give this person this gift? Write that down.

Now, think of a container to hide the object in. However, there is one rule, you may not use a pre-fabricated box or envelope of any sort. You must think of some other means to contain the gift. Write down the item you would use to contain that gift.

Next, choose 15 items that you could use to decorate your gift. Each item must be unique. No cheating by saying blue paper, purple paper, red paper, blue ribbon, white ribbon, masking tape, duct tape, etc. Use completely unique and different items. Write these items down. Now using all of these items, write a paragraph or two describing how you would wrap your present and what it would finally look like with all the of the items you selected.

The final present can look any way you want it to (comical, romantic, carefree), but it must look appropriate for the person and the type of gift it is. For example, if you're writing about giving your wife a present for your 50th wedding anniversary, would you give her a wedding ring wrapped in two ceramic bowls with their rims super glued together, wrapped in fat bubble wrap and had a honking clown nose? Take pride in your present, wrap it suitably for the recipient, the event and the gift itself.

# A Christmas Carol

By Charles Dickens

(1812-1870)

## THE SECOND OF THE THREE SPIRITS.

Awaking in the middle of a prodigiously tough snore, and sitting up in bed to get his thoughts together, Scrooge had no occasion to be told that the bell was again upon the stroke of One. He felt that he was restored to consciousness in the right nick of time, for the especial purpose of holding a conference with the second messenger despatched to him through Jacob Marley's intervention. But finding that he turned uncomfortably cold when he began to wonder which of his curtains this new spectre would draw back, he put them every one aside with his own hands; and lying down again, established a sharp look-out all round the bed. For he wished to challenge the Spirit on the moment of its appearance, and did not wish to be taken by surprise, and made nervous.

Gentlemen of the free-and-easy sort, who plume themselves on being acquainted with a move or two, and being usually equal to the time-of-day, express the wide range of their capacity for adventure by observing that they are good for anything from pitch-and-toss to manslaughter; between which opposite extremes, no doubt, there lies a tolerably wide and comprehensive range of subjects. Without venturing for Scrooge quite as hardily as this, I don't mind calling on you to believe that he was ready for a good broad field of strange appearances, and that nothing between a baby and rhinoceros would have astonished him very much.

Now, being prepared for almost anything, he was not by any means prepared for nothing; and, consequently, when the Bell struck One, and no shape appeared, he was taken with a violent fit of trembling. Five minutes, ten minutes, a quarter of an hour went by, yet nothing came. All this time, he lay upon his bed, the very core and centre of a blaze of ruddy light, which streamed upon it when the clock proclaimed the hour; and which, being only light, was more alarming than a dozen ghosts, as he was powerless to make out what it meant, or would be at; and was sometimes apprehensive that he might be at that very moment an interesting case of spontaneous combustion, without having the consolation of knowing it. At last, however, he began to think—as you or I would have thought at first; for it is always the person not in the predicament who knows what ought to have been done in it, and would unquestionably have done it too—at last, I say, he began to think that the source and secret of this ghostly light might be in the adjoining room, from whence, on further tracing it, it seemed to shine. This idea taking full possession of his mind, he got up softly and shuffled in his slippers to the door.

The moment Scrooge's hand was on the lock, a strange voice called him by his name, and bade him enter. He obeyed.

It was his own room. There was no doubt about that. But it had undergone a surprising transformation. The walls and ceiling were so hung with living green, that it looked a perfect grove; from every part of which, bright gleaming berries glistened. The crisp leaves of holly, mistletoe, and ivy reflected back the light, as if so many little mirrors had been scattered there; and such a mighty blaze went roaring up the chimney, as that dull petrification of a hearth had never known in Scrooge's time, or Marley's, or for many and many a winter season gone. Heaped up on the floor, to form a kind of throne, were turkeys, geese, game, poultry, brawn, great joints of meat, sucking-pigs, long wreaths of sausages, mince-pies, plum-puddings, barrels of oysters, red-hot chestnuts, cherry-cheeked apples, juicy oranges, luscious pears, immense twelfth-cakes, and seething bowls of punch, that made the chamber dim with their delicious steam. In easy state upon this couch, there sat a jolly Giant, glorious to see; who bore a glowing torch, in shape not unlike Plenty's horn, and held it up, high up, to shed its light on Scrooge, as he came peeping round the door.

"Come in!" exclaimed the Ghost. "Come in! and know me better, man!"

Scrooge entered timidly, and hung his head before this Spirit. He was not the dogged Scrooge he had been; and though the Spirit's eyes were clear and kind, he did not like to meet them.

"I am the Ghost of Christmas Present," said the Spirit. "Look upon me!"

Scrooge reverently did so. It was clothed in one simple green robe, or mantle, bordered with white fur. This garment hung so loosely on the figure, that its capacious breast was bare, as if disdaining to be warded or concealed by any artifice. Its feet, observable beneath the ample folds of the garment, were also bare; and on its head it wore no other covering than a holly wreath, set here and there with shining icicles. Its dark brown curls were long and free; free as its genial face, its sparkling eye, its open hand, its cheery voice, its unconstrained demeanour, and its joyful air. Girded round its middle was an antique scabbard; but no sword was in it, and the ancient sheath was eaten up with rust.

"You have never seen the like of me before!" exclaimed the Spirit.

"Never," Scrooge made answer to it.

"Have never walked forth with the younger members of my family; meaning (for I am very young) my elder brothers born in these later years?" pursued the Phantom.

"I don't think I have," said Scrooge. "I am afraid I have not. Have you had many brothers, Spirit?"

"More than eighteen hundred," said the Ghost.

"A tremendous family to provide for!" muttered Scrooge.

The Ghost of Christmas Present rose.

"Spirit," said Scrooge submissively, "conduct me where you will. I went forth last night on compulsion, and I learnt a lesson which is working now. To-night, if you have aught to teach me, let me profit by it."

"Touch my robe!"

Scrooge did as he was told, and held it fast.

Holly, mistletoe, red berries, ivy, turkeys, geese, game, poultry, brawn, meat, pigs, sausages, oysters, pies, puddings, fruit, and punch, all vanished instantly. So did the room, the fire, the ruddy glow, the hour of night, and they stood in the city streets on Christmas morning, where (for the weather was severe) the people made a rough, but brisk and not unpleasant kind of music, in scraping the snow from the pavement in front of their dwellings, and from the tops of their houses, whence it was mad delight to the boys to see it come plumping down into the road below, and splitting into artificial little snow-storms.

The house fronts looked black enough, and the windows blacker, contrasting with the smooth white sheet of snow upon the roofs, and with the dirtier snow upon the ground; which last deposit had been ploughed up in deep furrows by the heavy wheels of carts and waggons; furrows that crossed and re-crossed each other hundreds of times where the great streets branched off; and made intricate channels, hard to trace in the thick yellow mud and icy water. The sky was gloomy, and the shortest streets were choked up with a dingy mist, half thawed, half frozen, whose heavier particles descended in a shower of sooty atoms, as if all the chimneys in Great Britain had, by one consent, caught fire, and were blazing away to their dear hearts' content. There was nothing very cheerful in the climate or the town, and yet was there an air of cheerfulness abroad that the clearest summer air and brightest summer sun might have endeavoured to diffuse in vain.

For, the people who were shovelling away on the housetops were jovial and full of glee; calling out to one another from the parapets, and now and then exchanging a facetious snowball—better-natured missile far than many a wordy jest—laughing heartily if it went right and not less heartily if it went wrong. The poulterers' shops were still half open, and the fruiterers' were radiant in their glory. There were great, round, pot-bellied baskets of chestnuts, shaped like the waistcoats of jolly old gentlemen, lolling at the doors, and tumbling out into the street in their apoplectic opulence. There were ruddy, brown-faced, broad-girthed Spanish Onions, shining in the fatness of their growth like Spanish Friars, and winking from their shelves in wanton slyness at the girls as they went by, and glanced demurely at the hung-up mistletoe. There were pears and apples, clustered high in blooming pyramids; there were bunches of grapes, made, in the shopkeepers' benevolence to dangle from conspicuous hooks, that people's mouths might water gratis as they passed; there were piles of filberts, mossy and brown, recalling, in their fragrance, ancient walks among the woods, and pleasant shufflings ankle deep through withered leaves; there were Norfolk Biffins, squat and swarthy, setting off the yellow of the oranges and lemons, and, in the great compactness of their juicy persons, urgently entreating and beseeching to be carried home in paper bags and eaten after dinner. The very gold and silver fish, set forth among these choice fruits in a bowl, though members of a dull and stagnant-blooded race, appeared to know that there was something going on; and, to a fish, went gasping round and round their little world in slow and passionless excitement.

The Grocers'! oh, the Grocers'! nearly closed, with perhaps two shutters down, or one; but through those gaps such glimpses! It was not alone that the scales descending on the counter made a merry sound, or that the twine and roller parted company so briskly, or that the canisters were rattled up and down like juggling tricks, or even that the blended scents of tea and coffee were so grateful to the nose, or even that the raisins were so plentiful and rare, the almonds so extremely white, the sticks of cinnamon so long and straight, the other spices so delicious, the candied fruits so caked and spotted with molten sugar as to make the coldest lookers-on feel faint and subsequently bilious. Nor was it that the figs were moist and pulpy, or that the French plums blushed in modest tartness from their highly-decorated boxes, or that everything was good to eat and in its Christmas dress; but the customers were all so hurried and so eager in the hopeful promise of the day, that they tumbled up against each other at the door, crashing their wicker baskets wildly, and left their purchases upon the counter, and came running back to fetch them, and committed hundreds of the like mistakes, in the best humour possible; while the Grocer and his people were so frank and fresh that the polished hearts with which they fastened their aprons behind might have been their own, worn outside for general inspection, and for Christmas daws to peck at if they chose.

But soon the steeples called good people all, to church and chapel, and away they came, flocking through the streets in their best clothes, and with their gayest faces. And at the same time there emerged from scores of bye-streets, lanes, and nameless turnings, innumerable people, carrying their dinners to the bakers' shops. The sight of these poor revellers appeared to interest the Spirit very much, for he stood with Scrooge beside him in a baker's doorway, and taking off the covers as their bearers passed, sprinkled incense on their dinners from his torch. And it was a very uncommon kind of torch, for once or twice when there were angry words between some dinner-carriers who had jostled each other, he shed a few drops of water on them from it, and their good humour was restored directly. For they said, it was a shame to quarrel upon Christmas Day. And so it was! God love it, so it was!

In time the bells ceased, and the bakers were shut up; and yet there was a genial shadowing forth of all these dinners and the progress of their cooking, in the thawed blotch of wet above each baker's oven; where the pavement smoked as if its stones were cooking too.

"Is there a peculiar flavour in what you sprinkle from your torch?" asked Scrooge.

"There is. My own."

"Would it apply to any kind of dinner on this day?" asked Scrooge.

"To any kindly given. To a poor one most."

"Why to a poor one most?" asked Scrooge.

"Because it needs it most."

"Spirit," said Scrooge, after a moment's thought, "I wonder you, of all the beings in the many worlds about us, should desire to cramp these people's opportunities of innocent enjoyment."

"I!" cried the Spirit.

"You would deprive them of their means of dining every seventh day, often the only day on which they can be said to dine at all," said Scrooge. "Wouldn't you?"

"I!" cried the Spirit.

"You seek to close these places on the Seventh Day?" said Scrooge. "And it comes to the same thing."

"I seek!" exclaimed the Spirit.

"Forgive me if I am wrong. It has been done in your name, or at least in that of your family," said Scrooge.

"There are some upon this earth of yours," returned the Spirit, "who lay claim to know us, and who do their deeds of passion, pride, ill-will, hatred, envy, bigotry, and selfishness in our name, who are as strange to us and all our kith and kin, as if they had never lived. Remember that, and charge their doings on themselves, not us."

Scrooge promised that he would; and they went on, invisible, as they had been before, into the suburbs of the town. It was a remarkable quality of the Ghost (which Scrooge had observed at the baker's), that notwithstanding his gigantic size, he could accommodate himself to any place with ease; and that he stood beneath a low roof quite as gracefully and like a supernatural creature, as it was possible he could have done in any lofty hall.

And perhaps it was the pleasure the good Spirit had in showing off this power of his, or else it was his own kind, generous, hearty nature, and his sympathy with all poor men, that led him straight to Scrooge's clerk's; for there he went, and took Scrooge with him, holding to his robe; and on the threshold of the door the Spirit smiled, and stopped to bless Bob Cratchit's dwelling with the sprinkling of his torch. Think of that! Bob had but fifteen "Bob" a-week himself; he pocketed on Saturdays but fifteen copies of his Christian name; and yet the Ghost of Christmas Present blessed his four-roomed house!

Then up rose Mrs. Cratchit, Cratchit's wife, dressed out but poorly in a twice-turned gown, but brave in ribbons, which are cheap and make a goodly show for sixpence; and she laid the cloth, assisted by Belinda Cratchit, second of her daughters, also brave in ribbons; while Master Peter Cratchit plunged a fork into the saucepan of potatoes, and getting the corners of his monstrous shirt collar (Bob's private property, conferred upon his son and heir in honour of the day) into his mouth, rejoiced to find himself so gallantly attired, and yearned to show his linen in the fashionable Parks. And now two smaller Cratchits, boy and girl, came tearing in, screaming that outside the baker's they had smelt the goose, and known it for their own; and basking in luxurious thoughts of sage and onion, these young Cratchits danced about the table, and exalted Master Peter Cratchit to the skies, while he (not proud, although his collars nearly choked him) blew the fire, until the slow potatoes bubbling up, knocked loudly at the saucepan-lid to be let out and peeled.

"What has ever got your precious father then?" said Mrs. Cratchit. "And your brother, Tiny Tim! And Martha warn't as late last Christmas Day by half-an-hour?"

"Here's Martha, mother!" said a girl, appearing as she spoke.

"Here's Martha, mother!" cried the two young Cratchits. "Hurrah! There's such a goose, Martha!"

"Why, bless your heart alive, my dear, how late you are!" said Mrs. Cratchit, kissing her a dozen times, and taking off her shawl and bonnet for her with officious zeal.

"We'd a deal of work to finish up last night," replied the girl, "and had to clear away this morning, mother!"

"Well! Never mind so long as you are come," said Mrs. Cratchit. "Sit ye down before the fire, my dear, and have a warm, Lord bless ye!"

"No, no! There's father coming," cried the two young Cratchits, who were everywhere at once. "Hide, Martha, hide!"

So Martha hid herself, and in came little Bob, the father, with at least three feet of comforter exclusive of the fringe, hanging down before him; and his threadbare clothes darned up and brushed, to look seasonable; and Tiny Tim upon his shoulder. Alas for Tiny Tim, he bore a little crutch, and had his limbs supported by an iron frame!

"Why, where's our Martha?" cried Bob Cratchit, looking round.

"Not coming," said Mrs. Cratchit.

"Not coming!" said Bob, with a sudden declension in his high spirits; for he had been Tim's blood horse all the way from church, and had come home rampant. "Not coming upon Christmas Day!"

Martha didn't like to see him disappointed, if it were only in joke; so she came out prematurely from behind the closet door, and ran into his arms, while the two young Cratchits hustled Tiny Tim, and bore him off into the wash-house, that he might hear the pudding singing in the copper.

"And how did little Tim behave?" asked Mrs. Cratchit, when she had rallied Bob on his credulity, and Bob had hugged his daughter to his heart's content.

"As good as gold," said Bob, "and better. Somehow he gets thoughtful, sitting by himself so much, and thinks the strangest things you ever heard. He told me, coming home, that he hoped the people saw him in the church, because he was a cripple, and it might be pleasant to them to remember upon Christmas Day, who made lame beggars walk, and blind men see."

Bob's voice was tremulous when he told them this, and trembled more when he said that Tiny Tim was growing strong and hearty.

His active little crutch was heard upon the floor, and back came Tiny Tim before another word was spoken, escorted by his brother and sister to his stool before the fire; and while Bob, turning up his cuffs—as if, poor fellow, they were capable of being made more shabby—compounded some hot mixture in a jug with gin and lemons, and stirred it round and round and put it on the hob to simmer; Master Peter, and the two ubiquitous young Cratchits went to fetch the goose, with which they soon returned in high procession.

Such a bustle ensued that you might have thought a goose the rarest of all birds; a feathered phenomenon, to which a black swan was a matter of course—and in truth it was something very like it in that house. Mrs. Cratchit made the gravy (ready beforehand in a little saucepan) hissing hot; Master Peter mashed the potatoes with incredible vigour; Miss Belinda sweetened up the apple-sauce; Martha dusted the hot plates; Bob took Tiny Tim beside him in a tiny corner at the table; the two young Cratchits set chairs for everybody, not forgetting themselves, and mounting guard upon their posts, crammed spoons into their mouths, lest they should shriek for goose before their turn came to be helped. At last the dishes were set on, and grace was said. It was succeeded by a breathless pause, as Mrs. Cratchit, looking slowly all along the carving-knife, prepared to plunge it in the breast; but when she did, and when the long expected gush of stuffing issued forth, one murmur of delight arose all round the board, and even Tiny Tim, excited by the two young Cratchits, beat on the table with the handle of his knife, and feebly cried Hurrah!

There never was such a goose. Bob said he didn't believe there ever was such a goose cooked. Its tenderness and flavour, size and cheapness, were the themes of universal admiration. Eked out by apple-sauce and mashed potatoes, it was a sufficient dinner for the whole family; indeed, as Mrs. Cratchit said with great delight (surveying one small atom of a bone upon the dish), they hadn't ate it all at last! Yet every one had had enough, and the youngest Cratchits in particular, were steeped in sage and onion to the eyebrows! But now, the plates being changed by Miss Belinda, Mrs. Cratchit left the room alone—too nervous to bear witnesses—to take the pudding up and bring it in.

Suppose it should not be done enough! Suppose it should break in turning out! Suppose somebody should have got over the wall of the back-yard, and stolen it, while they were merry with the goose—a supposition at which the two young Cratchits became livid! All sorts of horrors were supposed.

Hallo! A great deal of steam! The pudding was out of the copper. A smell like a washing-day! That was the cloth. A smell like an eating-house and a pastrycook's next door to each other, with a laundress's next door to that! That was the pudding! In half a minute Mrs. Cratchit entered—flushed, but smiling proudly—with the pudding, like a speckled cannon-ball, so hard and firm, blazing in half of half-a-quartern of ignited brandy, and bedight with Christmas holly stuck into the top.

Oh, a wonderful pudding! Bob Cratchit said, and calmly too, that he regarded it as the greatest success achieved by Mrs. Cratchit since their marriage. Mrs. Cratchit said that now the weight was off her mind, she would confess she had had her doubts about the quantity of flour. Everybody had something to say about it, but nobody said or thought it was at all a small pudding for a large family. It would have been flat heresy to do so. Any Cratchit would have blushed to hint at such a thing.

At last the dinner was all done, the cloth was cleared, the hearth swept, and the fire made up. The compound in the jug being tasted, and considered perfect, apples and oranges were put upon the table, and a shovel-full of chestnuts on the fire. Then all the Cratchit family drew round the hearth, in what Bob Cratchit called a circle, meaning half a one; and at Bob Cratchit's elbow stood the family display of glass. Two tumblers, and a custard-cup without a handle.

These held the hot stuff from the jug, however, as well as golden goblets would have done; and Bob served it out with beaming looks, while the chestnuts on the fire sputtered and cracked noisily. Then Bob proposed:

"A Merry Christmas to us all, my dears. God bless us!"

Which all the family re-echoed.

"God bless us every one!" said Tiny Tim, the last of all.

He sat very close to his father's side upon his little stool. Bob held his withered little hand in his, as if he loved the child, and wished to keep him by his side, and dreaded that he might be taken from him.

"Spirit," said Scrooge, with an interest he had never felt before, "tell me if Tiny Tim will live."

"I see a vacant seat," replied the Ghost, "in the poor chimney-corner, and a crutch without an owner, carefully preserved. If these shadows remain unaltered by the Future, the child will die."

"No, no," said Scrooge. "Oh, no, kind Spirit! say he will be spared."

"If these shadows remain unaltered by the Future, none other of my race," returned the Ghost, "will find him here. What then? If he be like to die, he had better do it, and decrease the surplus population."

Scrooge hung his head to hear his own words quoted by the Spirit, and was overcome with penitence and grief.

"Man," said the Ghost, "if man you be in heart, not adamant, forbear that wicked cant until you have discovered What the surplus is, and Where it is. Will you decide what men shall live, what men shall die? It may be, that in the sight of Heaven, you are more worthless and less fit to live than millions like this poor man's child. Oh God! to hear the Insect on the leaf pronouncing on the too much life among his hungry brothers in the dust!"

Scrooge bent before the Ghost's rebuke, and trembling cast his eyes upon the ground. But he raised them speedily, on hearing his own name.

"Mr. Scrooge!" said Bob; "I'll give you Mr. Scrooge, the Founder of the Feast!"

"The Founder of the Feast indeed!" cried Mrs. Cratchit, reddening. "I wish I had him here. I'd give him a piece of my mind to feast upon, and I hope he'd have a good appetite for it."

"My dear," said Bob, "the children! Christmas Day."

"It should be Christmas Day, I am sure," said she, "on which one drinks the health of such an odious, stingy, hard, unfeeling man as Mr. Scrooge. You know he is, Robert! Nobody knows it better than you do, poor fellow!"

"My dear," was Bob's mild answer, "Christmas Day."

"I'll drink his health for your sake and the Day's," said Mrs. Cratchit, "not for his. Long life to him! A merry Christmas and a happy new year! He'll be very merry and very happy, I have no doubt!"

The children drank the toast after her. It was the first of their proceedings which had no heartiness. Tiny Tim drank it last of all, but he didn't care twopence for it. Scrooge was the Ogre of the family. The mention of his name cast a dark shadow on the party, which was not dispelled for full five minutes.

After it had passed away, they were ten times merrier than before, from the mere relief of Scrooge the Baleful being done with. Bob Cratchit told them how he had a situation in his eye for Master Peter, which would bring in, if obtained, full five-and-sixpence weekly. The two young Cratchits laughed tremendously at the idea of Peter's being a man of business; and Peter himself looked thoughtfully at the fire from between his collars, as if he were deliberating what particular investments he should favour when he came into the receipt of that bewildering income. Martha, who was a poor apprentice at a milliner's, then told them what kind of work she had to do, and how many hours she worked at a stretch, and how she meant to lie abed to-morrow morning for a good long rest; to-morrow being a holiday she passed at home. Also how she had seen a countess and a lord some days before, and how the lord "was much about as tall as Peter;" at which Peter pulled up his collars so high that you couldn't have seen his head if you had been there. All this time the chestnuts and the jug went round and round; and by-and-bye they had a song, about a lost child travelling in the snow, from Tiny Tim, who had a plaintive little voice, and sang it very well indeed.

There was nothing of high mark in this. They were not a handsome family; they were not well dressed; their shoes were far from being water-proof; their clothes were scanty; and Peter might have known, and very likely did, the inside of a pawnbroker's. But, they were happy, grateful, pleased with one another, and contented with the time; and when they faded, and looked happier yet in the bright sprinklings of the Spirit's torch at parting, Scrooge had his eye upon them, and especially on Tiny Tim, until the last.

By this time it was getting dark, and snowing pretty heavily; and as Scrooge and the Spirit went along the streets, the brightness of the roaring fires in kitchens, parlours, and all sorts of rooms, was wonderful. Here, the flickering of the blaze showed preparations for a cosy dinner, with hot plates baking through and through before the fire, and deep red curtains, ready to be drawn to shut out cold and darkness. There all the children of the house were running out into the snow to meet their married sisters, brothers, cousins, uncles, aunts, and be the first to greet them. Here, again, were shadows on the window-blind of guests assembling; and there a group of handsome girls, all hooded and fur-booted, and all chattering at once, tripped lightly off to some near neighbour's house; where, woe upon the single man who saw them enter—artful witches, well they knew it—in a glow!

But, if you had judged from the numbers of people on their way to friendly gatherings, you might have thought that no one was at home to give them welcome when they got there, instead of every house expecting company, and piling up its fires half-chimney high. Blessings on it, how the Ghost exulted! How it bared its breadth of breast, and opened its capacious palm, and floated on, outpouring, with a generous hand, its bright and harmless mirth on everything within its reach! The very lamplighter, who ran on before, dotting the dusky street with specks of light, and who was dressed to spend the evening somewhere, laughed out loudly as the Spirit passed, though little kenned the lamplighter that he had any company but Christmas!

And now, without a word of warning from the Ghost, they stood upon a bleak and desert moor, where monstrous masses of rude stone were cast about, as though it were the burial-place of giants; and water spread itself wheresoever it listed, or would have done so, but for the frost that held it prisoner; and nothing grew but moss and furze, and coarse rank grass. Down in the west the setting sun had left a streak of fiery red, which glared upon the desolation for an instant, like a sullen eye, and frowning lower, lower, lower yet, was lost in the thick gloom of darkest night.

"What place is this?" asked Scrooge.

"A place where Miners live, who labour in the bowels of the earth," returned the Spirit. "But they know me. See!"

A light shone from the window of a hut, and swiftly they advanced towards it. Passing through the wall of mud and stone, they found a cheerful company assembled round a glowing fire. An old, old man and woman, with their children and their children's children, and another generation beyond that, all decked out gaily in their holiday attire. The old man, in a voice that seldom rose above the howling of the wind upon the barren waste, was singing them a Christmas song—it had been a very old song when he was a boy—and from time to time they all joined in the chorus. So surely as they raised their voices, the old man got quite blithe and loud; and so surely as they stopped, his vigour sank again.

The Spirit did not tarry here, but bade Scrooge hold his robe, and passing on above the moor, sped—whither? Not to sea? To sea. To Scrooge's horror, looking back, he saw the last of the land, a frightful range of rocks, behind them; and his ears were deafened by the thundering of water, as it rolled and roared, and raged among the dreadful caverns it had worn, and fiercely tried to undermine the earth.

Built upon a dismal reef of sunken rocks, some league or so from shore, on which the waters chafed and dashed, the wild year through, there stood a solitary lighthouse. Great heaps of sea-weed clung to its base, and storm-birds—born of the wind one might suppose, as sea-weed of the water—rose and fell about it, like the waves they skimmed.

But even here, two men who watched the light had made a fire, that through the loophole in the thick stone wall shed out a ray of brightness on the awful sea. Joining their horny hands over the rough table at which they sat, they wished each other Merry Christmas in their can of grog; and one of them: the elder, too, with his face all damaged and scarred with hard weather, as the figure-head of an old ship might be: struck up a sturdy song that was like a Gale in itself.

Again the Ghost sped on, above the black and heaving sea—on, on—until, being far away, as he told Scrooge, from any shore, they lighted on a ship. They stood beside the helmsman at the wheel, the look-out in the bow, the officers who had the watch; dark, ghostly figures in their several stations; but every man among them hummed a Christmas tune, or had a Christmas thought, or spoke below his breath to his companion of some bygone Christmas Day, with homeward hopes belonging to it. And every man on board, waking or sleeping, good or bad, had had a kinder word for another on that day than on any day in the year; and had shared to some extent in its festivities; and had remembered those he cared for at a distance, and had known that they delighted to remember him.

It was a great surprise to Scrooge, while listening to the moaning of the wind, and thinking what a solemn thing it was to move on through the lonely darkness over an unknown abyss, whose depths were secrets as profound as Death: it was a great surprise to Scrooge, while thus engaged, to hear a hearty laugh. It was a much greater surprise to Scrooge to recognise it as his own nephew's and to find himself in a bright, dry, gleaming room, with the Spirit standing smiling by his side, and looking at that same nephew with approving affability!

"Ha, ha!" laughed Scrooge's nephew. "Ha, ha, ha!"

If you should happen, by any unlikely chance, to know a man more blest in a laugh than Scrooge's nephew, all I can say is, I should like to know him too. Introduce him to me, and I'll cultivate his acquaintance.

It is a fair, even-handed, noble adjustment of things, that while there is infection in disease and sorrow, there is nothing in the world so irresistibly contagious as laughter and good-humour. When Scrooge's nephew laughed in this way: holding his sides, rolling his head, and twisting his face into the most extravagant contortions: Scrooge's niece, by marriage, laughed as heartily as he. And their assembled friends being not a bit behindhand, roared out lustily.

"Ha, ha! Ha, ha, ha, ha!"

"He said that Christmas was a humbug, as I live!" cried Scrooge's nephew. "He believed it too!"

"More shame for him, Fred!" said Scrooge's niece, indignantly. Bless those women; they never do anything by halves. They are always in earnest.

She was very pretty: exceedingly pretty. With a dimpled, surprised-looking, capital face; a ripe little mouth, that seemed made to be kissed—as no doubt it was; all kinds of good little dots about her chin, that melted into one another when she laughed; and the sunniest pair of eyes you ever saw in any little creature's head. Altogether she was what you would have called provoking, you know; but satisfactory, too. Oh, perfectly satisfactory.

"He's a comical old fellow," said Scrooge's nephew, "that's the truth: and not so pleasant as he might be. However, his offences carry their own punishment, and I have nothing to say against him."

"I'm sure he is very rich, Fred," hinted Scrooge's niece. "At least you always tell me so."

"What of that, my dear!" said Scrooge's nephew. "His wealth is of no use to him. He don't do any good with it. He don't make himself comfortable with it. He hasn't the satisfaction of thinking—ha, ha, ha!—that he is ever going to benefit US with it."

"I have no patience with him," observed Scrooge's niece. Scrooge's niece's sisters, and all the other ladies, expressed the same opinion.

"Oh, I have!" said Scrooge's nephew. "I am sorry for him; I couldn't be angry with him if I tried. Who suffers by his ill whims! Himself, always. Here, he takes it into his head to dislike us, and he won't come and dine with us. What's the consequence? He don't lose much of a dinner."

"Indeed, I think he loses a very good dinner," interrupted Scrooge's niece. Everybody else said the same, and they must be allowed to have been competent judges, because they had just had dinner; and, with the dessert upon the table, were clustered round the fire, by lamplight.

"Well! I'm very glad to hear it," said Scrooge's nephew, "because I haven't great faith in these young housekeepers. What do you say, Topper?"

Topper had clearly got his eye upon one of Scrooge's niece's sisters, for he answered that a bachelor was a wretched outcast, who had no right to express an opinion on the subject. Whereat Scrooge's niece's sister—the plump one with the lace tucker: not the one with the roses—blushed.

"Do go on, Fred," said Scrooge's niece, clapping her hands. "He never finishes what he begins to say! He is such a ridiculous fellow!"

Scrooge's nephew revelled in another laugh, and as it was impossible to keep the infection off; though the plump sister tried hard to do it with aromatic vinegar; his example was unanimously followed.

"I was only going to say," said Scrooge's nephew, "that the consequence of his taking a dislike to us, and not making merry with us, is, as I think, that he loses some pleasant moments, which could do him no harm. I am sure he loses pleasanter companions than he can find in his own thoughts, either in his mouldy old office, or his dusty chambers. I mean to give him the same chance every year, whether he likes it or not, for I pity him. He may rail at Christmas till he dies, but he can't help thinking better of it—I defy him—if he finds me going there, in good temper, year after year, and saying Uncle Scrooge, how are you? If it only puts him in the vein to leave his poor clerk fifty pounds, that's something; and I think I shook him yesterday."

It was their turn to laugh now at the notion of his shaking Scrooge. But being thoroughly good-natured, and not much caring what they laughed at, so that they laughed at any rate, he encouraged them in their merriment, and passed the bottle joyously.

After tea, they had some music. For they were a musical family, and knew what they were about, when they sung a Glee or Catch, I can assure you: especially Topper, who could growl away in the bass like a good one, and never swell the large veins in his forehead, or get red in the face over it. Scrooge's niece played well upon the harp; and played among other tunes a simple little air (a mere nothing: you might learn to whistle it in two minutes), which had been familiar to the child who fetched Scrooge from the boarding-school, as he had been reminded by the Ghost of Christmas Past. When this strain of music sounded, all the things that Ghost had shown him, came upon his mind; he softened more and more; and thought that if he could have listened to it often, years ago, he might have cultivated the kindnesses of life for his own happiness with his own hands, without resorting to the sexton's spade that buried Jacob Marley.

But they didn't devote the whole evening to music. After a while they played at forfeits; for it is good to be children sometimes, and never better than at Christmas, when its mighty Founder was a child himself. Stop! There was first a game at blind-man's buff. Of course there was. And I no more believe Topper was really blind than I believe he had eyes in his boots. My opinion is, that it was a done thing between him and Scrooge's nephew; and that the Ghost of Christmas Present knew it. The way he went after that plump sister in the lace tucker, was an outrage on the credulity of human nature. Knocking down the fire-irons, tumbling over the chairs, bumping against the piano, smothering himself among the curtains, wherever she went, there went he! He always knew where the plump sister was. He wouldn't catch anybody else. If you had fallen up against him (as some of them did), on purpose, he would have made a feint of endeavouring to seize you, which would have been an affront to your understanding, and would instantly have sidled off in the direction of the plump sister. She often cried out that it wasn't fair; and it really was not. But when at last, he caught her; when, in spite of all her silken rustlings, and her rapid flutterings past him, he got her into a corner whence there was no escape; then his conduct was the most execrable. For his pretending not to know her; his pretending that it was necessary to touch her head-dress, and further to assure himself of her identity by pressing a certain ring upon her finger, and a certain chain about her neck; was vile, monstrous! No doubt she told him her opinion of it, when, another blind-man being in office, they were so very confidential together, behind the curtains.

Scrooge's niece was not one of the blind-man's buff party, but was made comfortable with a large chair and a footstool, in a snug corner, where the Ghost and Scrooge were close behind her. But she joined in the forfeits, and loved her love to admiration with all the letters of the alphabet. Likewise at the game of How, When, and Where, she was very great, and to the secret joy of Scrooge's nephew, beat her sisters hollow: though they were sharp girls too, as Topper could have told you. There might have been twenty people there, young and old, but they all played, and so did Scrooge; for wholly forgetting in the interest he had in what was going on, that his voice made no sound in their ears, he sometimes came out with his guess quite loud, and very often guessed quite right, too; for the sharpest needle, best Whitechapel, warranted not to cut in the eye, was not sharper than Scrooge; blunt as he took it in his head to be.

The Ghost was greatly pleased to find him in this mood, and looked upon him with such favour, that he begged like a boy to be allowed to stay until the guests departed. But this the Spirit said could not be done.

"Here is a new game," said Scrooge. "One half hour, Spirit, only one!"

It was a Game called Yes and No, where Scrooge's nephew had to think of something, and the rest must find out what; he only answering to their questions yes or no, as the case was. The brisk fire of questioning to which he was exposed, elicited from him that he was thinking of an animal, a live animal, rather a disagreeable animal, a savage animal, an animal that growled and grunted sometimes, and talked sometimes, and lived in London, and walked about the streets, and wasn't made a show of, and wasn't led by anybody, and didn't live in a menagerie, and was never killed in a market, and was not a horse, or an ass, or a cow, or a bull, or a tiger, or a dog, or a pig, or a cat, or a bear. At every fresh question that was put to him, this nephew burst into a fresh roar of laughter; and was so inexpressibly tickled, that he was obliged to get up off the sofa and stamp. At last the plump sister, falling into a similar state, cried out:

"I have found it out! I know what it is, Fred! I know what it is!"

"What is it?" cried Fred.

"It's your Uncle Scro-o-o-o-oge!"

Which it certainly was. Admiration was the universal sentiment, though some objected that the reply to "Is it a bear?" ought to have been "Yes;" inasmuch as an answer in the negative was sufficient to have diverted their thoughts from Mr. Scrooge, supposing they had ever had any tendency that way.

"He has given us plenty of merriment, I am sure," said Fred, "and it would be ungrateful not to drink his health. Here is a glass of mulled wine ready to our hand at the moment; and I say, 'Uncle Scrooge!' "

"Well! Uncle Scrooge!" they cried.

"A Merry Christmas and a Happy New Year to the old man, whatever he is!" said Scrooge's nephew. "He wouldn't take it from me, but may he have it, nevertheless. Uncle Scrooge!"

Uncle Scrooge had imperceptibly become so gay and light of heart, that he would have pledged the unconscious company in return, and thanked them in an inaudible speech, if the Ghost had given him time. But the whole scene passed off in the breath of the last word spoken by his nephew; and he and the Spirit were again upon their travels.

Much they saw, and far they went, and many homes they visited, but always with a happy end. The Spirit stood beside sick beds, and they were cheerful; on foreign lands, and they were close at home; by struggling men, and they were patient in their greater hope; by poverty, and it was rich. In almshouse, hospital, and jail, in misery's every refuge, where vain man in his little brief authority had not made fast the door, and barred the Spirit out, he left his blessing, and taught Scrooge his precepts.

It was a long night, if it were only a night; but Scrooge had his doubts of this, because the Christmas Holidays appeared to be condensed into the space of time they passed together.

It was strange, too, that while Scrooge remained unaltered in his outward form, the Ghost grew older, clearly older. Scrooge had observed this change, but never spoke of it, until they left a children's Twelfth Night party, when, looking at the Spirit as they stood together in an open place, he noticed that its hair was grey.

"Are spirits' lives so short?" asked Scrooge.

"My life upon this globe, is very brief," replied the Ghost. "It ends to-night."

"To-night!" cried Scrooge.

"To-night at midnight. Hark! The time is drawing near."

The chimes were ringing the three quarters past eleven at that moment.

"Forgive me if I am not justified in what I ask," said Scrooge, looking intently at the Spirit's robe, "but I see something strange, and not belonging to yourself, protruding from your skirts. Is it a foot or a claw?"

"It might be a claw, for the flesh there is upon it," was the Spirit's sorrowful reply. "Look here."

From the foldings of its robe, it brought two children; wretched, abject, frightful, hideous, miserable. They knelt down at its feet, and clung upon the outside of its garment.

"Oh, Man! look here. Look, look, down here!" exclaimed the Ghost.

They were a boy and girl. Yellow, meagre, ragged, scowling, wolfish; but prostrate, too, in their humility. Where graceful youth should have filled their features out, and touched them with its freshest tints, a stale and shrivelled hand, like that of age, had pinched, and twisted them, and pulled them into shreds. Where angels might have sat enthroned, devils lurked, and glared out menacing. No change, no degradation, no perversion of humanity, in any grade, through all the mysteries of wonderful creation, has monsters half so horrible and dread.

Scrooge started back, appalled. Having them shown to him in this way, he tried to say they were fine children, but the words choked themselves, rather than be parties to a lie of such enormous magnitude.

"Spirit! are they yours?" Scrooge could say no more.

"They are Man's," said the Spirit, looking down upon them. "And they cling to me, appealing from their fathers. This boy is Ignorance. This girl is Want. Beware them both, and all of their degree, but most of all beware this boy, for on his brow I see that written which is Doom, unless the writing be erased. Deny it!" cried the Spirit, stretching out its hand towards the city. "Slander those who tell it ye! Admit it for your factious purposes, and make it worse. And bide the end!"

"Have they no refuge or resource?" cried Scrooge.

"Are there no prisons?" said the Spirit, turning on him for the last time with his own words. "Are there no workhouses?"

The bell struck twelve.

Scrooge looked about him for the Ghost, and saw it not. As the last stroke ceased to vibrate, he remembered the prediction of old Jacob Marley, and lifting up his eyes, beheld a solemn Phantom, draped and hooded, coming, like a mist along the ground, towards him.

# A Deeper Look:

1.          How would you describe the feeling of this scene where
            Scrooge first meets the ghost of Christmas present?

2.          What kind of details did the author use to "wrap" this
            scene with? How did those details add or detract from the
            overall feeling that you described in question one?

3.          How might changing the items, which you originally
            wrote about using to wrap a present, change the mood of
            giving that present  away?

# Where's the Blood

Sometimes, simple visuals can say a lot about what happened to a character or in a setting before ever hearing a word about what happened—sometimes, without ever having to say a single word. A visual can show an extreme struggle or it might be something that the character wasn't even aware of.

In this exercise, we're going to practice painting a simple picture about a character and his, her or its story, by putting blood on it.

For now, pick a subject. It can be a person, an animal or even an object. Write that object down.

Next, pick a spot anywhere on that subject and imagine blood on it. Write down where the blood is on that subject.

Now decide how much blood there is. Is there only a small drop? A smudge? A smear? Or more?

Write a few sentences describing what the blood looks like and only what the blood looks like.

Got it?

Blood can say so much about urgency. For example if a person walks into an emergency room and he has a few drops of blood falling from his fingers, what does that say about this person's situation? Could it say he accidentally cut himself on a sharp tool? A female character who suddenly appears in the same emergency room with the front of her shirt completely stained in blood could suggest that someone important may have died in her arms after a truly horrible accident.

So now that you have a subject; picked a spot where the blood appears; and written down how much blood appears, write a few paragraphs describing what this person looks like walking into the emergency room. What other hints can you include in this scene to show what might have happened to this person without ever having to come out and say what actually happened?

# Les Misérables
By Victor Hugo
(1802-1885)

## The Agony of Death After
## The Agony of Life

A peculiarity of this species of war is, that the attack of the barricades is almost always made from the front, and that the assailants generally abstain from turning the position, either because they fear ambushes, or because they are afraid of getting entangled in the tortuous streets. The insurgents' whole attention had been directed, therefore, to the grand barricade, which was, evidently, the spot always menaced, and there the struggle would infallibly recommence. But Marius thought of the little barricade, and went thither. It was deserted and guarded only by the fire-pot which trembled between the paving-stones. Moreover, the Mondetour alley, and the branches of the Rue de la Petite Truanderie and the Rue du Cygne were profoundly calm.

As Marius was withdrawing, after concluding his inspection, he heard his name pronounced feebly in the darkness.

"Monsieur Marius!"

He started, for he recognized the voice which had called to him two hours before through the gate in the Rue Plumet.

Only, the voice now seemed to be nothing more than a breath.

He looked about him, but saw no one.

Marius thought he had been mistaken, that it was an illusion added by his mind to the extraordinary realities which were clashing around him. He advanced a step, in order to quit the distant recess where the barricade lay.

"Monsieur Marius!" repeated the voice.

This time he could not doubt that he had heard it distinctly; he looked and saw nothing.

"At your feet," said the voice.

He bent down, and saw in the darkness a form which was dragging itself towards him. It was crawling along the pavement. It was this that had spoken to him.

The fire-pot allowed him to distinguish a blouse, torn trousers of coarse velvet, bare feet, and something which resembled a pool of blood. Marius indistinctly made out a pale head which was lifted towards him and which was saying to him:--

"You do not recognize me?"

"No."

"Eponine."

Marius bent hastily down. It was, in fact, that unhappy child. She was dressed in men's clothes.

"How come you here? What are you doing here?"

"I am dying," said she.

There are words and incidents which arouse dejected beings. Marius cried out with a start:--

"You are wounded! Wait, I will carry you into the room! They will attend to you there. Is it serious? How must I take hold of you in order not to hurt you? Where do you suffer? Help! My God! But why did you come hither?"

And he tried to pass his arm under her, in order to raise her.

She uttered a feeble cry.

"Have I hurt you?" asked Marius.

"A little."

"But I only touched your hand."

She raised her hand to Marius, and in the middle of that hand Marius saw a black hole.

"What is the matter with your hand?" said he.

"It is pierced."

"Pierced?"

"Yes."

"What with?"

"A bullet."

"How?"

"Did you see a gun aimed at you?"

"Yes, and a hand stopping it."

"It was mine."

Marius was seized with a shudder.

"What madness! Poor child! But so much the better, if that is all, it is nothing, let me carry you to a bed. They will dress your wound; one does not die of a pierced hand."

She murmured:--

"The bullet traversed my hand, but it came out through my back. It is useless to remove me from this spot. I will tell you how you can care for me better than any surgeon. Sit down near me on this stone."

He obeyed; she laid her head on Marius' knees, and, without looking at him, she said:--

"Oh! How good this is! How comfortable this is! There; I no longer suffer."

She remained silent for a moment, then she turned her face with an effort, and looked at Marius.

"Do you know what, Monsieur Marius? It puzzled me because you entered that garden; it was stupid, because it was I who showed you that house; and then, I ought to have said to myself that a young man like you--"

She paused, and overstepping the sombre transitions that undoubtedly existed in her mind, she resumed with a heartrending smile:--

"You thought me ugly, didn't you?"

She continued:--

"You see, you are lost! Now, no one can get out of the barricade. It was I who led you here, by the way! You are going to die, I count upon that. And yet, when I saw them taking aim at you, I put my hand on the muzzle of the gun. How queer it is! But it was because I wanted to die before you. When I received that bullet, I dragged myself here, no one saw me, no one picked me up, I was waiting for you, I said: `So he is not coming!' Oh, if you only knew. I bit my blouse, I suffered so! Now I am well. Do you remember the day I entered your chamber and when I looked at myself in your mirror, and the day when I came to you on the boulevard near the washerwomen? How the birds sang! That was a long time ago. You gave me a hundred sous, and I said to you: `I don't want your money.' I hope you picked up your coin? You are not rich. I did not think to tell you to pick it up. The sun was shining bright, and it was not cold. Do you remember, Monsieur Marius? Oh! How happy I am! Every one is going to die."

She had a mad, grave, and heart-breaking air. Her torn blouse disclosed her bare throat.

As she talked, she pressed her pierced hand to her breast, where there was another hole, and whence there spurted from moment to moment a stream of blood, like a jet of wine from an open bung-hole.

Marius gazed at this unfortunate creature with profound compassion.

"Oh!" she resumed, "it is coming again, I am stifling!"

She caught up her blouse and bit it, and her limbs stiffened on the pavement.

At that moment the young cock's crow executed by little Gavroche resounded through the barricade.

The child had mounted a table to load his gun, and was singing gayly the song then so popular:--

"En voyant Lafayette,   "On beholding Lafayette,
Le gendarme repete:--      The gendarme repeats:--
Sauvons nous! sauvons nous!   Let us flee! let us flee!
   sauvons nous!"        let us flee!

Eponine raised herself and listened; then she murmured:--

"It is he."

And turning to Marius:--

"My brother is here. He must not see me. He would scold me."

"Your brother?" inquired Marius, who was meditating in the most bitter and sorrowful depths of his heart on the duties to the Thenardiers which his father had bequeathed to him; "who is your brother?"

"That little fellow."

"The one who is singing?"

"Yes."

Marius made a movement.

"Oh! don't go away," said she, "it will not be long now."

She was sitting almost upright, but her voice was very low and broken by hiccoughs.

At intervals, the death rattle interrupted her. She put her face as near that of Marius as possible. She added with a strange expression:--

"Listen, I do not wish to play you a trick. I have a letter in my pocket for you. I was told to put it in the post. I kept it. I did not want to have it reach you. But perhaps you will be angry with me for it when we meet again presently? Take your letter."

She grasped Marius' hand convulsively with her pierced hand, but she no longer seemed to feel her sufferings. She put Marius' hand in the pocket of her blouse. There, in fact, Marius felt a paper.

"Take it," said she.

Marius took the letter.

She made a sign of satisfaction and contentment.

"Now, for my trouble, promise me--"

And she stopped.

"What?" asked Marius.

"Promise me!"

"I promise."

"Promise to give me a kiss on my brow when I am dead.--I shall feel it."

She dropped her head again on Marius' knees, and her eyelids closed. He thought the poor soul had departed. Eponine remained motionless. All at once, at the very moment when Marius fancied her asleep forever, she slowly opened her eyes in which appeared the sombre profundity of death, and said to him in a tone whose sweetness seemed already to proceed from another world:--

"And by the way, Monsieur Marius, I believe that I was a little bit in love with you."

She tried to smile once more and expired

# A Deeper Look:

1.      Which character(s) was/were bleeding in this story? What
        do you think the blood says about the struggle that
        this/these character(s) endured?

2.      Did the author let the blood speak more than his own
        words about what transpired with this character? How so?

3.      Besides blood, can you think of anything else that might
        instantly tell a story about a person without having to say
        a word? How would you present that to your reader?

# Favorite Instrument

One of the most effective tools in connecting with readers is being able to recognize active details (the little details that pull at their humanity and dig into their souls). Detail alone is just detail. It bears no life. It has no soul. We can build mountains upon mountains of detail for any reader to see, but if those mountains have no life, our readers have no way to justify their own emotional connection with our work. And a work without emotional connection is an empty work.

Imagine standing in front of two paintings in a museum. One is an impressive 20-foot panoramic scene of a woodland area with flourishing green trees, tall mountains with jagged cliffs and all sorts of wildlife running around a cabin with a smoky chimney and a little old man with greying hair setting a steaming apple pie on the windowsill to cool. The other painting is a single, thick and jagged stroke of bright, fire-engine red paint slashed across a 24-inch by 18-inch canvas. It's not difficult to judge that visually the woodland scenery is much more detailed and artistic than the single red paint stroke on an otherwise empty canvas.

Now imagine reading the placards next to these works of art. The woodland scene's placard says that that it was created in color pencil by a 27 year old last week in his garage, it's titled "My Dream World." Upon reading the placard for the stroke of red paint, we learn that the artist is an injured Iraqi War veteran who lost his sight in a bomb blast, and that his best friend lost his life shielding the artist from the explosion. This is the artist's first painting ever and he created it after a three-year struggle with depression,while wishing that his friend were alive and that he, himself, were dead instead. The title of this work is "Blind-sided: Portrait of a fallen hero."

Which of these paintings seems more meaningful now?

For this assignment, choose an instrument that you like the sound of when you hear it. Or, if you can't hear, choose an instrument that you enjoy watching someone play.

Make a list of ten reasons this particular instrument means so much to you. Here's the catch, the items you list cannot be directly about the instrument itself. For example, instead of saying "I just think it looks cool," try instead listing where you were the first time you realized how it looked. Instead of, "I just think it sounds soothing," list a specific instance when you did find the music soothing.

Now, list five reasons why you don't like it. What are its flaws? Follow the same rules as when you created the list of reasons you like the instrument.

# Two Bugle Calls

### By O. W. Norton
### (1839-1920)

The bugle was much used in the army. The carrying quality of its tones made it possible to convey commands to a great distance in times of quiet, and even in the roar of battle its shrill notes could be distinctly heard. The reveille which waked the soldier from his slumber in camp or bivouac and the order to put out the lights at night were sounded on the bugle. There were calls to breakfast, dinner and supper. Men in camp unfit for duty were summoned to the surgeon's tent by the sick call. The skirmish line in battle was ordered to deploy, to advance, to commence fir- ing, to lie down, to cease firing, to retreat, to rally on the reserve, and to execute many other movements by various calls on the bugle. There were calls for sergeants to report to the adjutant, for officers to report to the colonel, for companies to form for roll-call, for regiments to form line of battle on the colors, to advance in line of battle and to re- treat, to change direction in marching, to strike tents and prepare to march, and many others. No cavalryman will ever forget the stirring call of ''Boots and Saddles.''

When General McClellan was organizing the Army of the Potomac near Washington in the autumn of 1861, the camps along the line were very near together, and the constant drilling, to the sound of the bugle, of the various regiments and brigades often caused confusion in understanding orders. General Daniel Butterfield, who organized a brigade at this time, known at first as ''Butterfield's Brigade,'' saw at an early date the necessity of doing something to prevent this confusion. Butterfield had a genius for military matters, which later secured for him high rank in the Army of the Potomac and in the western armies. He could himself sound the bugle calls when occasion required. Shortly after he assumed command of the brigade, he composed, and taught the writer, then serving as his brigade bugler, a bugle call for his brigade. This consisted of three long notes on one key, and a catch repeated. It was sound- ed twice before each call for any operation or movement, and indicated to the officers and men that the call to follow was for the troops of this brigade. General Butterfield also prepared different calls for the regimental bugler of each regiment in his brigade. The men were accustomed to sing various w^ords to the accompaniment of the bugle calls when they heard them. Most of these words were explanatory of the meaning of the call, or were jocose comments on the command. When the reveille was sounded men could be heard through the camps singing:

I can't wake 'em up, I can't wake 'em up, I can't wake 'em up
in the morning,
I can't wake 'em up. T can't wake 'em up, I can't wake 'em
up at all.
The corporal's worse than the private, the sergeant's worse
than the corporal.
The lieutenant's w^orse than the sergeant and the captain's
worst of all.
I can't w^ake 'em up, I can't wake 'em up, I can't wake 'em
up in the morning,
I can't wake 'em up. I can't wake 'em up, I can't wake 'em
up at all.''

These words exactly fitted the notes of the bugle. When the sick call sounded, the men sang, "All ye sick men, all ye sick men, get your calomel, get your calomel, get your calomel, get your calomel." Sometimes they sang, "Doctor Jones says, Doctor Jones says, come and

get your quinine,

quinine, quinine, come and get your quinine, qui-i-ni-i-ine."

When, on the march, the general halted his brigade intending to give the men an opportunity for a few moment's rest, the brigade call was sounded, then the call to halt, then a most welcome call of three short notes repeated, to which the great chorus responded along the line, "All lie down, all lie down." When the march was to be resumed the brigade call was again sounded, followed by the less wel- come call, ''Attention !" To this the men responded in words well suited to the music:

"Fall in ye poor devils as fast as ye can,

And when ye get tired I'll rest you again."

Words were set to many other calls, but one which lasted from Arlington Heights to Appomattox, was the interpretation of the brigade call. To this the men sang :

"Dan, Dan, Dan Butterfield, Butterfield,

Dan, Dan, Dan Butterfield, Butterfield."

The general used to say that sometimes in trying circum- stances when the brigade was called up from a too short rest, he thought he could distinguish the words, "Damn, Damn, Damn Butterfield." This is not very probable. The men

of that old brigade so much admired their gallant leader that nothing he could do would cause them to use such disrespectful language.

The general calls were used throughout the Union army. The music of the calls was printed in the Tactics where they could be studied and learned by officers whose duty it was to understand them and repeat in words to the men under their command the orders indicated by the bugle. This brigade call was used only by Butterfield's brigade and was not printed in the Tactics.

BUTTERFIELD'S BRIGADE CALL:

## BUTTERFIELD'S BRIGADE CALL.

Dan.    Dan.    Dan.    Butterfield,    Butterfield.

This special call for an organization was useful in many ways. It had no small effect in arousing and maintaining an esprit de corps in this brigade, second to none in the army. It was known by all troops of the Army of the Potomac, and the brigade which marched to its music was always respected and welcomed by its comrades in arms as an orqanization to be trusted, and sure to give a good account of itself under all circumstances.

The rout of the Union army at the second battle of Bull Run was for a time much greater than that which occurred at the first battle, although the men having become veterans, order was more quickly restored. After making a gallant charge which was received by masked batteries and musketry in front, the line also being enfiladed by a large part of Longstreet's artillery, the men fell back in confusion. At the turnpike all trace of organization was lost. Darkness came on and the blockade at the Stone Bridge broke up whatever semblance of order remained. Between the Stone Bridge and Centreville the turnpike was filled with a disorganized mass of infantry, artillery, ambulance and wagon trains. General Butterfield, riding in the midst of the melee, ordered his bugler to sound at short intervals his brigade call. It was received with shouts from all directions, and the men of this brigade, rallying to that call in the darkness, were formed into column, and marched into Centreville in better order than that prevailing in almost any other command.

In September, 1889, one of the regiments of this brigade met on Little Round Top, Gettysburg, to dedicate its regimental monument and to hold the annual reunion of the survivors of the regiment. Few of them had seen the battlefield since July, 1863. The writer, attending this reunion, took with him a bugle, and standing among the rocks and trees sounded once more the old Dan Butterfield Call. The men were scattered about over the hill and in the lower ground at its foot, some seeking the rocks where they fought, others going further to see how the position looked from the place where the enemy advanced. When the bugle sounded a great shout came up from the men, who recognized the old familiar call, although many of them had not heard it for a quarter of a century. They came charging up to the spot where the bugler stood, some with tears in their eyes, asking to have it repeated. That familiar sound echoing among the rocks where thev had fought brought back, perhaps more vividly than words could do, the memories of the days when they had answered so often to its sound. Few men of the old Third Brigade can hear that call to-day without emotion.

One day in July, 1862, when the Army of the Potomac was in camp at Harrison's Landing- on the James river, Virginia, resting and recruiting from its losses in the seven days of battle before Richmond, General Butterfield summoned the writer, his brigade bugler, to his tent, and whistling some new tune asked the bugler to sound it for him. This was done, not quite to his satisfaction at first, but after repeated trials, changing the time of some of the notes. which were scribbled on the back of an envelope, the call was finally arranged to suit the general. He then ordered that it should be substituted in his brigade for the regulation "Taps" (extinguish lights) which was printed in the Tactics and used by the whole army. This was done for the first time that night. The next day buglers from near-by brigades came over to the camp of Butterlield's brigade to ask the meaning of this new call. They liked it, and copying the music returned to their camps, but it was not until some time later, when generals of other commands had heard its melodious notes, that orders were issued, or permission given, to substitute it throughout the Army of the Potomac for the time-honored call which came down from West Point.

In the western armies the regulation call was in use until the autumn of 1863. At that time the Eleventh and Twelfth corps were detached from the Army of the Potomac and sent under command of General Hooker to reinforce the Union army at Chattanooga. Through its use in these corps it became known in the western armies and was adopted by them. From that time it became and remains to this day the official call for "Taps." It is printed in the present Tactics and is used throughout the United States Army, the National Guard, and all organizations of veteran soldiers.

General Butterfield in speaking of the reason for changing the call for "Taps," said that the regulation call was not very musical and not appropriate to the order which it conveyed. He wanted a call which in its music should have some suggestion of putting out tlic lights and lying down to rest in the silence of the camp, and musing over airs and musical phrases which might better represent this idea, he composed this call and directed its use in the camps of his brigade, the only troops over which he had at that time any authority. It made its way by its intrinsic beauty to a permanent place in the minds and hearts of the soldiers.

In accordance with the custom of attaching words to such calls as had a significance to which words were adapted, the men soon began to sing to this call, "Go to sleep, go to sleep, go to sleep, go to sleep, go to sleep. You may now go to sleep, go to sleep." This was the last regular call of the day or night in camp. About half an hour after the formation of a company for evening roll-call, to which it was summoned by the "Tattoo," this call was sounded as a signal to put out all lights in tents, stop all loud conversation, and everything which would interfere with the quiet rest and sleep of the men. Sometimes they sang, "Put out the lights, go to sleep, go to sleep, go to sleep, go to sleep. Put out the lights, go to sleep, go to sleep."

General Butterfield in composing this call and directing that it be used for "Taps" in his brigade, could not have foreseen its popularity and the use for another purpose into which it w^ould grow. To-day whenever a man is buried with military honors anywhere in the United States, the ceremony is concluded by firing three volleys of musketry over the grave, and sounding with the trumpet or bugle, "Put out the lights. Go to sleep." At the Soldiers' Homes, when the w^orn-out veterans of the Grand Army of the Re- public lie down to their last rest, while their comrades stand about the grave with bared heads, some comrade bids farewell by sounding on the bugle this call to "Go to sleep." At all posts of our little regular army, whether at garrisons or at the distant frontier camps, a soldier who is buried by his comrades receives this last salute. When General Butterfield was buried at West Point a few months ago, the solemn strains of this call bade the last farewell to its author. It consigned to their last rest Sheridan at Arlington, Sherman at St. Louis, Grant at New York and McKinley at Canton.

There is something singularly beautiful and appropriate in the music of this wonderful call. Its strains are melancholy, yet full of rest and peace. Its echoes linger in the heart long after its tones have ceased to vibrate in the air. Like Handel's Largo, it is immortal.

Put out the lights. Go to sleep. Go to sleep. Go to sleep. Go to

sleep. Put out the lights, Go to sleep, Go to sleep.

# A Deeper Look:

1.          What is the bugle's role in this story?

2.          What tools does the author use to present this instrument
            to the reader in an interesting way?

3.          For this exercise, you were asked to choose an instrument.
            What might be some unique approaches you might try to
            show that instrument to your own readers?

# Cause and Consequence:

## From buildup
## to aftermath

4

# Ingredients for Setup

Anticipation can be a great tool to build suspense. It can help frighten your readers about what's behind a door; make them wonder if a car will start in time; or keep them on edge as a character decides to kiss the villain.

For this exercise, let's begin by imagining a water balloon.

First, let's give it a color. Choose and write down a color.

Next, let's imagine what's in the balloon? Choose any substance, you wish: water, orange juice, nails,etc. It can be anything at all. We only want these items in the balloon, we're not concerned with how they get in the balloon at this point. Have you picked an item or items?

Write it down.

Now, decide how full this balloon will be. In other words, how will it feel? Will it be so full that the balloon feels almost solid? Will the balloon be pliable? Will the balloon be mushy? Or will it be somewhere between any of these previous examples?

In a sentence or two, describe the texture of your filled balloon.

Now, for the fun part.

Imagine holding that balloon between your hands and squeezing it until either it breaks or you have to give up.

Write down ten words that describe how you think you might feel when it does break.

Write down three different sentences that describe what you might be thinking right before the breaking point happens.

Write two different sentences that describe responses from two different people who might be watching you as you squeeze your balloon.

Now, imagine that moment right before the balloon breaks. It hasn't broken yet, it's just about to.

Using your ten words and your five sentences, write a few paragraphs describing the scene right up to the point before the balloon breaks, including how you feel about it, but don't let the balloon pop.

# The Jungle

By Upton Sinclair
(1839-1920)

Chapter seven
(beginning excerpt)

Now the dreadful winter was come upon them. In the forests, all summer long, the branches of the trees do battle for light, and some of them lose and die; and then come the raging blasts, and the storms of snow and hail, and strew the ground with these weaker branches. Just so it was in Packingtown; the whole district braced itself for the struggle that was an agony, and those whose time was come died off in hordes. All the year round they had been serving as cogs in the great packing machine; and now was the time for the renovating of it, and the replacing of damaged parts. There came pneumonia and grippe, stalking among them, seeking for weakened constitutions; there was the annual harvest of those whom tuberculosis had been dragging down. There came cruel, cold, and biting winds, and blizzards of snow, all testing relentlessly for failing muscles and impoverished blood. Sooner or later came the day when the unfit one did not report for work; and then, with no time lost in waiting, and no inquiries or regrets, there was a chance for a new hand.

The new hands were here by the thousands. All day long the gates of the packing houses were besieged by starving and penniless men; they came, literally, by the thousands every single morning, fighting with each other for a chance for life. Blizzards and cold made no difference to them, they were always on hand; they were on hand two hours before the sun rose, an hour before the work began. Sometimes their faces froze, sometimes their feet and their hands; sometimes they froze all together—but still they came, for they had no other place to go. One day Durham advertised in the paper for two hundred men to cut ice; and all that day the homeless and starving of the city came trudging through the snow from all over its two hundred square miles. That night forty score of them crowded into the station house of the stockyards district—they filled the rooms, sleeping in each other's laps, toboggan fashion, and they piled on top of each other in the corridors, till the police shut the doors and left some to freeze outside. On the morrow, before daybreak, there were three thousand at Durham's, and the police reserves had to be sent for to quell the riot. Then Durham's bosses picked out twenty of the biggest; the "two hundred" proved to have been a printer's error.

Four or five miles to the eastward lay the lake, and over this the bitter winds came raging. Sometimes the thermometer would fall to ten or twenty degrees below zero at night, and in the morning the streets would be piled with snowdrifts up to the first-floor windows. The streets through which our friends had to go to their work were all unpaved and full of deep holes and gullies; in summer, when it rained hard, a man might have to wade to his waist to get to his house; and now in winter it was no joke getting through these places, before light in the morning and after dark at night. They would wrap up in all they owned, but they could not wrap up against exhaustion; and many a man gave out in these battles with the snowdrifts, and lay down and fell asleep.

And if it was bad for the men, one may imagine how the women and children fared. Some would ride in the cars, if the cars were running; but when you are making only five cents an hour, as was little Stanislovas, you do not like to spend that much to ride two miles. The children would come to the yards with great shawls about their ears, and so tied up that you could hardly find them—and still there would be accidents. One bitter morning in February the little boy who worked at the lard machine with Stanislovas came about an hour late, and screaming with pain. They unwrapped him, and a man began vigorously rubbing his ears; and as they were frozen stiff, it took only two or three rubs to break them short off. As a result of this, little Stanislovas conceived a terror of the cold that was almost a mania. Every morning, when it came time to start for the yards, he would begin to cry and protest. Nobody knew quite how to manage him, for threats did no good—it seemed to be something that he could not control, and they feared sometimes that he would go into convulsions. In the end it had to be arranged that he always went with Jurgis, and came home with him again; and often, when the snow was deep, the man would carry him the whole way on his shoulders. Sometimes Jurgis would be working until late at night, and then it was pitiful, for there was no place for the little fellow to wait, save in the doorways or in a corner of the killing beds, and he would all but fall asleep there, and freeze to death.

There was no heat upon the killing beds; the men might exactly as well have worked out of doors all winter. For that matter, there was very little heat anywhere in the building, except in the cooking rooms and such places—and it was the men who worked in these who ran the most risk of all, because whenever they had to pass to another room they had to go through ice-cold corridors, and sometimes with nothing on above the waist except a sleeveless undershirt. On the killing beds you were apt to be covered with blood, and it would freeze solid; if you leaned against a pillar, you would freeze to that, and if you put your hand upon the blade of your knife, you would run a chance of leaving your skin on it. The men would tie up their feet in newspapers and old sacks, and these would be soaked in blood and frozen, and then soaked again, and so on, until by nighttime a man would be walking on great lumps the size of the feet of an elephant. Now and then, when the bosses were not looking, you would see them plunging their feet and ankles into the steaming hot carcass of the steer, or darting across the room to the hot-water jets. The cruelest thing of all was that nearly all of them—all of those who used knives—were unable to wear gloves, and their arms would be white with frost and their hands would grow numb, and then of course there would be accidents. Also the air would be full of steam, from the hot water and the hot blood, so that you could not see five feet before you; and then, with men rushing about at the speed they kept up on the killing beds, and all with butcher knives, like razors, in their hands—well, it was to be counted as a wonder that there were not more men slaughtered than cattle.

# A Deeper Look:

1.      How effective do you think this passage is in setting up the environment, character and setting?

2.      What specific "ingredients" did the author mention that you believe help set up this scene?

3.      Looking at this story, are there any particular words or passages that intrigued you as a writer? Why?

# Explosive Research

In the previous lesson, we imagined what a balloon would be like. Now let's compare it to reality. Following a scene of anticipation, a climactic event brings a burst of energy to the setting. But how do we control this energy or give it the respect it deserves? If this energy happens too fast, readers can gloss over the climax. If we spend too much time exposing that energy, we can belittle the climax and it can become boring. One reason that this can happen is because a climax itself is like a sudden explosion. So much detail and action can suddenly spew forth that it can become tempting to describe absolutely everything that happens. On the other hand, it can be easy to focus on one or two dominating details that it causes us to miss other important elements.

For this exercise, have some fun. Get yourself a water balloon and fill it with water. Now let's go outside to conduct some writer research. Wear clothing that can get wet. And don't forget your safety glasses.

Next, take a moment to inspect it. Come up with five words that could describe the balloon itself.

Now, inspect what you can see inside the balloon. Write as many words or phrases as you can that describe the contents of the balloon. Don't be afraid to play with the balloon, and make notes of any of the changes that happen to the contents. Try not to let the balloon pop.

Once you have all your thoughts written down, grip your balloon between your hands and squeeze the balloon until it pops. Take a mental picture and answer the following questions:

Where did the balloon break?
Which way did the water escape?
Did it spray, gush or fall?
Think of ten words that describe what it looked like.
Write down ten words that describes how it felt.
Did the water get on you? If so, where did it get on you?
What happened to the ballon?
What kind of scars (evidence of its existence) did it leave behind?

Using your answers and details that you've described, write    a five-sentence paragraph describing the explosion.

From your list, which details did you use?
Which details did you choose not to use?
How did you use those details?
Why did you choose to use these details over the others?

# The Jungle
By Upton Sinclair
(1839-1920)

## Chapter Seven
(continued)

The newspapers had been full of this scandal—once there had even been an investigation, and an actual uncovering of the pipes; but nobody had been punished, and the thing went right on. And then there was the condemned meat industry, with its endless horrors. The people of Chicago saw the government inspectors in Packingtown, and they all took that to mean that they were protected from diseased meat; they did not understand that these hundred and sixty-three inspectors had been appointed at the request of the packers, and that they were paid by the United States government to certify that all the diseased meat was kept in the state. They had no authority beyond that; for the inspection of meat to be sold in the city and state the whole force in Packingtown consisted of three henchmen of the local political machine!*

(*Rules and Regulations for the Inspection of Livestock and Their Products. United States Department of Agriculture, Bureau of Animal Industries, Order No. 125:—

Section 1. Proprietors of slaughterhouses, canning, salting, packing, or rendering establishments engaged in the slaughtering of cattle, sheep, or swine, or the packing of any of their products, the carcasses or products of which are to become subjects of interstate or foreign commerce, shall make application to the Secretary of Agriculture for inspection of said animals and their products....

Section 15. Such rejected or condemned animals shall at once be removed by the owners from the pens containing animals which have been inspected and found to be free from disease and fit for human food, and shall be disposed of in accordance with the laws, ordinances, and regulations of the state and municipality in which said rejected or condemned animals are located....

Section 25. A microscopic examination for trichinae shall be made of all swine products exported to countries requiring such examination. No microscopic examination will be made of hogs slaughtered for interstate trade, but this examination shall be confined to those intended for the export trade.)

And shortly afterward one of these, a physician, made the discovery that the carcasses of steers which had been condemned as tubercular by the government inspectors, and which therefore contained ptomaines, which are deadly poisons, were left upon an open platform and carted away to be sold in the city; and so he insisted that these carcasses be treated with an injection of kerosene—and was ordered to resign the same week! So indignant were the packers that they went farther, and compelled the mayor to abolish the whole bureau of inspection; so that since then there has not been even a pretense of any interference with the graft. There was said to be two thousand dollars a week hush money from the tubercular steers alone; and as much again from the hogs which had died of cholera on the trains, and which you might see any day being loaded into boxcars and hauled away to a place called Globe, in Indiana, where they made a fancy grade of lard.

Jurgis heard of these things little by little, in the gossip of those who were obliged to perpetrate them. It seemed as if every time you met a person from a new department, you heard of new swindles and new crimes. There was, for instance, a Lithuanian who was a cattle butcher for the plant where Marija had worked, which killed meat for canning only; and to hear this man describe the animals which came to his place would have been worthwhile for a Dante or a Zola. It seemed that they must have agencies all over the country, to hunt out old and crippled and diseased cattle to be canned. There were cattle which had been fed on "whisky-malt," the refuse of the breweries, and had become what the men called "steerly"— which means covered with boils. It was a nasty job killing these, for when you plunged your knife into them they would burst and splash foul-smelling stuff into your face; and when a man's sleeves were smeared with blood, and his hands steeped in it, how was he ever to wipe his face, or to clear his eyes so that he could see? It was stuff such as this that made the "embalmed beef" that had killed several times as many United States soldiers as all the bullets of the Spaniards; only the army beef, besides, was not fresh canned, it was old stuff that had been lying for years in the cellars.

# A Deeper Look:

1.    What kind of explosion/climax is taking place in this passage?

2.    What kind of reach does this explosion have? Who's involved? Who's affected? How damaging is it?

3.    Some explosions (climaxes) are more profound than others. Would you say this is a strong explosion or a small one? What do you think would be needed to make it a bigger explosion? How about a smaller explosion?

# Consequences

Aftermath and consequences of any given event can be tempting to ignore. Aftermath can demonstrate an abrupt change in environment. While consequences can show how an event has affected others. Anticipation and climax can be fun to show readers, while the consequences and aftermath may feel slow. After building up so much energy for a strong climax, it can become difficult to focus on changing the tempo and taking extra effort to focus on some details that may seem mundane.

These details are important because they behave as a residual. They can act as a transition into human element, a new rotation of energy, or a means of foreshadow.

For this exercise, let's imagine another balloon.

Choose a color for this balloon.

Now, choose any kind of liquid that you would like it to be filled with. Next, think of a specific place in your home to pop this balloon.

Just as before, imagine squeezing the balloon between your hands, but this time, let it explode. Think about how it might explode. Where might the liquid go? What kind of mess might it create? What items might get hit by the contents of this imaginary balloon?

Now, list five different items that you would need to clean up the mess.

Write one sentence explaining why you would need each specific item.

Now, look at the list of following items:

Paper towel

Chamois

Lint cloth

Facial Tissue

Sponge

Write down whether each of these items would be a good tool or a bad one to clean up the mess. Take a moment and answer why.

Now, pick one item from the list you created describing what you would need to clean up the mess. Then pick one item from the list that the book provided and spend a couple paragraphs describing the event of cleaning up (or adding to) this mess with these two items.

# The Jungle

By Upton Sinclair
(1839-1920)

Chapter seven
(continued)

Then one Sunday evening, Jurgis sat puffing his pipe by the kitchen stove, and talking with an old fellow whom Jonas had introduced, and who worked in the canning rooms at Durham's; and so Jurgis learned a few things about the great and only Durham canned goods, which had become a national institution. They were regular alchemists at Durham's; they advertised a mushroom-catsup, and the men who made it did not know what a mushroom looked like. They advertised "potted chicken,"—and it was like the boardinghouse soup of the comic papers, through which a chicken had walked with rubbers on. Perhaps they had a secret process for making chickens chemically—who knows? said Jurgis' friend; the things that went into the mixture were tripe, and the fat of pork, and beef suet, and hearts of beef, and finally the waste ends of veal, when they had any. They put these up in several grades, and sold them at several prices; but the contents of the cans all came out of the same hopper. And then there was "potted game" and "potted grouse," "potted ham," and "deviled ham"—de-vyled, as the men called it. "De-vyled" ham was made out of the waste ends of smoked beef that were too small to be sliced by the machines; and also tripe, dyed with chemicals so that it would not show white; and trimmings of hams and corned beef; and potatoes, skins and all; and finally the hard cartilaginous gullets of beef, after the tongues had been cut out. All this ingenious mixture was ground up and flavored with spices to make it taste like something. Anybody who could invent a new imitation had been sure of a fortune from old Durham, said Jurgis' informant; but it was hard to think of anything new in a place where so many sharp wits had been at work for so long; where men welcomed tuberculosis in the cattle they were feeding, because it made them fatten more quickly; and where they bought up all the old rancid butter left over in the grocery stores of a continent, and "oxidized" it by a forced-air process, to take away the odor, rechurned it with skim milk, and sold it in bricks in the cities! Up to a year or two ago it had been the custom to kill horses in the yards—ostensibly for fertilizer; but after long agitation the newspapers had been able to make the public realize that the horses were being canned. Now it was against the law to kill horses in Packingtown, and the law was really complied with—for the present, at any rate. Any day, however, one might see sharp-horned and shaggy-haired creatures running with the sheep and yet what a job you would have to get the public to believe that a good part of what it buys for lamb and mutton is really goat's flesh!

There was another interesting set of statistics that a person might have gathered in Packingtown—those of the various afflictions of the workers. When Jurgis had first inspected the packing plants with Szedvilas, he had marveled while he listened to the tale of all the things that were made out of the carcasses of animals, and of all the lesser industries that were maintained there; now he found that each one of these lesser industries was a separate little inferno, in its way as horrible as the killing beds, the source and fountain of them all. The workers in each of them had their own peculiar diseases. And the wandering visitor might be skeptical about all the swindles, but he could not be skeptical about these, for the worker bore the evidence of them about on his own person—generally he had only to hold out his hand.

There were the men in the pickle rooms, for instance, where old Antanas had gotten his death; scarce a one of these that had not some spot of horror on his person. Let a man so much as scrape his finger pushing a truck in the pickle rooms, and he might have a sore that would put him out of the world; all the joints in his fingers might be eaten by the acid, one by one. Of the butchers and floorsmen, the beef-boners and trimmers, and all those who used knives, you could scarcely find a person who had the use of his thumb; time and time again the base of it had been slashed, till it was a mere lump of flesh against which the man pressed the knife to hold it. The hands of these men would be criss-crossed with cuts, until you could no longer pretend to count them or to trace them. They would have no nails,—they had worn them off pulling hides; their knuckles were swollen so that their fingers spread out like a fan. There were men who worked in the cooking rooms, in the midst of steam and sickening odors, by artificial light; in these rooms the germs of tuberculosis might live for two years, but the supply was renewed every hour. There were the beef-luggers, who carried two-hundred-pound quarters into the refrigerator-cars; a fearful kind of work, that began at four o'clock in the morning, and that wore out the most powerful men in a few years. There were those who worked in the chilling rooms, and whose special disease was rheumatism; the time limit that a man could work in the chilling rooms was said to be five years. There were the wool-pluckers, whose hands went to pieces even sooner than the hands of the pickle men; for the pelts of the sheep had to be painted with acid to loosen the wool, and then the pluckers had to pull out this wool with their bare hands, till the acid had eaten their fingers off. There were those who made the tins for the canned meat; and their hands, too, were a maze of cuts, and each cut represented a chance for blood poisoning. Some worked at the stamping machines, and it was very seldom that one could work long there at the pace that was set, and not give out and forget himself and have a part of his hand chopped off. There were the "hoisters," as they were called, whose task it was to press the lever which lifted the dead cattle off the floor. They ran along upon a rafter, peering down through the damp and the steam; and as old Durham's architects had not built the killing room for the convenience of the hoisters, at every few feet they would have to stoop under a beam, say four feet above the one they ran on; which got them into the habit of stooping, so that in a few years they would be walking like chimpanzees. Worst of any, however, were the fertilizer men, and those who served in the cooking rooms. These people could not be shown to the visitor,—for the odor of a fertilizer man would scare any ordinary visitor at a hundred yards, and as for the other men, who worked in tank rooms full of steam, and in some of which there were open vats near the level of the floor, their peculiar trouble was that they fell into the vats; and when they were fished out, there was never enough of them left to be worth exhibiting,—sometimes they would be overlooked for days, till all but the bones of them had gone out to the world as Durham's Pure Leaf Lard!

# A Deeper Look:

1.     What kind of residual is left behind after the climax of this scene?

2.     How would you describe the detail used to explain the effect of the climax on the people it affected? Why?

3.     Now, remember back to your own efforts in this exercise. Did you overlook any detail of the aftermath of your own explosion?

# Humanity:

Exercises to give
character life

## 5

# Single and Looking

At the core of every story, life must be present. Even if the character is not human, your audience will be and must be able to relate. Humans relate best when they have events in their own lives to compare their emotions to. Humans who have never experienced pain or loss may not be as likely to feel for someone else's pain or loss. They may try to fake an emotional connection, but without having their own similar experiences, it is often difficult to connect with other's lives (fictional or real). Therefore, when we create characters, we must be able to prepare them with a life that many living readers can relate to personally.

Often published authors will hear a critic say "I didn't find this character believable." Some authors get down on themselves, maybe even get mad for not being better writers. But it's also quite likely that the reader who didn't find it believable simply doesn't have the experience to measure the true reality about character or a situation. There is no way to please every reader, because not every reader is fully experienced in every little detail about humanity. As writers, we must do our best to find as much common ground as possible; or, if there is no common ground, we need to find common reference points to help readers understand a new experience.

For example, if we write a scene about a person getting so angry that she picks up a sledge hammer and uses it to punch holes in the side of a house, some readers who have never seen people get this angry may suggest "that would never happen," but people who have seen high degrees of anger might break into tears recalling similar situations.

Although we can't please everyone, there are some steps that we can take to ensure that we are doing all we can to create a solid core of humanity for any character. A common and cliché exercise is to write a biography of your character. It is one of the most common character building tools for writing and among actors. There's a reason that so many of us use this practice and you are welcome to give it a go for yourself. It's a wonderful exercise to ask questions about your character and then to answer those questions as a means to build up your character.

However, you don't need this book to stir that kind of creative thought.

Instead, this exercise calls for you to choose a favorite comic book character. It can be someone from one of the new, high-tech superhero movies that plague the big screen today. Or it can be someone from an almost forgotten old-time radio show, dime novel or serial comic strips.

Now, let's pretend that you're trying to help this comic book character get a date. Help them write a personal ad that will make them appear attractive enough for a response. The only rule that you need to follow is that everything you list in the ad, must be true. You cannot make up anything new about this character that doesn't already exist.

Now that you've done this with a comic book character, write one for a character that you're currently developing or a character that you've already developed.

# Narrative of the Life of Frederick Douglass, an American Slave

By Frederick Douglass
(1818-1895)

## CHAPTER I

I was born in Tuckahoe, near Hillsborough, and about twelve miles from Easton, in Talbot county, Maryland. I have no accurate knowledge of my age, never having seen any authentic record containing it. By far the larger part of the slaves know as little of their ages as horses know of theirs, and it is the wish of most masters within my knowledge to keep their slaves thus ignorant. I do not remember to have ever met a slave who could tell of his birthday. They seldom come nearer to it than planting-time, harvest-time, cherry-time, spring-time, or fall-time. A want of information concerning my own was a source of unhappiness to me even during childhood. The white children could tell their ages. I could not tell why I ought to be deprived of the same privilege. I was not allowed to make any inquiries of my master concerning it. He deemed all such inquiries on the part of a slave improper and impertinent, and evidence of a restless spirit. The nearest estimate I can give makes me now between twenty-seven and twenty-eight years of age. I come to this, from hearing my master say, some time during 1835, I was about seventeen years old.

My mother was named Harriet Bailey. She was the daughter of Isaac and Betsey Bailey, both colored, and quite dark. My mother was of a darker complexion than either my grandmother or grandfather.

My father was a white man. He was admitted to be such by all I ever heard speak of my parentage. The opinion was also whispered that my master was my father; but of the correctness of this opinion, I know nothing; the means of knowing was withheld from me. My mother and I were separated when I was but an infant—before I knew her as my mother. It is a common custom, in the part of Maryland from which I ran away, to part children from their mothers at a very early age. Frequently, before the child has reached its twelfth month, its mother is taken from it, and hired out on some farm a considerable distance off, and the child is placed under the care of an old woman, too old for field labor. For what this separation is done, I do not know, unless it be to hinder the development of the child's affection toward its mother, and to blunt and destroy the natural affection of the mother for the child. This is the inevitable result.

I never saw my mother, to know her as such, more than four or five times in my life; and each of these times was very short in duration, and at night. She was hired by a Mr. Stewart, who lived about twelve miles from my home. She made her journeys to see me in the night, travelling the whole distance on foot, after the performance of her day's work. She was a field hand, and a whipping is the penalty of not being in the field at sunrise, unless a slave has special permission from his or her master to the contrary—a permission which they seldom get, and one that gives to him that gives it the proud name of being a kind master. I do not recollect of ever seeing my mother by the light of day. She was with me in the night. She would lie down with me, and get me to sleep, but long before I waked she was gone. Very little communication ever took place between us. Death soon ended what little we could have while she lived, and with it her hardships and suffering. She died when I was about seven years old, on one of my master's farms, near Lee's Mill. I was not allowed to be present during her illness, at her death, or burial. She was gone long before I knew any thing about it. Never having enjoyed, to any considerable extent, her soothing presence, her tender and watchful care, I received the tidings of her death with much the same emotions I should have probably felt at the death of a stranger.

Called thus suddenly away, she left me without the slightest intimation of who my father was. The whisper that my master was my father, may or may not be true; and, true or false, it is of but little consequence to my purpose whilst the fact remains, in all its glaring odiousness, that slaveholders have ordained, and by law established, that the children of slave women shall in all cases follow the condition of their mothers; and this is done too obviously to administer to their own lusts, and make a gratification of their wicked desires profitable as well as pleasurable; for by this cunning arrangement, the slaveholder, in cases not a few, sustains to his slaves the double relation of master and father.

I know of such cases; and it is worthy of remark that such slaves invariably suffer greater hardships, and have more to contend with, than others. They are, in the first place, a constant offence to their mistress. She is ever disposed to find fault with them; they can seldom do any thing to please her; she is never better pleased than when she sees them under the lash, especially when she suspects her husband of showing to his mulatto children favors which he withholds from his black slaves. The master is frequently compelled to sell this class of his slaves, out of deference to the feelings of his white wife; and, cruel as the deed may strike any one to be, for a man to sell his own children to human flesh-mongers, it is often the dictate of humanity for him to do so; for, unless he does this, he must not only whip them himself, but must stand by and see one white son tie up his brother, of but few shades darker complexion than himself, and ply the gory lash to his naked back; and if he lisp one word of disapproval, it is set down to his parental partiality, and only makes a bad matter worse, both for himself and the slave whom he would protect and defend.

Every year brings with it multitudes of this class of slaves. It was doubtless in consequence of a knowledge of this fact, that one great statesman of the south predicted the downfall of slavery by the inevitable laws of population. Whether this prophecy is ever fulfilled or not, it is nevertheless plain that a very different-looking class of people are springing up at the south, and are now held in slavery, from those originally brought to this country from Africa; and if their increase do no other good, it will do away the force of the argument, that God cursed Ham, and therefore American slavery is right. If the lineal descendants of Ham are alone to be scripturally enslaved, it is certain that slavery at the south must soon become unscriptural; for thousands are ushered into the world, annually, who, like myself, owe their existence to white fathers, and those fathers most frequently their own masters.

I have had two masters. My first master's name was Anthony. I do not remember his first name. He was generally called Captain Anthony—a title which, I presume, he acquired by sailing a craft on the Chesapeake Bay. He was not considered a rich slaveholder. He owned two or three farms, and about thirty slaves. His farms and slaves were under the care of an overseer. The overseer's name was Plummer. Mr. Plummer was a miserable drunkard, a profane swearer, and a savage monster. He always went armed with a cowskin and a heavy cudgel. I have known him to cut and slash the women's heads so horribly, that even master would be enraged at his cruelty, and would threaten to whip him if he did not mind himself. Master, however, was not a humane slaveholder. It required extraordinary barbarity on the part of an overseer to affect him. He was a cruel man, hardened by a long life of slaveholding. He would at times seem to take great pleasure in whipping a slave. I have often been awakened at the dawn of day by the most heart-rending shrieks of an own aunt of mine, whom he used to tie up to a joist, and whip upon her naked back till she was literally covered with blood. No words, no tears, no prayers, from his gory victim, seemed to move his iron heart from its bloody purpose. The louder she screamed, the harder he whipped; and where the blood ran fastest, there he whipped longest. He would whip her to make her scream, and whip her to make her hush; and not until overcome by fatigue, would he cease to swing the blood-clotted cowskin. I remember the first time I ever witnessed this horrible exhibition. I was quite a child, but I well remember it. I never shall forget it whilst I remember any thing. It was the first of a long series of such outrages, of which I was doomed to be a witness and a participant. It struck me with awful force. It was the blood-stained gate, the entrance to the hell of slavery, through which I was about to pass. It was a most terrible spectacle. I wish I could commit to paper the feelings with which I beheld it.

This occurrence took place very soon after I went to live with my old master, and under the following circumstances. Aunt Hester went out one night,—where or for what I do not know,—and happened to be absent when my master desired her presence. He had ordered her not to go out evenings, and warned her that she must never let him catch her in company with a young man, who was paying attention to her belonging to Colonel Lloyd. The young man's name was Ned Roberts, generally called Lloyd's Ned. Why master was so careful of her, may be safely left to conjecture. She was a woman of noble form, and of graceful proportions, having very few equals, and fewer superiors, in personal appearance, among the colored or white women of our neighborhood.

Aunt Hester had not only disobeyed his orders in going out, but had been found in company with Lloyd's Ned; which circumstance, I found, from what he said while whipping her, was the chief offence. Had he been a man of pure morals himself, he might have been thought interested in protecting the innocence of my aunt; but those who knew him will not suspect him of any such virtue. Before he commenced whipping Aunt Hester, he took her into the kitchen, and stripped her from neck to waist, leaving her neck, shoulders, and back, entirely naked. He then told her to cross her hands, calling her at the same time a d——d b——-h. After crossing her hands, he tied them with a strong rope, and led her to a stool under a large hook in the joist, put in for the purpose. He made her get upon the stool, and tied her hands to the hook. She now stood fair for his infernal purpose. Her arms were stretched up at their full length, so that she stood upon the ends of her toes. He then said to her, "Now, you d——d b——-h, I'll learn you how to disobey my orders!" and after rolling up his sleeves, he commenced to lay on the heavy cowskin, and soon the warm, red blood (amid heart-rending shrieks from her, and horrid oaths from him) came dripping to the floor. I was so terrified and horror-stricken at the sight, that I hid myself in a closet, and dared not venture out till long after the bloody transaction was over. I expected it would be my turn next. It was all new to me. I had never seen any thing like it before. I had always lived with my grandmother on the outskirts of the plantation, where she was put to raise the children of the younger women. I had therefore been, until now, out of the way of the bloody scenes that often occurred on the plantation.

# A Deeper Look:

1.    Besides the fact that this story is about a historic human being, in what specific ways do you think the author makes this character believably real?

2.    What other human beings appear in this story? Does the author make them as real as the main character himself?

3.    If you were to write a narrative of your own life, what kind of behaviors or characteristics would you show the reader to prove that you were a real human being? How do you think you might present that to your reader?

# Criminal Record

One of the biggest mistakes that writers can make is to try and create an absolutely perfect character. Some authors may make their romantic leads monstrous abominations, but they'll still give them perfect tall, dark and handsome looks and charming personalities. These are the worst kind of characters because they can't endure the test of time. They become fads for some readers and jokes to others.

The greatest help you can give your character and help readers associate with him or her is to give it flaws. Perfect is boring. Flawed is intriguing. Why? Because your readers are all flawed, because they're human and being human is being believable.

For example, previously we shared personal ads for comic book characters.

Imagine this personal ad for Superman:

*SWM. Tall, dark and handsome. The perfect gentleman. Never curses. Never gets mad. Is friendly to people. Loves all of humanity. Loves his mother, sends all of his paychecks home to her. In other words, the perfect, momma's boy. Loves to fly. Travels a lot. Will help anyone in need at any time. Is better in every way than any human being alive.*

This ad has one word written all over it: BORING!
Now let's read this ad by another well-known superhero:

*Single male. Millionaire baby! Daredevil. Hates bullies. Parents were killed by bullies. LOVES high-tech toys. Loves to drink and party and socialize, the prettier you are, the better. Sly women who wear leather and carry whips are a plus. MEOW! Has a lot of luggage and scars. Works day and night hours (ahh the pains of being a celebrity philanthropist), but has really cool cars, a big mansion, a pilot's license (we can go anywhere), eats at all the best restaurants, dances at all the best clubs and knows how to have a really good time.*

Now that's an intriguing character! Why? Because he's not perfect. Just like every single reader out there. Everyone has flaws. Everyone. Readers relate to flaws. Perfect characters depress readers and make them ask "why can't I find someone perfect like that."

For this exercise, let's create a criminal background for your character. You will need the personal ad that your wrote for the previous exercise. This can be for the comic book character or the one for your own character (if you created one). Begin by reading the ad again. Then create a list of ten character flaws this person or thing could have. After you create your list, select three flaws and insert them into your current ad.

Read your ad once more. How does it sound? Does it sound like a real person? Yes? No? Maybe? As you may notice, simply having positive traits and negative traits might not make a character believable or even human. Luckily for us, we're not really writing dating ads. Next up, part III

# The Birthmark

By Nathaniel Hawthorne

(1804-1864)

In the latter part of the last century there lived a man of science, an eminent proficient in every branch of natural philosophy, who not long before our story opens had made experience of a spiritual affinity more attractive than any chemical one. He had left his laboratory to the care of an assistant, cleared his fine countenance from the furnace smoke, washed the stain of acids from his fingers, and persuaded a beautiful woman to become his wife. In those days when the comparatively recent discovery of electricity and other kindred mysteries of Nature seemed to open paths into the region of miracle, it was not unusual for the love of science to rival the love of woman in its depth and absorbing energy. The higher intellect, the imagination, the spirit, and even the heart might all find their congenial aliment in pursuits which, as some of their ardent votaries believed, would ascend from one step of powerful intelligence to another, until the philosopher should lay his hand on the secret of creative force and perhaps make new worlds for himself. We know not whether Aylmer possessed this degree of faith in man's ultimate control over Nature. He had devoted himself, however, too unreservedly to scientific studies ever to be weaned from them by any second passion. His love for his young wife might prove the stronger of the two; but it could only be by intertwining itself with his love of science, and uniting the strength of the latter to his own.

Such a union accordingly took place, and was attended with truly remarkable consequences and a deeply impressive moral. One day, very soon after their marriage, Aylmer sat gazing at his wife with a trouble in his countenance that grew stronger until he spoke.

"Georgiana," said he, "has it never occurred to you that the mark upon your cheek might be removed?"

"No, indeed," said she, smiling; but perceiving the seriousness of his manner, she blushed deeply. "To tell you the truth it has been so often called a charm that I was simple enough to imagine it might be so."

"Ah, upon another face perhaps it might," replied her husband; "but never on yours. No, dearest Georgiana, you came so nearly perfect from the hand of Nature that this slightest possible defect, which we hesitate whether to term a defect or a beauty, shocks me, as being the visible mark of earthly imperfection."

"Shocks you, my husband!" cried Georgiana, deeply hurt; at first reddening with momentary anger, but then bursting into tears. "Then why did you take me from my mother's side? You cannot love what shocks you!"

To explain this conversation it must be mentioned that in the centre of Georgiana's left cheek there was a singular mark, deeply interwoven, as it were, with the texture and substance of her face. In the usual state of her complexion--a healthy though delicate bloom--the mark wore a tint of deeper crimson, which imperfectly defined its shape amid the surrounding rosiness. When she blushed it gradually became more indistinct, and finally vanished amid the triumphant rush of blood that bathed the whole cheek with its brilliant glow. But if any shifting motion caused her to turn pale there was the mark again, a crimson stain upon the snow, in what Aylmer sometimes deemed an almost fearful distinctness. Its shape bore not a little similarity to the human hand, though of the smallest pygmy size. Georgiana's lovers were wont to say that some fairy at her birth hour had laid her tiny hand upon the infant's cheek, and left this impress there in token of the magic endowments that were to give her such sway over all hearts. Many a desperate swain would have risked life for the privilege of pressing his lips to the mysterious hand. It must not be concealed, however, that the impression wrought by this fairy sign manual varied exceedingly, according to the difference of temperament in the beholders. Some fastidious persons--but they were exclusively of her own sex--affirmed that the bloody hand, as they chose to call it, quite destroyed the effect of Georgiana's beauty, and rendered her countenance even hideous. But it would be as reasonable to say that one of those small blue stains which sometimes occur in the purest statuary marble would convert the Eve of Powers to a monster. Masculine observers, if the birthmark did not heighten their admiration, contented themselves with wishing it away, that the world might possess one living specimen of ideal loveliness without the semblance of a flaw. After his marriage,--for he thought little or nothing of the matter before,--Aylmer discovered that this was the case with himself.

Had she been less beautiful,--if Envy's self could have found aught else to sneer at,--he might have felt his affection heightened by the prettiness of this mimic hand, now vaguely portrayed, now lost, now stealing forth again and glimmering to and fro with every pulse of emotion that throbbed within her heart; but seeing her otherwise so perfect, he found this one defect grow more and more intolerable with every moment of their united lives. It was the fatal flaw of humanity which Nature, in one shape or another, stamps ineffaceably on all her productions, either to imply that they are temporary and finite, or that their perfection must be wrought by toil and pain. The crimson hand expressed the ineludible gripe in which mortality clutches the highest and purest of earthly mould, degrading them into kindred with the lowest, and even with the very brutes, like whom their visible frames return to dust. In this manner, selecting it as the symbol of his wife's liability to sin, sorrow, decay, and death, Aylmer's sombre imagination was not long in rendering the birthmark a frightful object, causing him more trouble and horror than ever Georgiana's beauty, whether of soul or sense, had given him delight.

At all the seasons which should have been their happiest, he invariably and without intending it, nay, in spite of a purpose to the contrary, reverted to this one disastrous topic. Trifling as it at first appeared, it so connected itself with innumerable trains of thought and modes of feeling that it became the central point of all. With the morning twilight Aylmer opened his eyes upon his wife's face and recognized the symbol of imperfection; and when they sat together at the evening hearth his eyes wandered stealthily to her cheek, and beheld, flickering with the blaze of the wood fire, the spectral hand that wrote mortality where he would fain have worshipped. Georgiana soon learned to shudder at his gaze. It needed but a glance with the peculiar expression that his face often wore to change the roses of her cheek into a deathlike paleness, amid which the crimson hand was brought strongly out, like a bass-relief of ruby on the whitest marble.

Late one night when the lights were growing dim, so as hardly to betray the stain on the poor wife's cheek, she herself, for the first time, voluntarily took up the subject.

"Do you remember, my dear Aylmer," said she, with a feeble attempt at a smile, "have you any recollection of a dream last night about this odious hand?"

"None! none whatever!" replied Aylmer, starting; but then he added, in a dry, cold tone, affected for the sake of concealing the real depth of his emotion, "I might well dream of it; for before I fell asleep it had taken a pretty firm hold of my fancy."

"And you did dream of it?" continued Georgiana, hastily; for she dreaded lest a gush of tears should interrupt what she had to say. "A terrible dream! I wonder that you can forget it. Is it possible to forget this one expression?--'It is in her heart now; we must have it out!' Reflect, my husband; for by all means I would have you recall that dream."

The mind is in a sad state when Sleep, the all-involving, cannot confine her spectres within the dim region of her sway, but suffers them to break forth, affrighting this actual life with secrets that perchance belong to a deeper one. Aylmer now remembered his dream. He had fancied himself with his servant Aminadab, attempting an operation for the removal of the birthmark; but the deeper went the knife, the deeper sank the hand, until at length its tiny grasp appeared to have caught hold of Georgiana's heart; whence, however, her husband was inexorably resolved to cut or wrench it away.

When the dream had shaped itself perfectly in his memory, Aylmer sat in his wife's presence with a guilty feeling. Truth often finds its way to the mind close muffled in robes of sleep, and then speaks with uncompromising directness of matters in regard to which we practise an unconscious self-deception during our waking moments. Until now he had not been aware of the tyrannizing influence acquired by one idea over his mind, and of the lengths which he might find in his heart to go for the sake of giving himself peace.

"Aylmer," resumed Georgiana, solemnly, "I know not what may be the cost to both of us to rid me of this fatal birthmark. Perhaps its removal may cause cureless deformity; or it may be the stain goes as deep as life itself. Again: do we know that there is a possibility, on any terms, of unclasping the firm gripe of this little hand which was laid upon me before I came into the world?"

"Dearest Georgiana, I have spent much thought upon the subject," hastily interrupted Aylmer. "I am convinced of the perfect practicability of its removal."

"If there be the remotest possibility of it," continued Georgiana, "let the attempt be made at whatever risk. Danger is nothing to me; for life, while this hateful mark makes me the object of your horror and disgust,--life is a burden which I would fling down with joy. Either remove this dreadful hand, or take my wretched life! You have deep science. All the world bears witness of it. You have achieved great wonders. Cannot you remove this little, little mark, which I cover with the tips of two small fingers? Is this beyond your power, for the sake of your own peace, and to save your poor wife from madness?"

"Noblest, dearest, tenderest wife," cried Aylmer, rapturously, "doubt not my power. I have already given this matter the deepest thought--thought which might almost have enlightened me to create a being less perfect than yourself. Georgiana, you have led me deeper than ever into the heart of science. I feel myself fully competent to render this dear cheek as faultless as its fellow; and then, most beloved, what will be my triumph when I shall have corrected what Nature left imperfect in her fairest work! Even Pygmalion, when his sculptured woman assumed life, felt not greater ecstasy than mine will be."

"It is resolved, then," said Georgiana, faintly smiling. "And, Aylmer, spare me not, though you should find the birthmark take refuge in my heart at last."

Her husband tenderly kissed her cheek--her right cheek--not that which bore the impress of the crimson hand.

The next day Aylmer apprised his wife of a plan that he had formed whereby he might have opportunity for the intense thought and constant watchfulness which the proposed operation would require; while Georgiana, likewise, would enjoy the perfect repose essential to its success. They were to seclude themselves in the extensive apartments occupied by Aylmer as a laboratory, and where, during his toilsome youth, he had made discoveries in the elemental powers of Nature that had roused the admiration of all the learned societies in Europe. Seated calmly in this laboratory, the pale philosopher had investigated the secrets of the highest cloud region and of the profoundest mines; he had satisfied himself of the causes that kindled and kept alive the fires of the volcano; and had explained the mystery of fountains, and how it is that they gush forth, some so bright and pure, and others with such rich medicinal virtues, from the dark bosom of the earth. Here, too, at an earlier period, he had studied the wonders of the human frame, and attempted to fathom the very process by which Nature assimilates all her precious influences from earth and air, and from the spiritual world, to create and foster man, her masterpiece. The latter pursuit, however, Aylmer had long laid aside in unwilling recognition of the truth--against which all seekers sooner or later stumble--that our great creative Mother, while she amuses us with apparently working in the broadest sunshine, is yet severely careful to keep her own secrets, and, in spite of her pretended openness, shows us nothing but results. She permits us, indeed, to mar, but seldom to mend, and, like a jealous patentee, on no account to make. Now, however, Aylmer resumed these half-forgotten investigations; not, of course, with such hopes or wishes as first suggested them; but because they involved much physiological truth and lay in the path of his proposed scheme for the treatment of Georgiana.

As he led her over the threshold of the laboratory, Georgiana was cold and tremulous. Aylmer looked cheerfully into her face, with intent to reassure her, but was so startled with the intense glow of the birthmark upon the whiteness of her cheek that he could not restrain a strong convulsive shudder. His wife fainted.

"Aminadab! Aminadab!" shouted Aylmer, stamping violently on the floor.

Forthwith there issued from an inner apartment a man of low stature, but bulky frame, with shaggy hair hanging about his visage, which was grimed with the vapors of the furnace. This personage had been Aylmer's underworker during his whole scientific career, and was admirably fitted for that office by his great mechanical readiness, and the skill with which, while incapable of comprehending a single principle, he executed all the details of his master's experiments. With his vast strength, his shaggy hair, his smoky aspect, and the indescribable earthiness that incrusted him, he seemed to represent man's physical nature; while Aylmer's slender figure, and pale, intellectual face, were no less apt a type of the spiritual element.

"Throw open the door of the boudoir, Aminadab," said Aylmer, "and burn a pastil."

"Yes, master," answered Aminadab, looking intently at the lifeless form of Georgiana; and then he muttered to himself, "If she were my wife, I'd never part with that birthmark."

When Georgiana recovered consciousness she found herself breathing an atmosphere of penetrating fragrance, the gentle potency of which had recalled her from her deathlike faintness. The scene around her looked like enchantment. Aylmer had converted those smoky, dingy, sombre rooms, where he had spent his brightest years in recondite pursuits, into a series of beautiful apartments not unfit to be the secluded abode of a lovely woman. The walls were hung with gorgeous curtains, which imparted the combination of grandeur and grace that no other species of adornment can achieve; and as they fell from the ceiling to the floor, their rich and ponderous folds, concealing all angles and straight lines, appeared to shut in the scene from infinite space. For aught Georgiana knew, it might be a pavilion among the clouds. And Aylmer, excluding the sunshine, which would have interfered with his chemical processes, had supplied its place with perfumed lamps, emitting flames of various hue, but all uniting in a soft, impurpled radiance. He now knelt by his wife's side, watching her earnestly, but without alarm; for he was confident in his science, and felt that he could draw a magic circle round her within which no evil might intrude.

"Where am I? Ah, I remember," said Georgiana, faintly; and she placed her hand over her cheek to hide the terrible mark from her husband's eyes.

"Fear not, dearest!" exclaimed he. "Do not shrink from me! Believe me, Georgiana, I even rejoice in this single imperfection, since it will be such a rapture to remove it."

"Oh, spare me!" sadly replied his wife. "Pray do not look at it again. I never can forget that convulsive shudder."

In order to soothe Georgiana, and, as it were, to release her mind from the burden of actual things, Aylmer now put in practice some of the light and playful secrets which science had taught him among its profounder lore. Airy figures, absolutely bodiless ideas, and forms of unsubstantial beauty came and danced before her, imprinting their momentary footsteps on beams of light. Though she had some indistinct idea of the method of these optical phenomena, still the illusion was almost perfect enough to warrant the belief that her husband possessed sway over the spiritual world. Then again, when she felt a wish to look forth from her seclusion, immediately, as if her thoughts were answered, the procession of external existence flitted across a screen. The scenery and the figures of actual life were perfectly represented, but with that bewitching, yet indescribable difference which always makes a picture, an image, or a shadow so much more attractive than the original. When wearied of this, Aylmer bade her cast her eyes upon a vessel containing a quantity of earth. She did so, with little interest at first; but was soon startled to perceive the germ of a plant shooting upward from the soil. Then came the slender stalk; the leaves gradually unfolded themselves; and amid them was a perfect and lovely flower.

"It is magical!" cried Georgiana. "I dare not touch it."

"Nay, pluck it," answered Aylmer,--"pluck it, and inhale its brief perfume while you may. The flower will wither in a few moments and leave nothing save its brown seed vessels; but thence may be perpetuated a race as ephemeral as itself."

But Georgiana had no sooner touched the flower than the whole plant suffered a blight, its leaves turning coal-black as if by the agency of fire.

"There was too powerful a stimulus," said Aylmer, thoughtfully.

To make up for this abortive experiment, he proposed to take her portrait by a scientific process of his own invention. It was to be effected by rays of light striking upon a polished plate of metal. Georgiana assented; but, on looking at the result, was affrighted to find the features of the portrait blurred and indefinable; while the minute figure of a hand appeared where the cheek should have been. Aylmer snatched the metallic plate and threw it into a jar of corrosive acid.

Soon, however, he forgot these mortifying failures. In the intervals of study and chemical experiment he came to her flushed and exhausted, but seemed invigorated by her presence, and spoke in glowing language of the resources of his art. He gave a history of the long dynasty of the alchemists, who spent so many ages in quest of the universal solvent by which the golden principle might be elicited from all things vile and base. Aylmer appeared to believe that, by the plainest scientific logic, it was altogether within the limits of possibility to discover this long-sought medium; "but," he added, "a philosopher who should go deep enough to acquire the power would attain too lofty a wisdom to stoop to the exercise of it." Not less singular were his opinions in regard to the elixir vitae. He more than intimated that it was at his option to concoct a liquid that should prolong life for years, perhaps interminably; but that it would produce a discord in Nature which all the world, and chiefly the quaffer of the immortal nostrum, would find cause to curse.

"Aylmer, are you in earnest?" asked Georgiana, looking at him with amazement and fear. "It is terrible to possess such power, or even to dream of possessing it."

"Oh, do not tremble, my love," said her husband. "I would not wrong either you or myself by working such inharmonious effects upon our lives; but I would have you consider how trifling, in comparison, is the skill requisite to remove this little hand."

At the mention of the birthmark, Georgiana, as usual, shrank as if a redhot iron had touched her cheek.

Again Aylmer applied himself to his labors. She could hear his voice in the distant furnace room giving directions to Aminadab, whose harsh, uncouth, misshapen tones were audible in response, more like the grunt or growl of a brute than human speech. After hours of absence, Aylmer reappeared and proposed that she should now examine his cabinet of chemical products and natural treasures of the earth. Among the former he showed her a small vial, in which, he remarked, was contained a gentle yet most powerful fragrance, capable of impregnating all the breezes that blow across a kingdom. They were of inestimable value, the contents of that little vial; and, as he said so, he threw some of the perfume into the air and filled the room with piercing and invigorating delight.

"And what is this?" asked Georgiana, pointing to a small crystal globe containing a gold-colored liquid. "It is so beautiful to the eye that I could imagine it the elixir of life."

"In one sense it is," replied Aylmer; "or, rather, the elixir of immortality. It is the most precious poison that ever was concocted in this world. By its aid I could apportion the lifetime of any mortal at whom you might point your finger. The strength of the dose would determine whether he were to linger out years, or drop dead in the midst of a breath. No king on his guarded throne could keep his life if I, in my private station, should deem that the welfare of millions justified me in depriving him of it."

"Why do you keep such a terrific drug?" inquired Georgiana in horror.

"Do not mistrust me, dearest," said her husband, smiling; "its virtuous potency is yet greater than its harmful one. But see! here is a powerful cosmetic. With a few drops of this in a vase of water, freckles may be washed away as easily as the hands are cleansed. A stronger infusion would take the blood out of the cheek, and leave the rosiest beauty a pale ghost."

"Is it with this lotion that you intend to bathe my cheek?" asked Georgiana, anxiously.

"Oh, no," hastily replied her husband; "this is merely superficial. Your case demands a remedy that shall go deeper."

In his interviews with Georgiana, Aylmer generally made minute inquiries as to her sensations and whether the confinement of the rooms and the temperature of the atmosphere agreed with her. These questions had such a particular drift that Georgiana began to conjecture that she was already subjected to certain physical influences, either breathed in with the fragrant air or taken with her food. She fancied likewise, but it might be altogether fancy, that there was a stirring up of her system--a strange, indefinite sensation creeping through her veins, and tingling, half painfully, half pleasurably, at her heart. Still, whenever she dared to look into the mirror, there she beheld herself pale as a white rose and with the crimson birthmark stamped upon her cheek. Not even Aylmer now hated it so much as she.

To dispel the tedium of the hours which her husband found it necessary to devote to the processes of combination and analysis, Georgiana turned over the volumes of his scientific library. In many dark old tomes she met with chapters full of romance and poetry. They were the works of philosophers of the middle ages, such as Albertus Magnus, Cornelius Agrippa, Paracelsus, and the famous friar who created the prophetic Brazen Head. All these antique naturalists stood in advance of their centuries, yet were imbued with some of their credulity, and therefore were believed, and perhaps imagined themselves to have acquired from the investigation of Nature a power above Nature, and from physics a sway over the spiritual world. Hardly less curious and imaginative were the early volumes of the Transactions of the Royal Society, in which the members, knowing little of the limits of natural possibility, were continually recording wonders or proposing methods whereby wonders might be wrought.

But to Georgiana the most engrossing volume was a large folio from her husband's own hand, in which he had recorded every experiment of his scientific career, its original aim, the methods adopted for its development, and its final success or failure, with the circumstances to which either event was attributable. The book, in truth, was both the history and emblem of his ardent, ambitious, imaginative, yet practical and laborious life. He handled physical details as if there were nothing beyond them; yet spiritualized them all, and redeemed himself from materialism by his strong and eager aspiration towards the infinite. In his grasp the veriest clod of earth assumed a soul. Georgiana, as she read, reverenced Aylmer and loved him more profoundly than ever, but with a less entire dependence on his judgment than heretofore. Much as he had accomplished, she could not but observe that his most splendid successes were almost invariably failures, if compared with the ideal at which he aimed. His brightest diamonds were the merest pebbles, and felt to be so by himself, in comparison with the inestimable gems which lay hidden beyond his reach. The volume, rich with achievements that had won renown for its author, was yet as melancholy a record as ever mortal hand had penned. It was the sad confession and continual exemplification of the shortcomings of the composite man, the spirit burdened with clay and working in matter, and of the despair that assails the higher nature at finding itself so miserably thwarted by the earthly part. Perhaps every man of genius in whatever sphere might recognize the image of his own experience in Aylmer's journal.

So deeply did these reflections affect Georgiana that she laid her face upon the open volume and burst into tears. In this situation she was found by her husband.

"It is dangerous to read in a sorcerer's books," said he with a smile, though his countenance was uneasy and displeased. "Georgiana, there are pages in that volume which I can scarcely glance over and keep my senses. Take heed lest it prove as detrimental to you."

"It has made me worship you more than ever," said she.

"Ah, wait for this one success," rejoined he, "then worship me if you will. I shall deem myself hardly unworthy of it. But come, I have sought you for the luxury of your voice. Sing to me, dearest."

So she poured out the liquid music of her voice to quench the thirst of his spirit. He then took his leave with a boyish exuberance of gayety, assuring her that her seclusion would endure but a little longer, and that the result was already certain. Scarcely had he departed when Georgiana felt irresistibly impelled to follow him. She had forgotten to inform Aylmer of a symptom which for two or three hours past had begun to excite her attention. It was a sensation in the fatal birthmark, not painful, but which induced a restlessness throughout her system. Hastening after her husband, she intruded for the first time into the laboratory.

The first thing that struck her eye was the furnace, that hot and feverish worker, with the intense glow of its fire, which by the quantities of soot clustered above it seemed to have been burning for ages. There was a distilling apparatus in full operation. Around the room were retorts, tubes, cylinders, crucibles, and other apparatus of chemical research. An electrical machine stood ready for immediate use. The atmosphere felt oppressively close, and was tainted with gaseous odors which had been tormented forth by the processes of science. The severe and homely simplicity of the apartment, with its naked walls and brick pavement, looked strange, accustomed as Georgiana had become to the fantastic elegance of her boudoir. But what chiefly, indeed almost solely, drew her attention, was the aspect of Aylmer himself.

He was pale as death, anxious and absorbed, and hung over the furnace as if it depended upon his utmost watchfulness whether the liquid which it was distilling should be the draught of immortal happiness or misery. How different from the sanguine and joyous mien that he had assumed for Georgiana's encouragement!

"Carefully now, Aminadab; carefully, thou human machine; carefully, thou man of clay!" muttered Aylmer, more to himself than his assistant. "Now, if there be a thought too much or too little, it is all over."

"Ho! ho!" mumbled Aminadab. "Look, master! look!"

Aylmer raised his eyes hastily, and at first reddened, then grew paler than ever, on beholding Georgiana. He rushed towards her and seized her arm with a gripe that left the print of his fingers upon it.

"Why do you come hither? Have you no trust in your husband?" cried he, impetuously. "Would you throw the blight of that fatal birthmark over my labors? It is not well done. Go, prying woman, go!"

"Nay, Aylmer," said Georgiana with the firmness of which she possessed no stinted endowment, "it is not you that have a right to complain. You mistrust your wife; you have concealed the anxiety with which you watch the development of this experiment. Think not so unworthily of me, my husband. Tell me all the risk we run, and fear not that I shall shrink; for my share in it is far less than your own."

"No, no, Georgiana!" said Aylmer, impatiently; "it must not be."

"I submit," replied she calmly. "And, Aylmer, I shall quaff whatever draught you bring me; but it will be on the same principle that would induce me to take a dose of poison if offered by your hand."

"My noble wife," said Aylmer, deeply moved, "I knew not the height and depth of your nature until now. Nothing shall be concealed. Know, then, that this crimson hand, superficial as it seems, has clutched its grasp into your being with a strength of which I had no previous conception. I have already administered agents powerful enough to do aught except to change your entire physical system. Only one thing remains to be tried. If that fail us we are ruined."

"Why did you hesitate to tell me this?" asked she.

"Because, Georgiana," said Aylmer, in a low voice, "there is danger."

"Danger? There is but one danger--that this horrible stigma shall be left upon my cheek!" cried Georgiana. "Remove it, remove it, whatever be the cost, or we shall both go mad!"

"Heaven knows your words are too true," said Aylmer, sadly. "And now, dearest, return to your boudoir. In a little while all will be tested."

He conducted her back and took leave of her with a solemn tenderness which spoke far more than his words how much was now at stake. After his departure Georgiana became rapt in musings. She considered the character of Aylmer, and did it completer justice than at any previous moment. Her heart exulted, while it trembled, at his honorable love--so pure and lofty that it would accept nothing less than perfection nor miserably make itself contented with an earthlier nature than he had dreamed of. She felt how much more precious was such a sentiment than that meaner kind which would have borne with the imperfection for her sake, and have been guilty of treason to holy love by degrading its perfect idea to the level of the actual; and with her whole spirit she prayed that, for a single moment, she might satisfy his highest and deepest conception. Longer than one moment she well knew it could not be; for his spirit was ever on the march, ever ascending, and each instant required something that was beyond the scope of the instant before.

The sound of her husband's footsteps aroused her. He bore a crystal goblet containing a liquor colorless as water, but bright enough to be the draught of immortality. Aylmer was pale; but it seemed rather the consequence of a highly-wrought state of mind and tension of spirit than of fear or doubt.

"The concoction of the draught has been perfect," said he, in answer to Georgiana's look. "Unless all my science have deceived me, it cannot fail."

"Save on your account, my dearest Aylmer," observed his wife, "I might wish to put off this birthmark of mortality by relinquishing mortality itself in preference to any other mode. Life is but a sad possession to those who have attained precisely the degree of moral advancement at which I stand. Were I weaker and blinder it might be happiness. Were I stronger, it might be endured hopefully. But, being what I find myself, methinks I am of all mortals the most fit to die."

"You are fit for heaven without tasting death!" replied her husband "But why do we speak of dying? The draught cannot fail. Behold its effect upon this plant."

On the window seat there stood a geranium diseased with yellow blotches, which had overspread all its leaves. Aylmer poured a small quantity of the liquid upon the soil in which it grew. In a little time, when the roots of the plant had taken up the moisture, the unsightly blotches began to be extinguished in a living verdure.

"There needed no proof," said Georgiana, quietly. "Give me the goblet I joyfully stake all upon your word."

"Drink, then, thou lofty creature!" exclaimed Aylmer, with fervid admiration. "There is no taint of imperfection on thy spirit. Thy sensible frame, too, shall soon be all perfect."

She quaffed the liquid and returned the goblet to his hand.

"It is grateful," said she with a placid smile. "Methinks it is like water from a heavenly fountain; for it contains I know not what of unobtrusive fragrance and deliciousness. It allays a feverish thirst that had parched me for many days. Now, dearest, let me sleep. My earthly senses are closing over my spirit like the leaves around the heart of a rose at sunset."

She spoke the last words with a gentle reluctance, as if it required almost more energy than she could command to pronounce the faint and lingering syllables. Scarcely had they loitered through her lips ere she was lost in slumber. Aylmer sat by her side, watching her aspect with the emotions proper to a man the whole value of whose existence was involved in the process now to be tested. Mingled with this mood, however, was the philosophic investigation characteristic of the man of science. Not the minutest symptom escaped him. A heightened flush of the cheek, a slight irregularity of breath, a quiver of the eyelid, a hardly perceptible tremor through the frame,--such were the details which, as the moments passed, he wrote down in his folio volume. Intense thought had set its stamp upon every previous page of that volume, but the thoughts of years were all concentrated upon the last.

While thus employed, he failed not to gaze often at the fatal hand, and not without a shudder. Yet once, by a strange and unaccountable impulse he pressed it with his lips. His spirit recoiled, however, in the very act, and Georgiana, out of the midst of her deep sleep, moved uneasily and murmured as if in remonstrance. Again Aylmer resumed his watch. Nor was it without avail. The crimson hand, which at first had been strongly visible upon the marble paleness of Georgiana's cheek, now grew more faintly outlined. She remained not less pale than ever; but the birthmark with every breath that came and went, lost somewhat of its former distinctness. Its presence had been awful; its departure was more awful still. Watch the stain of the rainbow fading out the sky, and you will know how that mysterious symbol passed away.

"By Heaven! it is well-nigh gone!" said Aylmer to himself, in almost irrepressible ecstasy. "I can scarcely trace it now. Success! success! And now it is like the faintest rose color. The lightest flush of blood across her cheek would overcome it. But she is so pale!"

He drew aside the window curtain and suffered the light of natural day to fall into the room and rest upon her cheek. At the same time he heard a gross, hoarse chuckle, which he had long known as his servant Aminadab's expression of delight.

"Ah, clod! ah, earthly mass!" cried Aylmer, laughing in a sort of frenzy, "you have served me well! Matter and spirit--earth and heaven --have both done their part in this! Laugh, thing of the senses! You have earned the right to laugh."

These exclamations broke Georgiana's sleep. She slowly unclosed her eyes and gazed into the mirror which her husband had arranged for that purpose. A faint smile flitted over her lips when she recognized how barely perceptible was now that crimson hand which had once blazed forth with such disastrous brilliancy as to scare away all their happiness. But then her eyes sought Aylmer's face with a trouble and anxiety that he could by no means account for.

"My poor Aylmer!" murmured she.

"Poor? Nay, richest, happiest, most favored!" exclaimed he. "My peerless bride, it is successful! You are perfect!"

"My poor Aylmer," she repeated, with a more than human tenderness, "you have aimed loftily; you have done nobly. Do not repent that with so high and pure a feeling, you have rejected the best the earth could offer. Aylmer, dearest Aylmer, I am dying!"

Alas! it was too true! The fatal hand had grappled with the mystery of life, and was the bond by which an angelic spirit kept itself in union with a mortal frame. As the last crimson tint of the birthmark--that sole token of human imperfection--faded from her cheek, the parting breath of the now perfect woman passed into the atmosphere, and her soul, lingering a moment near her husband, took its heavenward flight. Then a hoarse, chuckling laugh was heard again! Thus ever does the gross fatality of earth exult in its invariable triumph over the immortal essence which, in this dim sphere of half development, demands the completeness of a higher state. Yet, had Alymer reached a profounder wisdom, he need not thus have flung away the happiness which would have woven his mortal life of the selfsame texture with the celestial. The momentary circumstance was too strong for him; he failed to look beyond the shadowy scope of time, and, living once for all in eternity, to find the perfect future in the present.

# A Deeper Look:

1.      Who do you think is the most intriguing character in this story?

2.      What kind of flaws do they have? What do you think they would be like if they didn't have these flaws? Do you think you'd find them more interesting or less interesting? Why?

3.      As a writer, how many flaws do you think a character should have to be considered interesting?

# The Truth Shall Set You Free

In part one, we practiced identifying and presenting positive character traits. In Part II, we threw in some flaws and you were asked to identify ways that the flaws or negative character traits add to the humanity of a character.

These variances between positive and negative traits are the small details that often sell or sink believability. Positive character traits, show who the character wishes to be or pretends to be. Flaws show whether the character is weak or actively seeks to behave negatively. Variances in character behavior tell the truth about the character's moral fiber. Variances are the details that sell a character as either someone good or someone bad. Either way, these variances demonstrate the truth and reliability of your character.

For example, let us suppose that in our personal ad, we wrote that our character loves children (positive trait). But now let us suppose that in our criminal background section, we said that our character hates dogs. Alone, either of these traits is easy to prove, but what does one have to do with the other? And how can these traits build or destroy a character's believability?

Imagine a set of scales. One side of the scale represents the negative side of humanity while the opposite side reflects the positive. This is where we create a human link that can tip a character for either side of the scale. It's this tipping variance that tells the truth.

One of the easiest ways to show this is by asking why a statement is true. For instance, why does this character love children or why does this character hate dogs. We might find that we come up with answers such as he lost a child once. We might decide that he hates dogs because they bite. Our human connection is the direct experience that he has with children, which our character loves and dogs, which he hates. The tipping point comes from how we see our character acting should these two worlds collide.

For example, if this person lost a child and he hated dogs because they bite, a believable variance would be that if a dog came near a child, this character might beat the dog to protect the child. This is a variance that tips the scale to the positive side of human element, at the same time it reveals another flaw: this character can be violent (beating the dog). We have now begun a chain of character variances that can connect with other traits. If this character is willing to beat a dog, what else might this character be willing to beat? As a character grows, you will find yourself learning to balance more variances as they mingle with others that continue to appear.

Let's try another one, this time let's shift the balance. Suppose that the character hates dogs because they bark and are loud. But he loves children. However sometimes children can be loud. We establish a human connection with the character by demonstrating he has experiences hating loud animals. In this scenario, the variance might be that if the child were running around and screaming in the livingroom while the character was trying to sleep, maybe our character might charge in and beat the child for being noisy instead. Here our balance has shifted to the negative side and we may reveal this person is a villain. Or maybe we might open the door to demonstrate a character's struggle with the guilt of performing this misdeed. Maybe through this struggle, other variances allow us to present an accurate story of what may turn out to be a very good person in the long run.

For this exercise, break out your updated personal ad. Look at all of your positive traits and answer why each one is a positive trait. Write your answers down so you can see them in writing. Do the same for your three flaws.

According to the answers you have given, do you feel you may need to reword some of your ad whether positive or negative because of this new influence? Rewrite your ad with these changes.

How does it sound now? Believable yet?

So let's test it. Choose one positive and one negative trait from your ad and create a scenario where the two collide.

Show the scenario. Write three to five paragraphs showing the event. Be sure to demonstrate or mention the positive trait at least once and the negative trait at least once, then show the collision.

Once you have written it, look back to your personals ad and your other character traits. Would any of them have prevented this particular scenario or any part of it from happening? If so, at the end of your story, write down the traits that would have interfered or altered the situation. Briefly explain why.

If you'd like to take this exercise one step further, go back and revise the scenario. How believable does it appear now? Have you learned anything new about your character? Does your character seem more or less exciting than before?

# Frankenstein
By Mary Shelley
(1797-1851)


## Chapter 24
(excerpt)

His voice became fainter as he spoke, and at length, exhausted by his effort, he sank into silence. About half an hour afterwards he attempted again to speak but was unable; he pressed my hand feebly, and his eyes closed forever, while the irradiation of a gentle smile passed away from his lips.

Margaret, what comment can I make on the untimely extinction of this glorious spirit? What can I say that will enable you to understand the depth of my sorrow? All that I should express would be inadequate and feeble. My tears flow; my mind is overshadowed by a cloud of disappointment. But I journey towards England, and I may there find consolation.

I am interrupted. What do these sounds portend? It is midnight; the breeze blows fairly, and the watch on deck scarcely stir. Again there is a sound as of a human voice, but hoarser; it comes from the cabin where the remains of Frankenstein still lie. I must arise and examine. Good night, my sister.

Great God! what a scene has just taken place! I am yet dizzy with the remembrance of it. I hardly know whether I shall have the power to detail it; yet the tale which I have recorded would be incomplete without this final and wonderful catastrophe.

I entered the cabin where lay the remains of my ill-fated and admirable friend. Over him hung a form which I cannot find words to describe; gigantic in stature, yet uncouth and distorted in its proportions. As he hung over the coffin his face was concealed by long locks of ragged hair; but one vast hand was extended, in colour and apparent texture like that of a mummy. When he heard the sound of my approach he ceased to utter exclamations of grief and horror and sprung towards the window. Never did I behold a vision so horrible as his face, of such loathsome yet appalling hideousness. I shut my eyes involuntarily and endeavoured to recollect what were my duties with regard to this destroyer. I called on him to stay.

He paused, looking on me with wonder; and, again turning towards the lifeless form of his creator, he seemed to forget my presence, and every feature and gesture seemed instigated by the wildest rage of some uncontrollable passion.

"That is also my victim!" he exclaimed: "in his murder my crimes are consummated; the miserable series of my being is wound to its close! Oh, Frankenstein! generous and self-devoted being! what does it avail that I now ask thee to pardon me? I, who irretrievably destroyed thee by destroying all thou lovedst. Alas! he is cold, he cannot answer me."

His voice seemed suffocated; and my first impulses, which had suggested to me the duty of obeying the dying request of my friend, in destroying his enemy, were now suspended by a mixture of curiosity and compassion. I approached this tremendous being; I dared not again raise my eyes to his face, there was something so scaring and unearthly in his ugliness. I attempted to speak, but the words died away on my lips. The monster continued to utter wild and incoherent self-reproaches. At length I gathered resolution to address him in a pause of the tempest of his passion: "Your repentance," I said, "is now superfluous. If you had listened to the voice of conscience, and heeded the stings of remorse, before you had urged your diabolical vengeance to this extremity, Frankenstein would yet have lived.

"And do you dream?" said the damon; "do you think that I was then dead to agony and remorse?--He," he continued, pointing to the corpse, "he suffered not in the consummation of the deed--oh! not the ten-thousandth portion of the anguish that was mine during the lingering detail of its execution. A frightful selfishness hurried me on, while my heart was poisoned with remorse. Think you that the groans of Clerval were music to my ears? My heart was fashioned to be susceptible of love and sympathy; and when wrenched by misery to vice and hatred it did not endure the violence of the change without tone such as you cannot even imagine.

"After the murder of Clerval I returned to Switzerland heart-broken and overcome. I pitied Frankenstein; my pity amounted to horror: I abhorred myself. But when I discovered that he, the author at once of my existence and of its unspeakable torments, dared to hope for happiness; that while he accumulated wretchedness and despair upon me he sought his own enjoyment in feelings and passions from the indulgence of which I was for ever barred, then impotent envy and bitter indignation filled me with an insatiable thirst for vengeance. I recollected my threat and resolved that it should be accomplished. I knew that I was preparing for myself a deadly torture; but I was the slave, not the master, of an impulse which I detested, yet could not disobey. Yet when she died!--nay, then I was not miserable. I had cast off all feeling, subdued all anguish, to riot in the excess of my despair. Evil thenceforth became my good. Urged thus far, I had no choice but to adapt my nature to an element which I had willingly chosen. The completion of my demoniacal design became an insatiable passion. And now it is ended; there is my last victim!"

I was at first touched by the expressions of his misery; yet, when I called to mind what Frankenstein had said of his powers of eloquence and persuasion, and when I again cast my eyes on the lifeless form of my friend, indignation was rekindled within me. "Wretch!" I said, "it is well that you come here to whine over the desolation that you have made. You throw a torch into a pile of buildings; and when they are consumed you sit among the ruins and lament the fall. Hypocritical fiend! if he whom you mourn still lived, still would he be the object, again would he become the prey, of your accursed vengeance. It is not pity that you feel; you lament only because the victim of your malignity is withdrawn from your power."

"Oh, it is not thus--not thus," interrupted the being; "yet such must be the impression conveyed to you by what appears to be the purport of my actions. Yet I seek not a fellow-feeling in my misery. No sympathy may I ever find. When I first sought it, it was the love of virtue, the feelings of happiness and affection with which my whole being overflowed, that I wished to be participated. But now that virtue has become to me a shadow and that happiness and affection are turned into bitter and loathing despair, in what should I seek for sympathy? I am content to suffer alone while my sufferings shall endure: when I die, I am well satisfied that abhorrence and opprobrium should load my memory. Once my fancy was soothed with dreams of virtue, of fame, and of enjoyment. Once I falsely hoped to meet with beings who, pardoning my outward form, would love me for the excellent qualities which I was capable of unfolding. I was nourished with high thoughts of honour and devotion. But now crime has degraded me beneath the meanest animal. No guilt, no mischief, no malignity, no misery, can be found comparable to mine. When I run over the frightful catalogue of my sins, I cannot believe that I am the same creature whose thoughts were once filled with sublime and transcendent visions of the beauty and the majesty of goodness. But it is even so; the fallen angel becomes a malignant devil. Yet even that enemy of God and man had friends and associates in his desolation; I am alone.

"You, who call Frankenstein your friend, seem to have a knowledge of my crimes and his misfortunes. But in the detail which he gave you of them he could not sum up the hours and months of misery which I endured, wasting in impotent passions. For while I destroyed his hopes, I did not satisfy my own desires. They were for ever ardent and craving; still I desired love and fellowship, and I was still spurned. Was there no injustice in this? Am I to be thought the only criminal when all human kind sinned against me? Why do you not hate Felix who drove his friend from his door with contumely? Why do you not execrate the rustic who sought to destroy the saviour of his child? Nay, these are virtuous and immaculate beings! I, the miserable and the abandoned, am an abortion, to be spurned at, and kicked, and trampled on. Even now my blood boils at the recollection of this injustice.

"But it is true that I am a wretch. I have murdered the lovely and the helpless; I have strangled the innocent as they slept, and grasped to death his throat who never injured me or any other living thing. I have devoted my creator, the select specimen of all that is worthy of love and admiration among men, to misery; I have pursued him even to that irremediable ruin. There he lies, white and cold in death. You hate me; but your abhorrence cannot equal that with which I regard myself. I look on the hands which executed the deed; I think on the heart in which the imagination of it was conceived, and long for the moment when these hands will meet my eyes, when that imagination will haunt my thoughts no more.

"Fear not that I shall be the instrument of future mischief. My work is nearly complete. Neither yours nor any man's death is needed to consummate the series of my being, and accomplish that which must be done; but it requires my own. Do not think that I shall be slow to perform this sacrifice. I shall quit your vessel on the iceraft which brought me thither, and shall seek the most northern extremity of the globe; I shall collect my funeral pile and consume to ashes this miserable frame, that its remains may afford no light to any curious and unhallowed wretch who would create such another as I have been. I shall die. I shall no longer feel the agonies which now consume me, or be the prey of feelings unsatisfied, yet unquenched. He is dead who called me into being; and when I shall be no more the very remembrance of us both will speedily vanish. I shall no longer see the sun or stars, or feel the winds play on my cheeks. Light, feeling, and sense will pass away; and in this condition must I find my happiness. Some years ago, when the images which this world affords first opened upon me, when I felt the cheering warmth of summer, and heard the rustling of the leaves and the warbling of the birds, and these were all to me, I should have wept to die; now it is my only consolation. Polluted by crimes, and torn by the bitterest remorse, where can I find rest but in death?

"Farewell! I leave you, and in you the last of human kind whom these eyes will ever behold. Farewell, Frankenstein! If thou wert yet alive, and yet cherished a desire of revenge against me, it would be better satiated in my life than in my destruction. But it was not so; thou didst seek my extinction that I might not cause greater wretchedness; and if yet, in some mode unknown to me, thou hast not ceased to think and feel, thou wouldst not desire against me a vengeance greater than that which I feel. Blasted as thou wert, my agony was still superior to thine; for the bitter sting of remorse will not cease to rankle in my wounds until death shall close them for ever.

"But soon," he cried, with sad and solemn enthusiasm, "I shall die, and what I now feel be no longer felt. Soon these burning miseries will be extinct. I shall ascend my funeral pile triumphantly, and exult in the agony of the torturing flames. The light of that conflagration will fade away; my ashes will be swept into the sea by the winds. My spirit will sleep in peace; or if it thinks, it will not surely think thus. Farewell."

He sprung from the cabin-window, as he said this, upon the ice-raft which lay close to the vessel. He was soon borne away by the waves and lost in darkness and distance.

# A Deeper Look:

1.  You have just read about one of the most famous
    monsters in literary history. Based on what we've
    discussed in this section, would you call this
    character a monster or a human being? Why?

2.  What flaws did you see in this character? What positive
    traits did you see? What did the author do or say to show
    you these traits?

3.  Do you think it's possible for any character to be a good
    being and a monster at the same time? How is this
    possible or not possible?

# Dialogue:

## Giving it purpose and making it real

# 6

# Text Speak

This exercise is for all of the technical savvy authors.

For this exercise, let's go to the chat message boards.

Part I:

List ten different chatspeak terms that you might use in your chats with other people.

Now, write out what each one means next to the word itself.

Next, using the chat speak terms only, not what they stand for, write a short chat session that uses only one chatspeak term per response. There should be ten statements total shared between two or more people. Write down who is having the conversation. In fact, you can even model how it appears after how it might actually appear in the chatroom. Have fun with it. Try and make it an exciting conversation.

Part II:

Now that you've got your conversation, let's amend it a little. First, Let's get rid of the chatroom appearance and put these statements in quotation marks as all respectable dialogue should appear. Since we're using quotes, identify if someone said something (i.e. she said, John said, yelled John, etc.). This time, instead of using the chatspeak terms, replace the terms with what they stand for. Change only the terms, nothing else.

Now read your conversation. Does it flow? Does it make sense? Does it sound the way you might speak to a real person in a real face-to-face conversation? Why does this matter? Because one of the most important tools in writing is creating believable dialogue. Chatspeak trains writers to become lazy in how they can think about characters holding conversation. It leads to famous movies with cheesy lines that have teens swooning and educated adults rolling their eyes and wondering why they wasted their money on such horrible writing.

When a character speaks, it should be believable. It should show you respect your audience to acknowledge that they know a real conversation when they read one.

So let's step up our game a bit now.

Part III:

Using the same conversation of your previous two, rewrite your dialogue into a real conversation that two or more people might hold. Without changing the intent of each line of dialogue, rewrite it into something believable for a face to face setting.

# Dracula

## By Bram Stoker
## (1847-1912)

### CHAPTER XV

*DR. SEWARD'S DIARY—continued*

FOR a while sheer anger mastered me; it was as if he had during her life struck Lucy on the face. I smote the table hard and rose up as I said to him:—

"Dr. Van Helsing, are you mad?" He raised his head and looked at me, and somehow the tenderness of his face calmed me at once. "Would I were!" he said. "Madness were easy to bear compared with truth like this. Oh, my friend, why, think you, did I go so far round, why take so long to tell you so simple a thing? Was it because I hate you and have hated you all my life? Was it because I wished to give you pain? Was it that I wanted, now so late, revenge for that time when you saved my life, and from a fearful death? Ah no!"

"Forgive me," said I. He went on:—

"My friend, it was because I wished to be gentle in the breaking to you, for I know you have loved that so sweet lady. But even yet I do not expect you to believe. It is so hard to accept at once any abstract truth, that we may doubt such to be possible when we have always believed the 'no' of it; it is more hard still to accept so sad a concrete truth, and of such a one as Miss Lucy. To-night I go to prove it. Dare you come with me?"

This staggered me. A man does not like to prove such a truth; Byron excepted from the category, jealousy.

"And prove the very truth he most abhorred."

He saw my hesitation, and spoke:—

"The logic is simple, no madman's logic this time, jumping from tussock to tussock in a misty bog. If it be not true, then proof will be relief; at worst it will not harm. If it be true! Ah, there is the dread; yet very dread should help my cause, for in it is some need of belief. Come, I tell you what I propose: first, that we go off now and see that child in the hospital. Dr. Vincent, of the North Hospital, where the papers say the child is, is friend of mine, and I think of yours since you were in class at Amsterdam. He will let two scientists see his case, if he will not let two friends. We shall tell him nothing, but only that we wish to learn. And then——"

"And then?" He took a key from his pocket and held it up. "And then we spend the night, you and I, in the churchyard where Lucy lies. This is the key that lock the tomb. I had it from the coffin-man to give to Arthur." My heart sank within me, for I felt that there was some fearful ordeal before us. I could do nothing, however, so I plucked up what heart I could and said that we had better hasten, as the afternoon was passing....

We found the child awake. It had had a sleep and taken some food, and altogether was going on well. Dr. Vincent took the bandage from its throat, and showed us the punctures. There was no mistaking the similarity to those which had been on Lucy's throat. They were smaller, and the edges looked fresher; that was all. We asked Vincent to what he attributed them, and he replied that it must have been a bite of some animal, perhaps a rat; but, for his own part, he was inclined to think that it was one of the bats which are so numerous on the northern heights of London. "Out of so many harmless ones," he said, "there may be some wild specimen from the South of a more malignant species. Some sailor may have brought one home, and it managed to escape; or even from the Zoölogical Gardens a young one may have got loose, or one be bred there from a vampire. These things do occur, you know. Only ten days ago a wolf got out, and was, I believe, traced up in this direction. For a week after, the children were playing nothing but Red Riding Hood on the Heath and in every alley in the place until this 'bloofer lady' scare came along, since when it has been quite a gala-time with them. Even this poor little mite, when he woke up to-day, asked the nurse if he might go away. When she asked him why he wanted to go, he said he wanted to play with the 'bloofer lady.' "

"I hope," said Van Helsing, "that when you are sending the child home you will caution its parents to keep strict watch over it. These fancies to stray are most dangerous; and if the child were to remain out another night, it would probably be fatal. But in any case I suppose you will not let it away for some days?"

"Certainly not, not for a week at least; longer if the wound is not healed."

Our visit to the hospital took more time than we had reckoned on, and the sun had dipped before we came out. When Van Helsing saw how dark it was, he said:—

"There is no hurry. It is more late than I thought. Come, let us seek somewhere that we may eat, and then we shall go on our way."

We dined at "Jack Straw's Castle" along with a little crowd of bicyclists and others who were genially noisy. About ten o'clock we started from the inn. It was then very dark, and the scattered lamps made the darkness greater when we were once outside their individual radius. The Professor had evidently noted the road we were to go, for he went on unhesitatingly; but, as for me, I was in quite a mixup as to locality. As we went further, we met fewer and fewer people, till at last we were somewhat surprised when we met even the patrol of horse police going their usual suburban round. At last we reached the wall of the churchyard, which we climbed over. With some little difficulty—for it was very dark, and the whole place seemed so strange to us—we found the Westenra tomb. The Professor took the key, opened the creaky door, and standing back, politely, but quite unconsciously, motioned me to precede him. There was a delicious irony in the offer, in the courtliness of giving preference on such a ghastly occasion. My companion followed me quickly, and cautiously drew the door to, after carefully ascertaining that the lock was a falling, and not a spring, one. In the latter case we should have been in a bad plight. Then he fumbled in his bag, and taking out a matchbox and a piece of candle, proceeded to make a light. The tomb in the day-time, and when wreathed with fresh flowers, had looked grim and gruesome enough; but now, some days afterwards, when the flowers hung lank and dead, their whites turning to rust and their greens to browns; when the spider and the beetle had resumed their accustomed dominance; when time-discoloured stone, and dust-encrusted mortar, and rusty, dank iron, and tarnished brass, and clouded silver-plating gave back the feeble glimmer of a candle, the effect was more miserable and sordid than could have been imagined. It conveyed irresistibly the idea that life—animal life—was not the only thing which could pass away.

Van Helsing went about his work systematically. Holding his candle so that he could read the coffin plates, and so holding it that the sperm dropped in white patches which congealed as they touched the metal, he made assurance of Lucy's coffin. Another search in his bag, and he took out a turnscrew.

"What are you going to do?" I asked.

"To open the coffin. You shall yet be convinced." Straightway he began taking out the screws, and finally lifted off the lid, showing the casing of lead beneath. The sight was almost too much for me. It seemed to be as much an affront to the dead as it would have been to have stripped off her clothing in her sleep whilst living; I actually took hold of his hand to stop him. He only said: "You shall see," and again fumbling in his bag, took out a tiny fret-saw. Striking the turnscrew through the lead with a swift downward stab, which made me wince, he made a small hole, which was, however, big enough to admit the point of the saw. I had expected a rush of gas from the week-old corpse. We doctors, who have had to study our dangers, have to become accustomed to such things, and I drew back towards the door. But the Professor never stopped for a moment; he sawed down a couple of feet along one side of the lead coffin, and then across, and down the other side. Taking the edge of the loose flange, he bent it back towards the foot of the coffin, and holding up the candle into the aperture, motioned to me to look.

I drew near and looked. The coffin was empty.

It was certainly a surprise to me, and gave me a considerable shock, but Van Helsing was unmoved. He was now more sure than ever of his ground, and so emboldened to proceed in his task. "Are you satisfied now, friend John?" he asked.

I felt all the dogged argumentativeness of my nature awake within me as I answered him:—

"I am satisfied that Lucy's body is not in that coffin; but that only proves one thing."

"And what is that, friend John?"

"That it is not there."

"That is good logic," he said, "so far as it goes. But how do you—how can you—account for it not being there?"

"Perhaps a body-snatcher," I suggested. "Some of the undertaker's people may have stolen it." I felt that I was speaking folly, and yet it was the only real cause which I could suggest. The Professor sighed. "Ah well!" he said, "we must have more proof. Come with me."

He put on the coffin-lid again, gathered up all his things and placed them in the bag, blew out the light, and placed the candle also in the bag. We opened the door, and went out. Behind us he closed the door and locked it. He handed me the key, saying: "Will you keep it? You had better be assured." I laughed—it was not a very cheerful laugh, I am bound to say—as I motioned him to keep it. "A key is nothing," I said; "there may be duplicates; and anyhow it is not difficult to pick a lock of that kind." He said nothing, but put the key in his pocket. Then he told me to watch at one side of the churchyard whilst he would watch at the other. I took up my place behind a yew-tree, and I saw his dark figure move until the intervening headstones and trees hid it from my sight.

It was a lonely vigil. Just after I had taken my place I heard a distant clock strike twelve, and in time came one and two. I was chilled and unnerved, and angry with the Professor for taking me on such an errand and with myself for coming. I was too cold and too sleepy to be keenly observant, and not sleepy enough to betray my trust so altogether I had a dreary, miserable time.

Suddenly, as I turned round, I thought I saw something like a white streak, moving between two dark yew-trees at the side of the churchyard farthest from the tomb; at the same time a dark mass moved from the Professor's side of the ground, and hurriedly went towards it. Then I too moved; but I had to go round headstones and railed-off tombs, and I stumbled over graves. The sky was overcast, and somewhere far off an early cock crew. A little way off, beyond a line of scattered juniper-trees, which marked the pathway to the church, a white, dim figure flitted in the direction of the tomb. The tomb itself was hidden by trees, and I could not see where the figure disappeared. I heard the rustle of actual movement where I had first seen the white figure, and coming over, found the Professor holding in his arms a tiny child. When he saw me he held it out to me, and said:—

"Are you satisfied now?"

"No," I said, in a way that I felt was aggressive.

"Do you not see the child?"

"Yes, it is a child, but who brought it here? And is it wounded?" I asked.

"We shall see," said the Professor, and with one impulse we took our way out of the churchyard, he carrying the sleeping child.

When we had got some little distance away, we went into a clump of trees, and struck a match, and looked at the child's throat. It was without a scratch or scar of any kind.

"Was I right?" I asked triumphantly.

"We were just in time," said the Professor thankfully.

We had now to decide what we were to do with the child, and so consulted about it. If we were to take it to a police-station we should have to give some account of our movements during the night; at least, we should have had to make some statement as to how we had come to find the child. So finally we decided that we would take it to the Heath, and when we heard a policeman coming, would leave it where he could not fail to find it; we would then seek our way home as quickly as we could. All fell out well. At the edge of Hampstead Heath we heard a policeman's heavy tramp, and laying the child on the pathway, we waited and watched until he saw it as he flashed his lantern to and fro. We heard his exclamation of astonishment, and then we went away silently. By good chance we got a cab near the "Spaniards," and drove to town.

I cannot sleep, so I make this entry. But I must try to get a few hours' sleep, as Van Helsing is to call for me at noon. He insists that I shall go with him on another expedition.

*27 September*—It was two o'clock before we found a suitable opportunity for our attempt. The funeral held at noon was all completed, and the last stragglers of the mourners had taken themselves lazily away, when, looking carefully from behind a clump of alder-trees, we saw the sexton lock the gate after him. We knew then that we were safe till morning did we desire it; but the Professor told me that we should not want more than an hour at most. Again I felt that horrid sense of the reality of things, in which any effort of imagination seemed out of place; and I realised distinctly the perils of the law which we were incurring in our unhallowed work. Besides, I felt it was all so useless. Outrageous as it was to open a leaden coffin, to see if a woman dead nearly a week were really dead, it now seemed the height of folly to open the tomb again, when we knew, from the evidence of our own eyesight, that the coffin was empty. I shrugged my shoulders, however, and rested silent, for Van Helsing had a way of going on his own road, no matter who remonstrated. He took the key, opened the vault, and again courteously motioned me to precede. The place was not so gruesome as last night, but oh, how unutterably mean-looking when the sunshine streamed in. Van Helsing walked over to Lucy's coffin, and I followed. He bent over and again forced back the leaden flange; and then a shock of surprise and dismay shot through me.

There lay Lucy, seemingly just as we had seen her the night before her funeral. She was, if possible, more radiantly beautiful than ever; and I could not believe that she was dead. The lips were red, nay redder than before; and on the cheeks was a delicate bloom.

"Is this a juggle?" I said to him.

"Are you convinced now?" said the Professor in response, and as he spoke he put over his hand, and in a way that made me shudder, pulled back the dead lips and showed the white teeth.

"See," he went on, "see, they are even sharper than before. With this and this"—and he touched one of the canine teeth and that below it—"the little children can be bitten. Are you of belief now, friend John?" Once more, argumentative hostility woke within me. I could not accept such an overwhelming idea as he suggested; so, with an attempt to argue of which I was even at the moment ashamed, I said:—

"She may have been placed here since last night."

"Indeed? That is so, and by whom?"

"I do not know. Some one has done it."

"And yet she has been dead one week. Most peoples in that time would not look so."
I had no answer for this, so was silent. Van Helsing did not seem to notice my silence; at
any rate, he showed neither chagrin nor triumph. He was looking intently at the face of the
dead woman, raising the eyelids and looking at the eyes, and once more opening the lips and
examining the teeth. Then he turned to me and said:—

"Here, there is one thing which is different from all recorded; here is some dual life
that is not as the common. She was bitten by the vampire when she was in a trance, sleep-
walking—oh, you start; you do not know that, friend John, but you shall know it all later—and
in trance could he best come to take more blood. In trance she died, and in trance she is Un-
Dead, too. So it is that she differ from all other. Usually when the Un-Dead sleep at home"—
as he spoke he made a comprehensive sweep of his arm to designate what to a vampire was
"home"—"their face show what they are, but this so sweet that was when she not Un-Dead
she go back to the nothings of the common dead. There is no malign there, see, and so it make
hard that I must kill her in her sleep." This turned my blood cold, and it began to dawn upon
me that I was accepting Van Helsing's theories; but if she were really dead, what was there of
terror in the idea of killing her? He looked up at me, and evidently saw the change in my face,
for he said almost joyously:—

"Ah, you believe now?"

I answered: "Do not press me too hard all at once. I am willing to accept. How will you
do this bloody work?"

"I shall cut off her head and fill her mouth with garlic, and I shall drive a stake through
her body." It made me shudder to think of so mutilating the body of the woman whom I had
loved. And yet the feeling was not so strong as I had expected. I was, in fact, beginning to
shudder at the presence of this being, this Un-Dead, as Van Helsing called it, and to loathe it.
Is it possible that love is all subjective, or all objective?

I waited a considerable time for Van Helsing to begin, but he stood as if wrapped in
thought. Presently he closed the catch of his bag with a snap, and said:—

"I have been thinking, and have made up my mind as to what is best. If I did simply
follow my inclining I would do now, at this moment, what is to be done; but there are other
things to follow, and things that are thousand times more difficult in that them we do not
know. This is simple. She have yet no life taken, though that is of time; and to act now would
be to take danger from her for ever. But then we may have to want Arthur, and how shall we
tell him of this? If you, who saw the wounds on Lucy's throat, and saw the wounds so similar
on the child's at the hospital; if you, who saw the coffin empty last night and full to-day with a
woman who have not change only to be more rose and more beautiful in a whole week, after
she die—if you know of this and know of the white figure last night that brought the child
to the churchyard, and yet of your own senses you did not believe, how, then, can I expect
Arthur, who know none of those things, to believe? He doubted me when I took him from her
kiss when she was dying. I know he has forgiven me because in some mistaken idea I have
done things that prevent him say good-bye as he ought; and he may think that in some more
mistaken idea this woman was buried alive; and that in most mistake of all we have killed her.
He will then argue back that it is we, mistaken ones, that have killed her by our ideas; and so
he will be much unhappy always. Yet he never can be sure; and that is the worst of all. And
he will sometimes think that she he loved was buried alive, and that will paint his dreams
with horrors of what she must have suffered; and again, he will think that we may be right,
and that his so beloved was, after all, an Un-Dead. No! I told him once, and since then I learn
much. Now, since I know it is all true, a hundred thousand times more do I know that he must
pass through the bitter waters to reach the sweet. He, poor fellow, must have one hour that

will make the very face of heaven grow black to him; then we can act for good all round and send him peace. My mind is made up. Let us go. You return home for to-night to your asylum, and see that all be well. As for me, I shall spend the night here in this churchyard in my own way. To-morrow night you will come to me to the Berkeley Hotel at ten of the clock. I shall send for Arthur to come too, and also that so fine young man of America that gave his blood. Later we shall all have work to do. I come with you so far as Piccadilly and there dine, for I must be back here before the sun set."

So we locked the tomb and came away, and got over the wall of the churchyard, which was not much of a task, and drove back to Piccadilly.

*Note left by Van Helsing in his portmanteau, Berkeley Hotel directed to John Seward, M. D.*

*(Not delivered.)*

"27 September.

"Friend John,—

"I write this in case anything should happen. I go alone to watch in that churchyard. It pleases me that the Un-Dead, Miss Lucy, shall not leave to-night, that so on the morrow night she may be more eager. Therefore I shall fix some things she like not—garlic and a crucifix—and so seal up the door of the tomb. She is young as Un-Dead, and will heed. Moreover, these are only to prevent her coming out; they may not prevail on her wanting to get in; for then the Un-Dead is desperate, and must find the line of least resistance, whatsoever it may be. I shall be at hand all the night from sunset till after the sunrise, and if there be aught that may be learned I shall learn it. For Miss Lucy or from her, I have no fear; but that other to whom is there that she is Un-Dead, he have now the power to seek her tomb and find shelter. He is cunning, as I know from Mr. Jonathan and from the way that all along he have fooled us when he played with us for Miss Lucy's life, and we lost; and in many ways the Un-Dead are strong. He have always the strength in his hand of twenty men; even we four who gave our strength to Miss Lucy it also is all to him. Besides, he can summon his wolf and I know not what. So if it be that he come thither on this night he shall find me; but none other shall—until it be too late. But it may be that he will not attempt the place. There is no reason why he should; his hunting ground is more full of game than the churchyard where the Un-Dead woman sleep, and the one old man watch.

"Therefore I write this in case.... Take the papers that are with this, the diaries of Harker and the rest, and read them, and then find this great Un-Dead, and cut off his head and burn his heart or drive a stake through it, so that the world may rest from him.

"If it be so, farewell.

"Van Helsing."

*Dr. Seward's Diary.*

*28 September*—It is wonderful what a good night's sleep will do for one. Yesterday I was almost willing to accept Van Helsing's monstrous ideas; but now they seem to start out lurid before me as outrages on common sense. I have no doubt that he believes it all. I wonder if his mind can have become in any way unhinged. Surely there must be some rational explanation of all these mysterious things. Is it possible that the Professor can have done it himself? He is so abnormally clever that if he went off his head he would carry out his intent with regard to some fixed idea in a wonderful way. I am loath to think it, and indeed it would be almost as great a marvel as the other to find that Van Helsing was mad; but anyhow I shall watch him carefully. I may get some light on the mystery.

*29 September, morning.....* Last night, at a little before ten o'clock, Arthur and Quincey came into Van Helsing's room; he told us all that he wanted us to do, but especially addressing himself to Arthur, as if all our wills were centred in his. He began by saying that he hoped we would all come with him too, "for," he said, "there is a grave duty to be done there. You were doubtless surprised at my letter?" This query was directly addressed to Lord Godalming.

"I was. It rather upset me for a bit. There has been so much trouble around my house of late that I could do without any more. I have been curious, too, as to what you mean. Quincey and I talked it over; but the more we talked, the more puzzled we got, till now I can say for myself that I'm about up a tree as to any meaning about anything."

"Me too," said Quincey Morris laconically.

"Oh," said the Professor, "then you are nearer the beginning, both of you, than friend John here, who has to go a long way back before he can even get so far as to begin."

It was evident that he recognised my return to my old doubting frame of mind without my saying a word. Then, turning to the other two, he said with intense gravity:—

"I want your permission to do what I think good this night. It is, I know, much to ask; and when you know what it is I propose to do you will know, and only then, how much. Therefore may I ask that you promise me in the dark, so that afterwards, though you may be angry with me for a time—I must not disguise from myself the possibility that such may be—you shall not blame yourselves for anything."

"That's frank anyhow," broke in Quincey. "I'll answer for the Professor. I don't quite see his drift, but I swear he's honest; and that's good enough for me."

"I thank you, sir," said Van Helsing proudly. "I have done myself the honour of counting you one trusting friend, and such endorsement is dear to me." He held out a hand, which Quincey took.

Then Arthur spoke out:—

"Dr. Van Helsing, I don't quite like to 'buy a pig in a poke,' as they say in Scotland, and if it be anything in which my honour as a gentleman or my faith as a Christian is concerned, I cannot make such a promise. If you can assure me that what you intend does not violate either of these two, then I give my consent at once; though for the life of me, I cannot understand what you are driving at."

"I accept your limitation," said Van Helsing, "and all I ask of you is that if you feel it necessary to condemn any act of mine, you will first consider it well and be satisfied that it does not violate your reservations."

"Agreed!" said Arthur; "that is only fair. And now that the pourparlers are over, may I ask what it is we are to do?"

"I want you to come with me, and to come in secret, to the churchyard at Kingstead."

Arthur's face fell as he said in an amazed sort of way:—

"Where poor Lucy is buried?" The Professor bowed. Arthur went on: "And when there?"

"To enter the tomb!" Arthur stood up.

"Professor, are you in earnest; or it is some monstrous joke? Pardon me, I see that you are in earnest." He sat down again, but I could see that he sat firmly and proudly, as one who is on his dignity. There was silence until he asked again:—

"And when in the tomb?"

"To open the coffin."

"This is too much!" he said, angrily rising again. "I am willing to be patient in all things that are reasonable; but in this—this desecration of the grave—of one who——" He fairly choked with indignation. The Professor looked pityingly at him.

"If I could spare you one pang, my poor friend," he said, "God knows I would. But this night our feet must tread in thorny paths; or later, and for ever, the feet you love must walk in paths of flame!"

Arthur looked up with set white face and said:—

"Take care, sir, take care!"

"Would it not be well to hear what I have to say?" said Van Helsing. "And then you will at least know the limit of my purpose. Shall I go on?"

"That's fair enough," broke in Morris.

After a pause Van Helsing went on, evidently with an effort:—

"Miss Lucy is dead; is it not so? Yes! Then there can be no wrong to her. But if she be not dead——"

Arthur jumped to his feet.

"Good God!" he cried. "What do you mean? Has there been any mistake; has she been buried alive?" He groaned in anguish that not even hope could soften.

"I did not say she was alive, my child; I did not think it. I go no further than to say that she might be Un-Dead."

"Un-Dead! Not alive! What do you mean? Is this all a nightmare, or what is it?"

"There are mysteries which men can only guess at, which age by age they may solve only in part. Believe me, we are now on the verge of one. But I have not done. May I cut off the head of dead Miss Lucy?"

"Heavens and earth, no!" cried Arthur in a storm of passion. "Not for the wide world will I consent to any mutilation of her dead body. Dr. Van Helsing, you try me too far. What have I done to you that you should torture me so? What did that poor, sweet girl do that you should want to cast such dishonour on her grave? Are you mad that speak such things, or am I mad to listen to them? Don't dare to think more of such a desecration; I shall not give my consent to anything you do. I have a duty to do in protecting her grave from outrage; and, by God, I shall do it!"

Van Helsing rose up from where he had all the time been seated, and said, gravely and sternly:—

"My Lord Godalming, I, too, have a duty to do, a duty to others, a duty to you, a duty to the dead; and, by God, I shall do it! All I ask you now is that you come with me, that you look and listen; and if when later I make the same request you do not be more eager for its fulfilment even than I am, then—then I shall do my duty, whatever it may seem to me. And then, to follow of your Lordship's wishes I shall hold myself at your disposal to render an account to you, when and where you will." His voice broke a little, and he went on with a voice full of pity:—

"But, I beseech you, do not go forth in anger with me. In a long life of acts which were often not pleasant to do, and which sometimes did wring my heart, I have never had so heavy a task as now. Believe me that if the time comes for you to change your mind towards me, one look from you will wipe away all this so sad hour, for I would do what a man can to save you from sorrow. Just think. For why should I give myself so much of labour and so much of sorrow? I have come here from my own land to do what I can of good; at the first to please my friend John, and then to help a sweet young lady, whom, too, I came to love. For her—I am ashamed to say so much, but I say it in kindness—I gave what you gave; the blood of my veins; I gave it, I, who was not, like you, her lover, but only her physician and her friend. I gave to her my nights and days—before death, after death; and if my death can do her good even now, when she is the dead Un-Dead, she shall have it freely." He said this with a very grave, sweet pride, and Arthur was much affected by it. He took the old man's hand and said in a broken voice:—

"Oh, it is hard to think of it, and I cannot understand; but at least I shall go with you and wait."

# A Deeper Look:

1. How does the dialogue in this story come across to you? Why?

2. Do you think the dialogue works for this story? Why? Or Why not?

3. What do you think might be the most difficult aspect about writing dialogue? How could you practice making your dialogue stronger and more effective?

# Facebook Page

Nothing runs as rampant today as the heated and controversial arguments, which flood the countless public forums and litter the Internet today. Your friend posts on Facebook that he hates a popular movie that has no story and a million people all have to take offense.

It's easy to get upset and to form our own opinions. It's easy to argue our own opinions—but let's face it, the characters we create don't all agree with each other. They don't all agree with us for that matter. If all we create are characters that agree with us or share our philosophies, then we become preachers and not story tellers. If we only have a villain to make an audience hate him, while every other character agrees with our personal opinions, then all we've done is masked that we're preaching.

But when we can create a world of characters that don't agree with us, bicker among themselves and can't possibly come together in a common purpose, then we have the makings of a real story world.

This exercise is all about seeing through someone else's eyes and making your readers believe that person, even if you don't.

To start, pick a controversial topic that you have a strong opinion about. It has to be controversial and it has to be one that can be debated. Are you pro-life? Are you a gun rights advocate? Do you believe in teacher unions? Do you believe democrats follow each other off of cliffs after drinking the red punch? Do you believe in torture? Do you protest death penalties? Do you believe in spanking a child? Do you believe in God? Do you believe God should be left out of this discussion?

Whatever the topic, pick one.

Now, if you had one question that you could ask the president of the biggest organization that opposed your opinion, what would it be?

Let's pretend we're on Facebook now. Pretend you've posted your question. Now, as any character that you have created, answer and debate that question.

Rule #1: Many writers make the mistake of masking an argument with character stupidity. You cannot make a weak argument against your question simply by making your character too stupid. Every human being is intelligent in some way, just as every character is stupid to some degree. We are all stupid to some degree, even on topics we are highly connected to and educated within.

Let your characters behave accordingly. If your character is an intelligent person, let him behave like an intelligent person. Don't fill his mouth with faulty information that an intelligent person wouldn't accept. You have to give an honest answer. Imagine that this character is going to be a main character and will have to persuade your audience to their kind of thinking if they're going to support a climax led by that character.

For instance, if you're personally against the death penalty, imagine how, if your character was a lawyer in your book (and the entire story was about him) your character might speak that would persuade your readers to agree in reaching a climax where the villain deserved the death penalty.

Using this information, stir up an argument between you and your character in a way you might see it unfold on someone's acebook page.

Rule #2: Your character must win the debate.

Rule #3: Your character can't simply win because you refuse to argue or quit. Your character must lose because it's not possible to win. Only after losing the debate can you quit or leave the argument.

In other words, you have to provide your character the unique genius it needs that matches its intelligence and common sense approach to outwit yourself.

As you argue, notice if any new character traits jump out at you that could help mold who your character is or could be.

Have fun arguing with yourself.

There is no length for this exercise because, who knows, maybe you might want to come back later and revisit this argument when you discover a new piece of information. This is an exercise that can last only a few lines or one that can continue for as long as you use a specific character throughout your own various writings.

# Alice's Adventures in Wonderland

By Lewis Carroll

(1832-1898)

## CHAPTER VII
### A Mad Tea-Party

There was a table set out under a tree in front of the house, and the March Hare and the Hatter were having tea at it: a Dormouse was sitting between them, fast asleep, and the other two were using it as a cushion, resting their elbows on it, and talking over its head. 'Very uncomfortable for the Dormouse,' thought Alice; 'only, as it's asleep, I suppose it doesn't mind.'

The table was a large one, but the three were all crowded together at one corner of it: 'No room! No room!' they cried out when they saw Alice coming. 'There's PLENTY of room!' said Alice indignantly, and she sat down in a large arm-chair at one end of the table.

'Have some wine,' the March Hare said in an encouraging tone.

Alice looked all round the table, but there was nothing on it but tea. 'I don't see any wine,' she remarked.

'There isn't any,' said the March Hare.

'Then it wasn't very civil of you to offer it,' said Alice angrily.

'It wasn't very civil of you to sit down without being invited,' said the March Hare.

'I didn't know it was YOUR table,' said Alice; 'it's laid for a great many more than three.'

'Your hair wants cutting,' said the Hatter. He had been looking at Alice for some time with great curiosity, and this was his first speech.

'You should learn not to make personal remarks,' Alice said with some severity; 'it's very rude.'

The Hatter opened his eyes very wide on hearing this; but all he SAID was, 'Why is a raven like a writing-desk?'

'Come, we shall have some fun now!' thought Alice. 'I'm glad they've begun asking riddles.—I believe I can guess that,' she added aloud.

'Do you mean that you think you can find out the answer to it?' said the March Hare.

'Exactly so,' said Alice.

'Then you should say what you mean,' the March Hare went on.

'I do,' Alice hastily replied; 'at least—at least I mean what I say—that's the same thing, you know.'

'Not the same thing a bit!' said the Hatter. 'You might just as well say that "I see what I eat" is the same thing as "I eat what I see"!'

'You might just as well say,' added the March Hare, 'that "I like what I get" is the same thing as "I get what I like"!'

'You might just as well say,' added the Dormouse, who seemed to be talking in his sleep, 'that "I breathe when I sleep" is the same thing as "I sleep when I breathe"!'

'It IS the same thing with you,' said the Hatter, and here the conversation dropped, and the party sat silent for a minute, while Alice thought over all she could remember about ravens and writing-desks, which wasn't much.

The Hatter was the first to break the silence. 'What day of the month is it?' he said, turning to Alice: he had taken his watch out of his pocket, and was looking at it uneasily, shaking it every now and then, and holding it to his ear.

Alice considered a little, and then said 'The fourth.'

'Two days wrong!' sighed the Hatter. 'I told you butter wouldn't suit the works!' he added looking angrily at the March Hare.

'It was the BEST butter,' the March Hare meekly replied.

'Yes, but some crumbs must have got in as well,' the Hatter grumbled: 'you shouldn't have put it in with the bread-knife.'

The March Hare took the watch and looked at it gloomily: then he dipped it into his cup of tea, and looked at it again: but he could think of nothing better to say than his first remark, 'It was the BEST butter, you know.'

Alice had been looking over his shoulder with some curiosity. 'What a funny watch!' she remarked. 'It tells the day of the month, and doesn't tell what o'clock it is!'

'Why should it?' muttered the Hatter. 'Does YOUR watch tell you what year it is?'

'Of course not,' Alice replied very readily: 'but that's because it stays the same year for such a long time together.'

'Which is just the case with MINE,' said the Hatter.

Alice felt dreadfully puzzled. The Hatter's remark seemed to have no sort of meaning in it, and yet it was certainly English. 'I don't quite understand you,' she said, as politely as she could.

'The Dormouse is asleep again,' said the Hatter, and he poured a little hot tea upon its nose.

The Dormouse shook its head impatiently, and said, without opening its eyes, 'Of course, of course; just what I was going to remark myself.'

'Have you guessed the riddle yet?' the Hatter said, turning to Alice again.

'No, I give it up,' Alice replied: 'what's the answer?'

'I haven't the slightest idea,' said the Hatter.

'Nor I,' said the March Hare.

Alice sighed wearily. 'I think you might do something better with the time,' she said, 'than waste it in asking riddles that have no answers.'

'If you knew Time as well as I do,' said the Hatter, 'you wouldn't talk about wasting IT. It's HIM.'

'I don't know what you mean,' said Alice.

'Of course you don't!' the Hatter said, tossing his head contemptuously. 'I dare say you never even spoke to Time!'

'Perhaps not,' Alice cautiously replied: 'but I know I have to beat time when I learn music.'

'Ah! that accounts for it,' said the Hatter. 'He won't stand beating. Now, if you only kept on good terms with him, he'd do almost anything you liked with the clock. For instance, suppose it were nine o'clock in the morning, just time to begin lessons: you'd only have to whisper a hint to Time, and round goes the clock in a twinkling! Half-past one, time for dinner!'

('I only wish it was,' the March Hare said to itself in a whisper.)

'That would be grand, certainly,' said Alice thoughtfully: 'but then—I shouldn't be hungry for it, you know.'

'Not at first, perhaps,' said the Hatter: 'but you could keep it to half-past one as long as you liked.'

'Is that the way YOU manage?' Alice asked.

The Hatter shook his head mournfully. 'Not I!' he replied. 'We quarrelled last March— just before HE went mad, you know—' (pointing with his tea spoon at the March Hare,) '—it was at the great concert given by the Queen of Hearts, and I had to sing

    "Twinkle, twinkle, little bat!

    How I wonder what you're at!"

You know the song, perhaps?'

'I've heard something like it,' said Alice.

'It goes on, you know,' the Hatter continued, 'in this way:—

  "Up above the world you fly,
  Like a tea-tray in the sky.
   Twinkle, twinkle—'"

Here the Dormouse shook itself, and began singing in its sleep 'Twinkle, twinkle, twinkle, twinkle—' and went on so long that they had to pinch it to make it stop.

'Well, I'd hardly finished the first verse,' said the Hatter, 'when the Queen jumped up and bawled out, "He's murdering the time! Off with his head!"'

'How dreadfully savage!' exclaimed Alice.

'And ever since that,' the Hatter went on in a mournful tone, 'he won't do a thing I ask! It's always six o'clock now.'

A bright idea came into Alice's head. 'Is that the reason so many tea-things are put out here?' she asked.

'Yes, that's it,' said the Hatter with a sigh: 'it's always tea-time, and we've no time to wash the things between whiles.'

'Then you keep moving round, I suppose?' said Alice.

'Exactly so,' said the Hatter: 'as the things get used up.'

'But what happens when you come to the beginning again?' Alice ventured to ask.

'Suppose we change the subject,' the March Hare interrupted, yawning. 'I'm getting tired of this. I vote the young lady tells us a story.'

'I'm afraid I don't know one,' said Alice, rather alarmed at the proposal.

'Then the Dormouse shall!' they both cried. 'Wake up, Dormouse!' And they pinched it on both sides at once.

The Dormouse slowly opened his eyes. 'I wasn't asleep,' he said in a hoarse, feeble voice: 'I heard every word you fellows were saying.'

'Tell us a story!' said the March Hare.

'Yes, please do!' pleaded Alice.

'And be quick about it,' added the Hatter, 'or you'll be asleep again before it's done.'

'Once upon a time there were three little sisters,' the Dormouse began in a great hurry; 'and their names were Elsie, Lacie, and Tillie; and they lived at the bottom of a well—'

'What did they live on?' said Alice, who always took a great interest in questions of eating and drinking.

'They lived on treacle,' said the Dormouse, after thinking a minute or two.

'They couldn't have done that, you know,' Alice gently remarked; 'they'd have been ill.'

'So they were,' said the Dormouse; 'VERY ill.'

Alice tried to fancy to herself what such an extraordinary ways of living would be like, but it puzzled her too much, so she went on: 'But why did they live at the bottom of a well?'

'Take some more tea,' the March Hare said to Alice, very earnestly.

'I've had nothing yet,' Alice replied in an offended tone, 'so I can't take more.'

'You mean you can't take LESS,' said the Hatter: 'it's very easy to take MORE than nothing.'

'Nobody asked YOUR opinion,' said Alice.

'Who's making personal remarks now?' the Hatter asked triumphantly.

Alice did not quite know what to say to this: so she helped herself to some tea and bread-and-butter, and then turned to the Dormouse, and repeated her question. 'Why did they live at the bottom of a well?'

The Dormouse again took a minute or two to think about it, and then said, 'It was a treacle-well.'

'There's no such thing!' Alice was beginning very angrily, but the Hatter and the March Hare went 'Sh! sh!' and the Dormouse sulkily remarked, 'If you can't be civil, you'd better finish the story for yourself.'

'No, please go on!' Alice said very humbly; 'I won't interrupt again. I dare say there may be ONE.'

'One, indeed!' said the Dormouse indignantly. However, he consented to go on. 'And so these three little sisters—they were learning to draw, you know—'

'What did they draw?' said Alice, quite forgetting her promise.

'Treacle,' said the Dormouse, without considering at all this time.

'I want a clean cup,' interrupted the Hatter: 'let's all move one place on.'

He moved on as he spoke, and the Dormouse followed him: the March Hare moved into the Dormouse's place, and Alice rather unwillingly took the place of the March Hare. The Hatter was the only one who got any advantage from the change: and Alice was a good deal worse off than before, as the March Hare had just upset the milk-jug into his plate.

Alice did not wish to offend the Dormouse again, so she began very cautiously: 'But I don't understand. Where did they draw the treacle from?'

'You can draw water out of a water-well,' said the Hatter; 'so I should think you could draw treacle out of a treacle-well—eh, stupid?'

'But they were IN the well,' Alice said to the Dormouse, not choosing to notice this last remark.

'Of course they were', said the Dormouse; '—well in.'

This answer so confused poor Alice, that she let the Dormouse go on for some time without interrupting it.

'They were learning to draw,' the Dormouse went on, yawning and rubbing its eyes, for it was getting very sleepy; 'and they drew all manner of things—everything that begins with an M—'

'Why with an M?' said Alice.

'Why not?' said the March Hare.

Alice was silent.

The Dormouse had closed its eyes by this time, and was going off into a doze; but, on being pinched by the Hatter, it woke up again with a little shriek, and went on: '—that begins with an M, such as mouse-traps, and the moon, and memory, and muchness—you know you say things are "much of a muchness"—did you ever see such a thing as a drawing of a muchness?'

'Really, now you ask me,' said Alice, very much confused, 'I don't think—'

'Then you shouldn't talk,' said the Hatter.

This piece of rudeness was more than Alice could bear: she got up in great disgust, and walked off; the Dormouse fell asleep instantly, and neither of the others took the least notice of her going, though she looked back once or twice, half hoping that they would call after her: the last time she saw them, they were trying to put the Dormouse into the teapot.

'At any rate I'll never go THERE again!' said Alice as she picked her way through the wood. 'It's the stupidest tea-party I ever was at in all my life!'

Just as she said this, she noticed that one of the trees had a door leading right into it. 'That's very curious!' she thought. 'But everything's curious today. I think I may as well go in at once.' And in she went.

Once more she found herself in the long hall, and close to the little glass table. 'Now, I'll manage better this time,' she said to herself, and began by taking the little golden key, and unlocking the door that led into the garden. Then she went to work nibbling at the mushroom (she had kept a piece of it in her pocket) till she was about a foot high: then she walked down the little passage: and THEN—she found herself at last in the beautiful garden, among the bright flower-beds and the cool fountains.

# A Deeper Look:

1.          What kind of conversation was this? Organized? Frustrating? Some other kind? Why?

2.          Who was in control of this conversation?

3.          Alice walked away from this conversation to end it. What are some other approaches Alice or any of the other characters might take to end this conversation?

# Spectator

Authors can present action in many different ways.

To demonstrate one of these ways, let's go to our elementary school playground.

Some of you kept sports equipment in your classrooms. Some of you may have had a school sports locker where you checked out bats and balls.

For this exercise, remember what recess was like, or try to recall running out the door after school to play with friends. The first item you'll need for this exercise is a ball. Choose a ball. What kind of ball is it? Football? Basketball? Gigantic four-square ball? Tether ball? What was your favorite ball?

Write it down.

Now, write a list of 20 actions that you can take with that specific ball. Can you bounce it? Can you kick it? Can you hurl it at great speed? Can you use the ball with other people? Or only by yourself?

Write your list down.

Choose one action on your list and write down five possible outcomes from that action.

For this exercise, we are going to use dialogue to show these actions.

Dialogue is one of the most abused and misused tools available to any writer. Some writers and filmmakers swear off dialogue all together. Some writers think dialogue must be used at every turn. Make no mistake, dialogue can be an effective tool, but how do we make it so to begin with?

This section focuses on using dialogue to strengthen your story.

Generally speaking, how we speak to others depends greatly on our own observations. For instance, if we're speaking to someone and they yawn or keep looking away, we may decide to stop talking, change topic, or even leave the conversation.

Additionally, we don't speak to people as though we're on an old-time radio program: "Bob, hand me that knife. Not that knife, the one with the sharp edge and silver handle, the one sitting there on the counter just waiting to stab someone. Oh, I see you already found it. Show it to me. Yeah, that's the one. See how it glistens under these bright kitchen lights?"

Instead, we speak based on what we notice about the person we're speaking to: "Hand me a knife. No, the one with the—yeah, that's it."

This kind of dialogue allows authors to show action without saying a single word about it. For instance, from the previous statement, we can see another character in the room scrambling to find a knife, finding the wrong knife, then finding the correct knife.

Now it's your turn. Pretend you are a spectator watching the action unfold at a national game. Using the action you chose and the five possible outcomes, show the action and outcome through what you shout from your seat in the stands. Write one sentence of dialogue that demonstrates the start of the action and another that shows the outcome. Think about what you would say in reality.

You probably wouldn't shout "Bounce pass the ball to Johnson. That's Burrows not Johnson" to show someone throwing the ball to the wrong player. Instead, you would probably find yourself shouting, "Throw it to Johnson! Throw it to John—Not him!" This dialogue can show not only the electricity of the fan who is getting into the action in the arena, but it can also show what just happened in the game, all without having to paint every detailed move of the game to the reader.

It's your turn now. What would you say to show the action you've chosen and the five possible outcomes?

For more practice, pick another item on your list; name five other possible outcomes; and create some new dialogue.

# Pride and Prejudice

By Jane Austen

(1775-1817)

## Chapter 10

The day passed much as the day before had done. Mrs. Hurst and Miss Bingley had spent some hours of the morning with the invalid, who continued, though slowly, to mend; and in the evening Elizabeth joined their party in the drawing-room. The loo-table, however, did not appear. Mr. Darcy was writing, and Miss Bingley, seated near him, was watching the progress of his letter and repeatedly calling off his attention by messages to his sister. Mr. Hurst and Mr. Bingley were at piquet, and Mrs. Hurst was observing their game.

Elizabeth took up some needlework, and was sufficiently amused in attending to what passed between Darcy and his companion. The perpetual commendations of the lady, either on his handwriting, or on the evenness of his lines, or on the length of his letter, with the perfect unconcern with which her praises were received, formed a curious dialogue, and was exactly in union with her opinion of each.

"How delighted Miss Darcy will be to receive such a letter!"

He made no answer.

"You write uncommonly fast."

"You are mistaken. I write rather slowly."

"How many letters you must have occasion to write in the course of a year! Letters of business, too! How odious I should think them!"

"It is fortunate, then, that they fall to my lot instead of yours."

"Pray tell your sister that I long to see her."

"I have already told her so once, by your desire."

"I am afraid you do not like your pen. Let me mend it for you. I mend pens remarkably well."

"Thank you—but I always mend my own."

"How can you contrive to write so even?"

He was silent.

"Tell your sister I am delighted to hear of her improvement on the harp; and pray let her know that I am quite in raptures with her beautiful little design for a table, and I think it infinitely superior to Miss Grantley's."

"Will you give me leave to defer your raptures till I write again? At present I have not room to do them justice."

"Oh! it is of no consequence. I shall see her in January. But do you always write such charming long letters to her, Mr. Darcy?"

"They are generally long; but whether always charming it is not for me to determine."

"It is a rule with me, that a person who can write a long letter with ease, cannot write ill."

"That will not do for a compliment to Darcy, Caroline," cried her brother, "because he does *not* write with ease. He studies too much for words of four syllables. Do not you, Darcy?"

"My style of writing is very different from yours."

"Oh!" cried Miss Bingley, "Charles writes in the most careless way imaginable. He leaves out half his words, and blots the rest."

"My ideas flow so rapidly that I have not time to express them—by which means my letters sometimes convey no ideas at all to my correspondents."

"Your humility, Mr. Bingley," said Elizabeth, "must disarm reproof."

"Nothing is more deceitful," said Darcy, "than the appearance of humility. It is often only carelessness of opinion, and sometimes an indirect boast."

"And which of the two do you call *my* little recent piece of modesty?"

"The indirect boast; for you are really proud of your defects in writing, because you consider them as proceeding from a rapidity of thought and carelessness of execution, which, if not estimable, you think at least highly interesting. The power of doing anything with quickness is always prized much by the possessor, and often without any attention to the imperfection of the performance. When you told Mrs. Bennet this morning that if you ever resolved upon quitting Netherfield you should be gone in five minutes, you meant it to be a sort of panegyric, of compliment to yourself—and yet what is there so very laudable in a precipitance which must leave very necessary business undone, and can be of no real advantage to yourself or anyone else?"

"Nay," cried Bingley, "this is too much, to remember at night all the foolish things that were said in the morning. And yet, upon my honour, I believe what I said of myself to be true, and I believe it at this moment. At least, therefore, I did not assume the character of needless precipitance merely to show off before the ladies."

"I dare say you believed it; but I am by no means convinced that you would be gone with such celerity. Your conduct would be quite as dependent on chance as that of any man I know; and if, as you were mounting your horse, a friend were to say, 'Bingley, you had better stay till next week,' you would probably do it, you would probably not go—and at another word, might stay a month."

"You have only proved by this," cried Elizabeth, "that Mr. Bingley did not do justice to his own disposition. You have shown him off now much more than he did himself."

"I am exceedingly gratified," said Bingley, "by your converting what my friend says into a compliment on the sweetness of my temper. But I am afraid you are giving it a turn which that gentleman did by no means intend; for he would certainly think better of me, if under such a circumstance I were to give a flat denial, and ride off as fast as I could."

"Would Mr. Darcy then consider the rashness of your original intentions as atoned for by your obstinacy in adhering to it?"

"Upon my word, I cannot exactly explain the matter; Darcy must speak for himself."

"You expect me to account for opinions which you choose to call mine, but which I have never acknowledged. Allowing the case, however, to stand according to your representation, you must remember, Miss Bennet, that the friend who is supposed to desire his return to the house, and the delay of his plan, has merely desired it, asked it without offering one argument in favour of its propriety."

"To yield readily—easily—to the *persuasion* of a friend is no merit with you."

"To yield without conviction is no compliment to the understanding of either."

"You appear to me, Mr. Darcy, to allow nothing for the influence of friendship and affection. A regard for the requester would often make one readily yield to a request, without waiting for arguments to reason one into it. I am not particularly speaking of such a case as you have supposed about Mr. Bingley. We may as well wait, perhaps, till the circumstance occurs before we discuss the discretion of his behaviour thereupon. But in general and ordinary cases between friend and friend, where one of them is desired by the other to change a resolution of no very great moment, should you think ill of that person for complying with the desire, without waiting to be argued into it?"

"Will it not be advisable, before we proceed on this subject, to arrange with rather more precision the degree of importance which is to appertain to this request, as well as the degree of intimacy subsisting between the parties?"

"By all means," cried Bingley; "let us hear all the particulars, not forgetting their comparative height and size; for that will have more weight in the argument, Miss Bennet, than you may be aware of. I assure you, that if Darcy were not such a great tall fellow, in comparison with myself, I should not pay him half so much deference. I declare I do not know a more awful object than Darcy, on particular occasions, and in particular places; at his own house especially, and of a Sunday evening, when he has nothing to do."

Mr. Darcy smiled; but Elizabeth thought she could perceive that he was rather offended, and therefore checked her laugh. Miss Bingley warmly resented the indignity he had received, in an expostulation with her brother for talking such nonsense.

"I see your design, Bingley," said his friend. "You dislike an argument, and want to silence this."

"Perhaps I do. Arguments are too much like disputes. If you and Miss Bennet will defer yours till I am out of the room, I shall be very thankful; and then you may say whatever you like of me."

"What you ask," said Elizabeth, "is no sacrifice on my side; and Mr. Darcy had much better finish his letter."

Mr. Darcy took her advice, and did finish his letter.

When that business was over, he applied to Miss Bingley and Elizabeth for an indulgence of some music. Miss Bingley moved with some alacrity to the pianoforte; and, after a polite request that Elizabeth would lead the way which the other as politely and more earnestly negatived, she seated herself.

Mrs. Hurst sang with her sister, and while they were thus employed, Elizabeth could not help observing, as she turned over some music-books that lay on the instrument, how frequently Mr. Darcy's eyes were fixed on her. She hardly knew how to suppose that she could be an object of admiration to so great a man; and yet that he should look at her because he disliked her, was still more strange. She could only imagine, however, at last that she drew his notice because there was something more wrong and reprehensible, according to his ideas of right, than in any other person present. The supposition did not pain her. She liked him too little to care for his approbation.

After playing some Italian songs, Miss Bingley varied the charm by a lively Scotch air; and soon afterwards Mr. Darcy, drawing near Elizabeth, said to her:

"Do not you feel a great inclination, Miss Bennet, to seize such an opportunity of dancing a reel?"

She smiled, but made no answer. He repeated the question, with some surprise at her silence.

"Oh!" said she, "I heard you before, but I could not immediately determine what to say in reply. You wanted me, I know, to say 'Yes,' that you might have the pleasure of despising my taste; but I always delight in overthrowing those kind of schemes, and cheating a person of their premeditated contempt. I have, therefore, made up my mind to tell you, that I do not want to dance a reel at all—and now despise me if you dare."

"Indeed I do not dare."

Elizabeth, having rather expected to affront him, was amazed at his gallantry; but there was a mixture of sweetness and archness in her manner which made it difficult for her to affront anybody; and Darcy had never been so bewitched by any woman as he was by her. He really believed, that were it not for the inferiority of her connections, he should be in some danger.

Miss Bingley saw, or suspected enough to be jealous; and her great anxiety for the recovery of her dear friend Jane received some assistance from her desire of getting rid of Elizabeth.

She often tried to provoke Darcy into disliking her guest, by talking of their supposed marriage, and planning his happiness in such an alliance.

"I hope," said she, as they were walking together in the shrubbery the next day, "you will give your mother-in-law a few hints, when this desirable event takes place, as to the advantage of holding her tongue; and if you can compass it, do cure the younger girls of running after officers. And, if I may mention so delicate a subject, endeavour to check that little something, bordering on conceit and impertinence, which your lady possesses."

"Have you anything else to propose for my domestic felicity?"

"Oh! yes. Do let the portraits of your uncle and aunt Phillips be placed in the gallery at Pemberley. Put them next to your great-uncle the judge. They are in the same profession, you know, only in different lines. As for your Elizabeth's picture, you must not have it taken, for what painter could do justice to those beautiful eyes?"

"It would not be easy, indeed, to catch their expression, but their colour and shape, and the eyelashes, so remarkably fine, might be copied."

At that moment they were met from another walk by Mrs. Hurst and Elizabeth herself.

"I did not know that you intended to walk," said Miss Bingley, in some confusion, lest they had been overheard.

"You used us abominably ill," answered Mrs. Hurst, "running away without telling us that you were coming out."

Then taking the disengaged arm of Mr. Darcy, she left Elizabeth to walk by herself. The path just admitted three. Mr. Darcy felt their rudeness, and immediately said:

"This walk is not wide enough for our party. We had better go into the avenue."

But Elizabeth, who had not the least inclination to remain with them, laughingly answered:

"No, no; stay where you are. You are charmingly grouped, and appear to uncommon advantage. The picturesque would be spoilt by admitting a fourth. Good-bye."

She then ran gaily off, rejoicing as she rambled about, in the hope of being at home again in a day or two. Jane was already so much recovered as to intend leaving her room for a couple of hours that evening.

# A Deeper Look:

1.      How is dialogue used in this story to show the action of a
        character who is not the one speaking?

2.      What actions did you see these characters taking?

3.      In what ways might you find it appropriate to use
        dialogue to show the behavior of other characters?

# Key to Growth:

## Exercises in being receptive to feedback

# 7

# It's Nothing Personal

A woman approached me as I sat in a book signing once, and upon learning that I studied writing in the university and had undergraduate and graduate degrees in writing, she made the comment: "Well, you have a lot to unlearn." She claimed it was because I had been trained to write as professors thought I should write. And that professors were bad teachers.

To all serious writers, nothing will advertise your amateur and inexperienced approach as saying "well, you have a lot to unlearn." Many authors suggest that you should never take classes, read books about writing or listen to other people tell you how to write. Anyone who says this should not be giving counsel.

Classes, books, workshops and other writing opportunities all add up to one important event, practice. Practice makes perfect. That's the saying, right? Writing is all about practice, but not just any practice, the right practice. If you are writing alone, without accepting anyone's feedback, you are doing it wrong. This is bad practice.

Good practice happens when you are able to learn how to write not just for yourself, but for others who represent your audience. If you don't learn what an audience wants to read, how do you expect to know how to write for them so they can understand you?

A professor, in a writing class, represents an audience of one. If you can't learn to write for an audience of one person, how can you expect to learn to write for an audience of ten, a hundred, or even a million?

Good practice occurs when you surround yourself with other serious writers who are all working on common goals. This can include working with teachers, groups of students, reading books or attending writing workshops. When a teacher is successfully published many times over, why wouldn't we want to learn from that teacher?

Sometimes words can hurt, but if you can't learn how to accept hurtful words from one professor, how do you think you'll hold up when blogs erupt with scathing reviews about something terrible you've written. This is all practice, not only to help you write, but also to help you understand the field of writing and to build a thick skin.

The majority of college professors are published. To become a college professor, publishing gets you the job. This idea that those who can, do and those who can't, teach couldn't be further from the truth. In writing, those who can, do, and that's why they're allowed to teach.

Those who can't, counsel others not to practice.

So if published teachers are teaching these classes in the university and these teachers know the world of submitting work, dealing with editors and how to make profits off of your writing, why shouldn't we put ourselves in that environment? And just what part of that valuable experience should we unlearn? The part that gets us published and helps us sell our work?

Here's what it comes down to: it takes discipline to be a writer. Serious writers have what it takes to sit through classes of someone saying "I don't like what you wrote." Writers who can't hack it, quit; go home to sulk behind their computer monitors; and suddenly think that they're writers. This offense occurs because writers don't learn how to separate themselves from their work. Critiquing an author's work, as a means to help that author learn how to create a clearer message, is not an attack on the author. Author's who take it as such, will put up barriers that prevent them from getting better. Critiquing opportunities, as university classes, books and workshops allow, are intended to help writers find and magnify their own voices. Authors who walk out on these opportunities are only walking out on themselves.

So how can we get past this? To take what scares us and do it anyway.

Here is a simple assignment that can help start you in the right direction.

On a piece of paper, write down ten details that you enjoy about writing. For each detail, write down why it is so important to you.

Now, write down ten fears that you have about writing. These can be thinking you're not good enough; fear of rejection; bad reviews; or something specific someone could say that might hurt your feelings.

Now for the liberating part, for each of your fears, write three tactics that you think you could use to overcome that fear.

Finally, choose one item from each list (what you enjoy and what you fear), and use these to write a four paragraph narrative that tells the story of your own writing process. This can be a true story or a fictional one. The first paragraph must address the item that you enjoy the most. The second paragraph must tell about the process of actually writing the story itself. The third paragraph must show one of your fears trying to stop you from writing. This could be mailing out a story and getting a rejection letter. This could be getting feedback from a friend that they hated your story. Just pick one and show it trying to stop you from writing. For the final paragraph, choose one of the tactics that you wrote down that could be used to overcome this fear and write about using that tactic to do just that.

By the time you are done, you will have accomplished many writing principles. You'll have written a full story about writing a story. You'll have practiced writing for an audience because you were given a specific outline. The majority of publishers will have their own general model that they know they can sell. This exercise will help you practice writing for those people who can put money in your pockets.

Most importantly, you'll have begun to visualize how to overcome an obstacle. The more you can prepare for, the better your chances of success are. In writing, there are more obstacles trying to keep you down than there are roads paved in gold walking you straight to a publishing contract. It's easy to feel overwhelmed, but once you prepare and PRACTICE, you won't be as likely to find you convincing yourself that the best approach to success is to try facing these obstacles on your own.

# David and Goliath

Holy Bible
King James Version
I Samuel

## Chapter 17

Now the Philistines gathered together their armies to battle, and were gathered together at Shochoh, which belongeth to Judah, and pitched between Shochoh and Azekah, in Ephesdammim.

² And Saul and the men of Israel were gathered together, and pitched by the valley of Elah, and set the battle in array against the Philistines.

³ And the Philistines stood on a mountain on the one side, and Israel stood on a mountain on the other side: and there was a valley between them.

⁴ And there went out a champion out of the camp of the Philistines, named Goliath, of Gath, whose height was six cubits and a span.

⁵ And he had an helmet of brass upon his head, and he was armed with a coat of mail; and the weight of the coat was five thousand shekels of brass.

⁶ And he had greaves of brass upon his legs, and a target of brass between his shoulders.

⁷ And the staff of his spear was like a weaver's beam; and his spear's head weighed six hundred shekels of iron: and one bearing a shield went before him.

⁸ And he stood and cried unto the armies of Israel, and said unto them, Why are ye come out to set your battle in array? am not I a Philistine, and ye servants to Saul? choose you a man for you, and let him come down to me.

⁹ If he be able to fight with me, and to kill me, then will we be your servants: but if I prevail against him, and kill him, then shall ye be our servants, and serve us.

¹⁰ And the Philistine said, I defy the armies of Israel this day; give me a man, that we may fight together.

¹¹ When Saul and all Israel heard those words of the Philistine, they were dismayed, and greatly afraid.

¹² Now David was the son of that Ephrathite of Bethlehemjudah, whose name was Jesse; and he had eight sons: and the man went among men for an old man in the days of Saul.

¹³ And the three eldest sons of Jesse went and followed Saul to the battle: and the names of his three sons that went to the battle were Eliab the firstborn, and next unto him Abinadab, and the third Shammah.

¹⁴ And David was the youngest: and the three eldest followed Saul.

¹⁵ But David went and returned from Saul to feed his father's sheep at Bethlehem.

¹⁶ And the Philistine drew near morning and evening, and presented himself forty days.

¹⁷ And Jesse said unto David his son, Take now for thy brethren an ephah of this parched corn, and these ten loaves, and run to the camp of thy brethren;

¹⁸ And carry these ten cheeses unto the captain of their thousand, and look how thy brethren fare, and take their pledge.

¹⁹ Now Saul, and they, and all the men of Israel, were in the valley of Elah, fighting with the Philistines.

²⁰ And David rose up early in the morning, and left the sheep with a keeper, and took, and went, as Jesse had commanded him; and he came to the trench, as the host was going forth to the fight, and shouted for the battle.

²¹ For Israel and the Philistines had put the battle in array, army against army.

²² And David left his carriage in the hand of the keeper of the carriage, and ran into the army,

and came and saluted his brethren.

²³ And as he talked with them, behold, there came up the champion, the Philistine of Gath, Goliath by name, out of the armies of the Philistines, and spake according to the same words: and David heard them.

²⁴ And all the men of Israel, when they saw the man, fled from him, and were sore afraid.

²⁵ And the men of Israel said, Have ye seen this man that is come up? surely to defy Israel is he come up: and it shall be, that the man who killeth him, the king will enrich him with great riches, and will give him his daughter, and make his father's house free in Israel.

²⁶ And David spake to the men that stood by him, saying, What shall be done to the man that killeth this Philistine, and taketh away the reproach from Israel? for who is this uncircumcised Philistine, that he should defy the armies of the living God?

²⁷ And the people answered him after this manner, saying, So shall it be done to the man that killeth him.

²⁸ And Eliab his eldest brother heard when he spake unto the men; and Eliab's anger was kindled against David, and he said, Why camest thou down hither? and with whom hast thou left those few sheep in the wilderness? I know thy pride, and the naughtiness of thine heart; for thou art come down that thou mightest see the battle.

²⁹ And David said, What have I now done? Is there not a cause?

³⁰ And he turned from him toward another, and spake after the same manner: and the people answered him again after the former manner.

³¹ And when the words were heard which David spake, they rehearsed them before Saul: and he sent for him.

³² And David said to Saul, Let no man's heart fail because of him; thy servant will go and fight with this Philistine.

³³ And Saul said to David, Thou art not able to go against this Philistine to fight with him: for thou art but a youth, and he a man of war from his youth.

³⁴ And David said unto Saul, Thy servant kept his father's sheep, and there came a lion, and a bear, and took a lamb out of the flock:

³⁵ And I went out after him, and smote him, and delivered it out of his mouth: and when he arose against me, I caught him by his beard, and smote him, and slew him.

³⁶ Thy servant slew both the lion and the bear: and this uncircumcised Philistine shall be as one of them, seeing he hath defied the armies of the living God.

³⁷ David said moreover, The Lord that delivered me out of the paw of the lion, and out of the paw of the bear, he will deliver me out of the hand of this Philistine. And Saul said unto David, Go, and the Lord be with thee.

³⁸ And Saul armed David with his armour, and he put an helmet of brass upon his head; also he armed him with a coat of mail.

³⁹ And David girded his sword upon his armour, and he assayed to go; for he had not proved it. And David said unto Saul, I cannot go with these; for I have not proved them. And David put them off him.

⁴⁰ And he took his staff in his hand, and chose him five smooth stones out of the brook, and put them in a shepherd's bag which he had, even in a scrip; and his sling was in his hand: and he drew near to the Philistine.

⁴¹ And the Philistine came on and drew near unto David; and the man that bare the shield went before him.

⁴² And when the Philistine looked about, and saw David, he disdained him: for he was but a youth, and ruddy, and of a fair countenance.

⁴³ And the Philistine said unto David, Am I a dog, that thou comest to me with staves? And the Philistine cursed David by his gods.

⁴⁴ And the Philistine said to David, Come to me, and I will give thy flesh unto the fowls of the

air, and to the beasts of the field.

[45] Then said David to the Philistine, Thou comest to me with a sword, and with a spear, and with a shield: but I come to thee in the name of the LORD of hosts, the God of the armies of Israel, whom thou hast defied.

[46] This day will the LORD deliver thee into mine hand; and I will smite thee, and take thine head from thee; and I will give the carcases of the host of the Philistines this day unto the fowls of the air, and to the wild beasts of the earth; that all the earth may know that there is a God in Israel.

[47] And all this assembly shall know that the LORD saveth not with sword and spear: for the battle is the LORD's, and he will give you into our hands.

[48] And it came to pass, when the Philistine arose, and came, and drew nigh to meet David, that David hastened, and ran toward the army to meet the Philistine.

[49] And David put his hand in his bag, and took thence a stone, and slang it, and smote the Philistine in his forehead, that the stone sunk into his forehead; and he fell upon his face to the earth.

[50] So David prevailed over the Philistine with a sling and with a stone, and smote the Philistine, and slew him; but there was no sword in the hand of David.

[51] Therefore David ran, and stood upon the Philistine, and took his sword, and drew it out of the sheath thereof, and slew him, and cut off his head therewith. And when the Philistines saw their champion was dead, they fled.

[52] And the men of Israel and of Judah arose, and shouted, and pursued the Philistines, until thou come to the valley, and to the gates of Ekron. And the wounded of the Philistines fell down by the way to Shaaraim, even unto Gath, and unto Ekron.

[53] And the children of Israel returned from chasing after the Philistines, and they spoiled their tents.

[54] And David took the head of the Philistine, and brought it to Jerusalem; but he put his armour in his tent.

[55] And when Saul saw David go forth against the Philistine, he said unto Abner, the captain of the host, Abner, whose son is this youth? And Abner said, As thy soul liveth, O king, I cannot tell.

[56] And the king said, Enquire thou whose son the stripling is.

[57] And as David returned from the slaughter of the Philistine, Abner took him, and brought him before Saul with the head of the Philistine in his hand.

[58] And Saul said to him, Whose son art thou, thou young man? And David answered, I am the son of thy servant Jesse the Bethlehemite

# A Deeper Look:

1.         What kind of feedback do we see David receive from
           others in this story?

2.         What feedback did he reject? What feedback did he
           accept?

3.         What are some ways that you can prepare yourself to hear
           difficult comments about your own work? What are some
           ways you might see yourself handling receiving harsh
           feedback or feedback that you disagree with?

# Hating to Say "Goodbye"

Let's stay on this idea of taking work personally.

It's very simple to feel that an attack on our work is an attack on our personal being. It's also easy to become attached to a phrase, set of words, entire chapter or even a story. It's all right to cherish your work, but it's also important to recognize when it's time to say goodbye to that work or some of that work.

As I worked on a novel once, I pitted two of my favorite characters against each other. The scene was amazing, an engaging dramedy that ended on a note that had tears running down my face from laughing so hard when it was over. I knew my readers would love it, but it didn't fit. I hated to remove the scene, but the story became stronger without it. I saved the story, thinking perhaps I could use it at another time. Now, it sits in a digital file gathering virtual dust.

Putting it there was the right decision. I still have it for if I ever need it

Sometimes, it's difficult to say goodbye to writing, but the very best of writers have all had to do it.

Ernest Hemingway himself rewrote the end of *A Farewell to Arms* nearly forty times, without a computer or spell check, before he decided which set of words provided the best fit for his novel.

It's not always easy to hear someone else say "this part doesn't fit." Writers who are new to this process will often put up barriers. More advanced writers may grumble too, but advanced writers also know that they can always save this work and maybe even use it in some future project where it might fit more appropriately.

For this exercise, let's practice saying some simple goodbyes. If you can say *goodbye* to a single word, you can learn to say goodbye to collections of words, whether you want to or not.

To start, choose a piece of your own writing. It can be an exercise you performed from this book. It can be something you've done on your own elsewhere.

Now, format your project into a regular 8.5" by 11" document. Make it single spaced. Go through your entire document and make sure any word greater than four letters long does not appear more than once per page of writing.

Use your thesaurus. Use your dictionary. Say goodbye to your repetitive words.

When you can do this, then you're on the path to allowing yourself to say the more difficult goodbyes, which you will have to make in writing.

# The Black Cat
By Edgar Allan Poe
(1809-1849)

FOR the most wild, yet most homely narrative which I am about to pen, I neither expect nor solicit belief. Mad indeed would I be to expect it, in a case where my very senses reject their own evidence. Yet, mad am I not - and very surely do I not dream. But to-morrow I die, and to-day I would unburthen my soul. My immediate purpose is to place before the world, plainly, succinctly, and without comment, a series of mere household events. In their consequences, these events have terrified - have tortured - have destroyed me. Yet I will not attempt to expound them. To me, they have presented little but Horror - to many they will seem less terrible than barroques. Hereafter, perhaps, some intellect may be found which will reduce my phantasm to the common-place - some intellect more calm, more logical, and far less excitable than my own, which will perceive, in the circumstances I detail with awe, nothing more than an ordinary succession of very natural causes and effects.

From my infancy I was noted for the docility and humanity of my disposition. My tenderness of heart was even so conspicuous as to make me the jest of my companions. I was especially fond of animals, and was indulged by my parents with a great variety of pets. With these I spent most of my time, and never was so happy as when feeding and caressing them. This peculiarity of character grew with my growth, and in my manhood, I derived from it one of my principal sources of pleasure. To those who have cherished an affection for a faithful and sagacious dog, I need hardly be at the trouble of explaining the nature or the intensity of the gratification thus derivable. There is something in the unselfish and self-sacrificing love of a brute, which goes directly to the heart of him who has had frequent occasion to test the paltry friendship and gossamer fidelity of mere Man .

I married early, and was happy to find in my wife a disposition not uncongenial with my own. Observing my partiality for domestic pets, she lost no opportunity of procuring those of the most agreeable kind. We had birds, gold-fish, a fine dog, rabbits, a small monkey, and a cat .

This latter was a remarkably large and beautiful animal, entirely black, and sagacious to an astonishing degree. In speaking of his intelligence, my wife, who at heart was not a little tinctured with superstition, made frequent allusion to the ancient popular notion, which regarded all black cats as witches in disguise. Not that she was ever serious upon this point - and I mention the matter at all for no better reason than that it happens, just now, to be remembered.

Pluto - this was the cat's name - was my favorite pet and playmate. I alone fed him, and he attended me wherever I went about the house. It was even with difficulty that I could prevent him from following me through the streets.

Our friendship lasted, in this manner, for several years, during which my general temperament and character - through the instrumentality of the Fiend Intemperance - had (I blush to confess it) experienced a radical alteration for the worse. I grew, day by day, more moody, more irritable, more regardless of the feelings of others. I suffered myself to use intemperate language to my wife. At length, I even offered her personal violence. My pets, of course, were made to feel the change in my disposition. I not only neglected, but ill-used them. For Pluto, however, I still retained sufficient regard to restrain me from maltreating him, as I made no scruple of maltreating the rabbits, the monkey, or even the dog, when by accident, or through affection, they came in my way. But my disease grew upon me - for what disease is like Alcohol! - and at length even Pluto, who was now becoming old, and consequently somewhat peevish - even Pluto began to experience the effects of my ill temper.

One night, returning home, much intoxicated, from one of my haunts about town, I fancied that the cat avoided my presence. I seized him; when, in his fright at my violence, he inflicted a slight wound upon my hand with his teeth. The fury of a demon instantly possessed me. I knew myself no longer. My original soul seemed, at once, to take its flight from my body and a more than fiendish malevolence, gin-nurtured, thrilled every fibre of my frame. I took from my waistcoat-pocket a pen-knife, opened it, grasped the poor beast by the throat, and deliberately cut one of its eyes from the socket! I blush, I burn, I shudder, while I pen the damnable atrocity.

When reason returned with the morning - when I had slept off the fumes of the night's debauch - I experienced a sentiment half of horror, half of remorse, for the crime of which I had been guilty; but it was, at best, a feeble and equivocal feeling, and the soul remained untouched. I again plunged into excess, and soon drowned in wine all memory of the deed.

In the meantime the cat slowly recovered. The socket of the lost eye presented, it is true, a frightful appearance, but he no longer appeared to suffer any pain. He went about the house as usual, but, as might be expected, fled in extreme terror at my approach. I had so much of my old heart left, as to be at first grieved by this evident dislike on the part of a creature which had once so loved me. But this feeling soon gave place to irritation. And then came, as if to my final and irrevocable overthrow, the spirit of PERVERSENESS. Of this spirit philosophy takes no account. Yet I am not more sure that my soul lives, than I am that perverseness is one of the primitive impulses of the human heart - one of the indivisible primary faculties, or sentiments, which give direction to the character of Man. Who has not, a hundred times, found himself committing a vile or a silly action, for no other reason than because he knows he should not? Have we not a perpetual inclination, in the teeth of our best judgment, to violate that which is Law , merely because we understand it to be such? This spirit of perverseness, I say, came to my final overthrow. It was this unfathomable longing of the soul to vex itself - to offer violence to its own nature - to do wrong for the wrong's sake only - that urged me to continue and finally to consummate the injury I had inflicted upon the unoffending brute. One morning, in cool blood, I slipped a noose about its neck and hung it to the limb of a tree; - hung it with the tears streaming from my eyes, and with the bitterest remorse at my heart; - hung it because I knew that it had loved me, and because I felt it had given me no reason of offence; - hung it because I knew that in so doing I was committing a sin - a deadly sin that would so jeopardize my immortal soul as to place it - if such a thing wore possible - even beyond the reach of the infinite mercy of the Most Merciful and Most Terrible God.

On the night of the day on which this cruel deed was done, I was aroused from sleep by the cry of fire. The curtains of my bed were in flames. The whole house was blazing. It was with great difficulty that my wife, a servant, and myself, made our escape from the conflagration. The destruction was complete. My entire worldly wealth was swallowed up, and I resigned myself thenceforward to despair.

I am above the weakness of seeking to establish a sequence of cause and effect, between the disaster and the atrocity. But I am detailing a chain of facts - and wish not to leave even a possible link imperfect. On the day succeeding the fire, I visited the ruins. The walls, with one exception, had fallen in. This exception was found in a compartment wall, not very thick, which stood about the middle of the house, and against which had rested the head of my bed. The plastering had here, in great measure, resisted the action of the fire - a fact which I attributed to its having been recently spread. About this wall a dense crowd were collected, and many persons seemed to be examining a particular portion of it with very minute and eager attention. The words "strange!" "singular!" and other similar expressions, excited my curiosity. I approached and saw, as if graven in bas relief upon the white surface, the figure of a gigantic cat. The impression was given with an accuracy truly marvellous. There was a rope about the animal's neck.

When I first beheld this apparition - for I could scarcely regard it as less - my wonder and my terror were extreme. But at length reflection came to my aid. The cat, I remembered, had been hung in a garden adjacent to the house. Upon the alarm of fire, this garden had been immediately filled by the crowd - by some one of whom the animal must have been cut from the tree and thrown, through an open window, into my chamber. This had probably been done with the view of arousing me from sleep. The falling of other walls had compressed the victim of my cruelty into the substance of the freshly-spread plaster; the lime of which, with the flames, and the ammonia from the carcass, had then accomplished the portraiture as I saw it.

Although I thus readily accounted to my reason, if not altogether to my conscience, for the startling fact just detailed, it did not the less fail to make a deep impression upon my fancy. For months I could not rid myself of the phantasm of the cat; and, during this period, there came back into my spirit a half-sentiment that seemed, but was not, remorse. I went so far as to regret the loss of the animal, and to look about me, among the vile haunts which I now habitually frequented, for another pet of the same species, and of somewhat similar appearance, with which to supply its place.

One night as I sat, half stupified, in a den of more than infamy, my attention was suddenly drawn to some black object, reposing upon the head of one of the immense hogsheads of Gin, or of Rum, which constituted the chief furniture of the apartment. I had been looking steadily at the top of this hogshead for some minutes, and what now caused me surprise was the fact that I had not sooner perceived the object thereupon. I approached it, and touched it with my hand. It was a black cat - a very large one - fully as large as Pluto, and closely resembling him in every respect but one. Pluto had not a white hair upon any portion of his body; but this cat had a large, although indefinite splotch of white, covering nearly the whole region of the breast. Upon my touching him, he immediately arose, purred loudly, rubbed against my hand, and appeared delighted with my notice. This, then, was the very creature of which I was in search. I at once offered to purchase it of the landlord; but this person made no claim to it - knew nothing of it - had never seen it before.

I continued my caresses, and, when I prepared to go home, the animal evinced a disposition to accompany me. I permitted it to do so; occasionally stooping and patting it as I proceeded. When it reached the house it domesticated itself at once, and became immediately a great favorite with my wife.

For my own part, I soon found a dislike to it arising within me. This was just the reverse of what I had anticipated; but - I know not how or why it was - its evident fondness for myself rather disgusted and annoyed. By slow degrees, these feelings of disgust and annoyance rose into the bitterness of hatred. I avoided the creature; a certain sense of shame, and the remembrance of my former deed of cruelty, preventing me from physically abusing it. I did not, for some weeks, strike, or otherwise violently ill use it; but gradually - very gradually - I came to look upon it with unutterable loathing, and to flee silently from its odious presence, as from the breath of a pestilence.

What added, no doubt, to my hatred of the beast, was the discovery, on the morning after I brought it home, that, like Pluto, it also had been deprived of one of its eyes. This circumstance, however, only endeared it to my wife, who, as I have already said, possessed, in a high degree, that humanity of feeling which had once been my distinguishing trait, and the source of many of my simplest and purest pleasures.

With my aversion to this cat, however, its partiality for myself seemed to increase. It followed my footsteps with a pertinacity which it would be difficult to make the reader comprehend. Whenever I sat, it would crouch beneath my chair, or spring upon my knees, covering me with its loathsome caresses. If I arose to walk it would get between my feet and thus nearly throw me down, or, fastening its long and sharp claws in my dress, clamber, in this manner, to my breast. At such times, although I longed to destroy it with a blow, I was yet withheld from so doing, partly by a memory of my former crime, but chiefly - let me confess it at once - by absolute dread of the beast.

This dread was not exactly a dread of physical evil - and yet I should be at a loss how otherwise to define it. I am almost ashamed to own - yes, even in this felon's cell, I am almost ashamed to own - that the terror and horror with which the animal inspired me, had been heightened by one of the merest chimaeras it would be possible to conceive. My wife had called my attention, more than once, to the character of the mark of white hair, of which I have spoken, and which constituted the sole visible difference between the strange beast and the one I had destroyed. The reader will remember that this mark, although large, had been originally very indefinite; but, by slow degrees - degrees nearly imperceptible, and which for a long time my Reason struggled to reject as fanciful - it had, at length, assumed a rigorous distinctness of outline. It was now the representation of an object that I shudder to name - and for this, above all, I loathed, and dreaded, and would have rid myself of the monster had I dared - it was now, I say, the image of a hideous - of a ghastly thing - of the GALLOWS ! - oh, mournful and terrible engine of Horror and of Crime - of Agony and of Death !

And now was I indeed wretched beyond the wretchedness of mere Humanity. And a brute beast - whose fellow I had contemptuously destroyed - a brute beast to work out for me - for me a man, fashioned in the image of the High God - so much of insufferable wo! Alas! neither by day nor by night knew I the blessing of Rest any more! During the former the creature left me no moment alone; and, in the latter, I started, hourly, from dreams of unutterable fear, to find the hot breath of the thing upon my face, and its vast weight - an incarnate Night-Mare that I had no power to shake off - incumbent eternally upon my heart !

Beneath the pressure of torments such as these, the feeble remnant of the good within me succumbed. Evil thoughts became my sole intimates - the darkest and most evil of thoughts. The moodiness of my usual temper increased to hatred of all things and of all mankind; while, from the sudden, frequent, and ungovernable outbursts of a fury to which I now blindly abandoned myself, my uncomplaining wife, alas! was the most usual and the most patient of sufferers.

One day she accompanied me, upon some household errand, into the cellar of the old building which our poverty compelled us to inhabit. The cat followed me down the steep stairs, and, nearly throwing me headlong, exasperated me to madness. Uplifting an axe, and forgetting, in my wrath, the childish dread which had hitherto stayed my hand, I aimed a blow at the animal which, of course, would have proved instantly fatal had it descended as I wished. But this blow was arrested by the hand of my wife. Goaded, by the interference, into a rage more than demoniacal, I withdrew my arm from her grasp and buried the axe in her brain. She fell dead upon the spot, without a groan.

This hideous murder accomplished, I set myself forthwith, and with entire deliberation, to the task of concealing the body. I knew that I could not remove it from the house, either by day or by night, without the risk of being observed by the neighbors. Many projects entered my mind. At one period I thought of cutting the corpse into minute fragments, and destroying them by fire. At another, I resolved to dig a grave for it in the floor of the cellar. Again, I deliberated about casting it in the well in the yard - about packing it in a box, as if merchandize, with the usual arrangements, and so getting a porter to take it from the house. Finally I hit upon what I considered a far better expedient than either of these. I determined to wall it up in the cellar - as the monks of the middle ages are recorded to have walled up their victims.

For a purpose such as this the cellar was well adapted. Its walls were loosely constructed, and had lately been plastered throughout with a rough plaster, which the dampness of the atmosphere had prevented from hardening. Moreover, in one of the walls was a projection, caused by a false chimney, or fireplace, that had been filled up, and made to resemble the red of the cellar. I made no doubt that I could readily displace the bricks at this point, insert the corpse, and wall the whole up as before, so that no eye could detect any thing suspicious. And in this calculation I was not deceived. By means of a crow-bar I easily dislodged the bricks, and, having carefully deposited the body against the inner wall, I propped it in that position, while, with little trouble, I re-laid the whole structure as it originally stood. Having procured mortar, sand, and hair, with every possible precaution, I prepared a plaster which could not be distinguished from the old, and with this I very carefully went over the new brickwork. When I had finished, I felt satisfied that all was right. The wall did not present the slightest appearance of having been disturbed. The rubbish on the floor was picked up with the minutest care. I looked around triumphantly, and said to myself - "Here at least, then, my labor has not been in vain."

My next step was to look for the beast which had been the cause of so much wretchedness; for I had, at length, firmly resolved to put it to death. Had I been able to meet with it, at the moment, there could have been no doubt of its fate; but it appeared that the crafty animal had been alarmed at the violence of my previous anger, and forebore to present itself in my present mood. It is impossible to describe, or to imagine, the deep, the blissful sense of relief which the absence of the detested creature occasioned in my bosom. It did not make its appearance during the night - and thus for one night at least, since its introduction into the house, I soundly and tranquilly slept; aye, slept even with the burden of murder upon my soul!

The second and the third day passed, and still my tormentor came not. Once again I breathed as a freeman. The monster, in terror, had fled the premises forever! I should behold it no more! My happiness was supreme! The guilt of my dark deed disturbed me but little. Some few inquiries had been made, but these had been readily answered. Even a search had been instituted - but of course nothing was to be discovered. I looked upon my future felicity as secured.

Upon the fourth day of the assassination, a party of the police came, very unexpectedly, into the house, and proceeded again to make rigorous investigation of the premises. Secure, however, in the inscrutability of my place of concealment, I felt no embarrassment whatever. The officers bade me accompany them in their search. They left no nook or corner unexplored. At length, for the third or fourth time, they descended into the cellar. I quivered not in a muscle. My heart beat calmly as that of one who slumbers in innocence. I walked the cellar from end to end. I folded my arms upon my bosom, and roamed easily to and fro. The police were thoroughly satisfied and prepared to depart. The glee at my heart was too strong to be restrained. I burned to say if but one word, by way of triumph, and to render doubly sure their assurance of my guiltlessness.

"Gentlemen," I said at last, as the party ascended the steps, "I delight to have allayed your suspicions. I wish you all health, and a little more courtesy. By the bye, gentlemen, this - this is a very well constructed house." [In the rabid desire to say something easily, I scarcely knew what I uttered at all.] - "I may say an excellently well constructed house. These walls are you going, gentlemen? - these walls are solidly put together;" and here, through the mere phrenzy of bravado, I rapped heavily, with a cane which I held in my hand, upon that very portion of the brick-work behind which stood the corpse of the wife of my bosom.

But may God shield and deliver me from the fangs of the Arch-Fiend ! No sooner had the reverberation of my blows sunk into silence, than I was answered by a voice from within the tomb! - by a cry, at first muffled and broken, like the sobbing of a child, and then quickly swelling into one long, loud, and continuous scream, utterly anomalous and inhuman - a howl - a wailing shriek, half of horror and half of triumph, such as might have arisen only out of hell, conjointly from the throats of the dammed in their agony and of the demons that exult in the damnation.

Of my own thoughts it is folly to speak. Swooning, I staggered to the opposite wall. For one instant the party upon the stairs remained motionless, through extremity of terror and of awe. In the next, a dozen stout arms were toiling at the wall. It fell bodily. The corpse, already greatly decayed and clotted with gore, stood erect before the eyes of the spectators. Upon its head, with red extended mouth and solitary eye of fire, sat the hideous beast whose craft had seduced me into murder, and whose informing voice had consigned me to the hangman. I had walled the monster up within the tomb!

# A Deeper Look:

---

1.          Does this author sound repetitive? Why? Why not?

2.          Are there any lines in this story that you can point to and
            say, "this sentence or word isn't needed?" If so, why isn't it
            needed?

3.          Pick any page in this story. How many words longer than
            four letters long repeat themselves? What are they? How
            does this strengthen or weaken the story?

# Don't Be Afraid, But Shut UP!

This exercise is a great refresher for anyone familiar with feedback groups. If you've never been a part of a feedback group, this exercise is for you.

During your practice in writing, hopefully you are surrounding yourself with other writers who are willing to learn and practice as much as you are. Writing groups can fail rather quickly if everyone within them doesn't learn the practice of one very important process: feedback.

It's a very simple process, but many writers have never learned it. Learning how to improve your abilities can't happen on your own, you need other sets of eyes helping you. Many great books never get shared because writers are afraid of having other people judge them. To these people, I say: I used to be one of you. My advice: find a serious group and try it once. If your group is a true writing group, it will be supportive and you will never again doubt how uplifting the experience can be. If it's not uplifting, then look for another group. One with similar interests and goals as yourself. Just don't work alone.

Also, some authors believe that if they share their work, someone will steal it. Copyright laws are such today that this is an extremely rare occurrence, and by that I mean, good luck ever actually finding a time it's happened in the past 30 years. It's only a fear that inexperienced writers face and that's only because they have heard too many paranoid people convince them of "what if something bad happens."

So first, we need to be open to allowing ourselves to receive feedback, otherwise there's no reason to continue writing.

Second, we need to learn the process itself and the roles we hold. Feedback only occurs correctly when everyone respects and understands its potential. Not everyone will give you exactly what you want to hear. It's easy, as authors, to expect our readers to always say something profound and if they don't then we say "how can we learn from feedback if the people giving it are as stupid as I am."

Feedback is really simple.

Here's how it works: The author writes a piece of work. The author presents that work to other people. Those people read the work and provide feedback. The author then decides which feedback to apply and which to disregard (not all feedback will be valid). Then the author uses the feedback to revise their work and begin a new feedback process.

There are two roles: the author and the reviewer.

The author writes the work and prepares any specific questions about their work that they would like the reviewers to pay special consideration to. At this point, the author's role is to SHUT UP! The only words that should come out of the author's mouth at this time is *thank you* and you should write down every comment that you receive whether you agree with it or not. Your role is not to argue, ever. I don't care what credentials you have or how important you think you are, if you can't shut up and listen when people are trying to help you, you're not a writer. When you argue, people stop providing feedback. No one has to give you feedback at all. They don't even have to read your work, so the least you can do is learn to shut up and listen. Otherwise, you run the risk of silencing feedback from others who learn that you're not willing to accept it. Accept or disregard the feedback on your own time, NEVER in the group. If you must ask a question, it should be confined of "where does this happen." That's the only question you should have to ask during the feedback process. Specific questions should be asked before the feedback process begins (for instance, when you hand out copies of your manuscript to your readers). If you have more questions, save them for the next round of feedback and present them when you present your document.

Believe it or not, the most difficult practice for authors to accept is to learn how to shut up. You reviewers may sound stupid and even miss your point completely, but you never call them out. If you don't like it consider two options: first, they represent your audience. If they find something unclear that you believe is perfectly written, your message might not be as clear as you think if your reviewers are all confused. Your second option, if you don't like what you're hearing, is to find another group. If you continue to hear the same comments, it may be time to break down and accept the feedback.

The second role in the process of feedback is that of the reviewer. The reviewer's purpose is to critique the work. It is not to critique the author. The reviewer's job is not to say "this is stupid." As reviewers, you're going to read a lot of writing that doesn't agree with you. That's OK. You might not be that particular audience, but it doesn't mean you can't still help the author prepare for their audience. The reviewer asks two questions: "What works," in which the reviewer highlights strengths of the project and "what doesn't work," in which the reviewer highlights areas that could be stronger. If you enter the process with an attitude of "I don't want to say anything bad that could hurt someone's feelings," then you have already done a disservice to the author. This is exactly the kind of behavior that does not belong in a feedback session. Positive feedback reinforces strengths, while negative feedback helps writers overcome weakness and grow. If you can't handle that, you may want to think of a different line of work because you'll help no writer if you're afraid to say that his or her work isn't perfect.

Serious writers will know enough that feedback is a science and a process required to help them improve. Encourage your group, but don't hold back information that you know can help them grow. It doesn't mean you have to be mean, but you should be honest even if it's not easy.

For this exercise, you will need a document that you have written. This can be a poem, a short story, an article or a chapter for a book. Your goal here is to ask someone you know if they would mind giving you some feedback. Take a moment and explain the role of feedback to them. Remind yourself of the rules. Take a breath and allow yourself to experience the process on a small scale.

A few rules to keep in mind. Don't ask someone who's a professional writer or editor unless you're willing to pay them. It's considered bad form. Your best bet is to find someone who you know won't mind or someone who will take your writing as seriously as you do. Second, avoid asking spouses. Many arguments have sprouted between spouses because of the written word. When you ask people for feedback who don't live with you, that conversation is likely to end when one of you leaves the other's presence. Spouses may continue to give feedback even after the conversation has ended, and it's easy for writer's patience to run out when that happens.

Find someone you trust and give feedback a try.

From your feedback, list two items that you plan to apply to rewriting and two pieces of feedback that you might ignore.

Feedback doesn't end with only one reading. It can take place again and again, each time with a stronger document. When you start to hear fewer and fewer comments about your work being weak, that's when you'll know you're probably ready to submit your work for publication.

# The Adventures of Pinocchio
By C. Collodi
(a.k.a Carlo Lorenzini)
(1826-1890)
*Translated by M. A. Murray*

## CHAPTER 4

*The story of Pinocchio and the Talking-cricket, from which we see that naughty boys cannot endure to be corrected by those who know more than they do.*

Well then, children, I must tell you that whilst poor Geppetto was being taken to prison for no fault of his, that imp Pinocchio, finding himself free from the clutches of the carabineer, ran off as fast as his legs could carry him. That he might reach home the quicker he rushed across the fields, and in his mad hurry he jumped high banks, thorn hedges, and ditches full of water, exactly as a kid or a leveret would have done if pursued by hunters.

Having arrived at the house he found the street door ajar. He pushed it open, went in, and having secured the latch threw himself seated on the ground and gave a great sigh of satisfaction.

But his satisfaction did not last long, for he heard some one in the room who was saying 'Cri-cri-cri!'

'Who calls me?' said Pinocchio in a fright.

'It is I!'

Pinocchio turned round and saw a big cricket crawling slowly up the wall.

'Tell me, Cricket, who may you be?'

'I am the Talking-cricket, and I have lived in this room a hundred years and more.'

'Now, however, this room is mine,' said the puppet, 'and if you would do me a pleasure go away at once, without even turning round.'

'I will not go,' answered the Cricket, 'until I have told you a great truth.'

'Tell it me, then and be quick about it.'

'Woe to those boys who rebel against their parents, and run away capriciously from home. They will never come to any good in the world, and sooner or later they will repent bitterly.'

'Sing away, Cricket, as you please, and as long as you please. For me, I have made up my mind to run away to-morrow at daybreak, because if I remain I shall not escape the fate of all other boys; I shall be sent to school and shall be made to study either by love or by force. To tell you in confidence, I have no wish to learn; it is much more amusing to run after butterflies, or to climb trees and to take the young birds out of their nest.'

'Poor little goose! But do you not know that in that way you will grow up a perfect donkey, and that every one will make game of you?'

'Hold your tongue, you wicked ill-omened croaker!' shouted Pinocchio.

But the Cricket, who was patient and philosophical, instead of becoming angry at this impertinence, continued in the same tone:

'But if you do not wish to go to school why not at least learn a trade, if only to enable you to earn honestly a piece of bread!'

'Do you want me to tell you?' replied Pinocchio, who was beginning to lose patience. 'Amonst all the trades in the world there is only one that really takes my fancy.'

'And that trade—what is it?'

'It is to eat, drink, sleep, and amuse myself, and to lead a vagabond life from morning to night.'

'As a rule,' said the Talking-cricket with the same composure, 'all those who follow that trade end almost always either in a hospital or in prison.'

'Take care, you wicked ill-omened croaker!. . . Woe to you if I fly into apassion!. . .'

'Poor Pinocchio! I really pity you!. . .'

'Why do you pity me?'

'Because you are a puppet and, what is worse, because you have a wooden head.'

At these last words Pinocchio jumped up in a rage, and snatching a wooden hammer from the bench he threw it at the Talking-cricket.

Perhaps he never meant to hit him; but unfortunately it struck him exactly on the head, so that the poor Cricket had scarcely breath to cry cri-cri-cri, and then he remained dried up and flattened against the wall.

# A Deeper Look:

1.          How can this metaphor be applied to how a person
            receives feedback from a peer?

2.          What effects can lashing out or arguing with people who
            want to give you feedback have on you and those giving
            the feedback?

3.          How do you think you'd react if an author you were
            giving feedback to lashed out at you? Would you give
            feedback to that person again? Why? Or Why Not? How
            might your own peers react to you if you argued their
            feedback with them? Do you think you'd get honest
            feedback from them in the future?

# Don't Stop!

As writers, we learn from our practice. We become more connected to not only the written word, but to humanity as well. We become more accurate in our observations of the world surrounding us. Above all, we learn how to grow.

By now, if you've invested yourselves honestly into these exercises, you should have developed a stronger understanding of your own abilities; become more comfortable with your voice; and discovered areas where you could improve and grow as a writer. Above all, you've hopefully learned that you don't have to be perfect.

Writers should seek to surround themselves with numerous exercises and opportunities to test their voices and to build their confidence. Don't stop just because you've read this book. These opportunities can come in many forms: from attending workshops at your local library to enrolling in advanced college writing classes; from letting someone just read your work to letting someone comment honestly about it; and from sitting in on writing lectures to reading books such as this one.

Keep practicing.

Accept feedback for what it is: the intention to help you improve and not a personal attack to show you how terrible you are.

Never stop practicing. And on the occasion that you ever come across someone who suggests that you should deny yourself these opportunities, remember that this is not what writing is about. Kick this bad advice to the gutter and write on.

Surround yourself with practice. Embrace practice. Practicing by yourself (alone) has its place, but it should always be part of a larger process that involves you working with others. This is the best and only way to get plenty of reliable feedback designed to help you improve. You don't know everything about writing and neither does any other person who has ever existed. Remember this, and you'll never forget that you can grow. Remember this, and instead of looking down on beginning, developing writers, you can help them grow instead. Encourage practice.

Ignore those who suggest you have something to unlearn because you've practiced with others. If you surround yourself with reliable peers who respect the goals and ambitions of the writer, you will find that practice isn't about having to unlearn what you've practiced, but it's about discovering how you can grow.

Seek practice and growth.

Embrace it.

Never stop.

Growing by yourself will never be as great as growing with others.

Anyone who tries to convince you otherwise, has never learned how to write.

Now, go find another opportunity to practice and master your voice.

# Credits

## TEXT CREDITS

Andersen: "The Little Match Girl," from *Hans Andersen's Story Book* by Hans Christian Andersen. Printed 1860 by C.S. Francis and Company. Public Domain.

Austen: "Chapter X," from *Pride and Prejudice: a Novel in Three Volumes*, Vol I, by Jane Austen. Printed 1813 by Egerton.

Carroll: "A Mad Tea Party," from Alice's Adventures in Wonderland by Lewis Carroll. Printed 1866 by Macmillan. Public domain.

Collodi: "Chapter IV," from *The Story of a Puppet or The Adventures of Pinocchio* by C. Collodi, translated by M. A. Murray. Printed 1892 by T. Fisher Unwin. Public domain.

Dickens: *A Christmas Carol in Prose. Being A Ghost Story of Christmas* by Charles Dickens. Printed 1843 by Chapman and Hall. Public domain.

Douglass: *Narrative of the Life of Frederick Douglass an American Slave* by Frederick Douglass. Printed 1845 by The Anti-slavery office. Public domain.

Doyle: "Chapter 1: The Science of Deduction," from *The Sign of Four* by Sir Arthur Conan Doyle. Printed 1890 by Spencer Blackett. Public domain

Gilbert: "A Nightmare," from *Songs of a Savoyard* by Sir W.S. Gilbert. Printed 1890 by George Routlege and Sons. Public domain.

Hawthorne: "The Birthmark," from *Mosses from an Old Manse* by Nathaniel Hawthorne. Printed 1871 by James R. Osgood.

Holy Bible: KJV, I Samuel, 17

Hugo: "The Bells," from *Notre Dame de Paris* by Victor Hugo, translated by Isabel F. Hapgood. Printed 1900 by Walter Scott. Public Domain. "The Agony of Death After the Agony of Life," from *Les Misérables* by Victor Hugo, translated by Isabel F. Hapgood. Printed 1887 by Thomas Y. Crowell. Public domain.

Keats: "Naughty Boy: A Song About Myself," from *The Complete Poetical Works and Letters of John Keats* by John Keats, edited by Horace E. Scudder. Published 1899 by Houghton, Mifflin. Public domain

Norton: "Two Bugle Calls," from *Army Letters* by Oliver Willcox Norton. Printed 1903 by O.W. Norton. Public Domain

Melville: *Moby Dick; or, The Whale* by Herman Melville. Printed 1851 by Harper and Brothers. Public domain.

Montgomery, Lucy Maud: "Matthew Insists on Puffed Sleeves," from *Anne of Green Gables* by L.M. Montgomery. First printed in 1908 by L.C. Page and Co. Public domain.

Poe: "The Black Cat," by Edgar Allan Poe from *The Saturday Evening Post*. Printed 1843. Public domain.

Saki: "The Open Window," from *Beasts and Super-Beasts* by Saki a.k.a. H.H. Munro. Printed in 1914 by John Lane—The Bodley Head.

Shelley: Excerpt from "Chapter 24," from *Frankenstein; or, The Modern Prometheus* by Mary Shelley. Printed 1818 by Lackington, Hughes, Harding, Mavor & Jones

Sinclair: Excerpts from *The Jungle* by Upton Sinclair. Printed 1906 by Doubleday. Public domain.

Stetson: "The Yellow Wallpaper" by Charlotte Perkins Stetson (Gilman) from *The New England Magazine*, January. Printed in 1892 by New England Magazine Corp. Public Domain.

Stoker: "Chapter XV," from *Dracula*, by Bram Stoker. Printed 1897 by Grosset & Dunlap. Public domain.

Twain: *The Adventures of Huckleberry Finn* by Mark Twain. Printed 1885 by Charles L. Webster. Public Domain.

# Index

# About the Author

*David Fairchild holds a bachelors and M.F.A. in Creative Writing as well as a bachelors in journalism. He is an author, editor and entertainer. Currently, he teaches English at Brigham Young University – Idaho. As a proponent of the individual's voice, he openly refutes anyone who provides counsel that stunts the growth of any aspiring author.*

www.ingramcontent.com/pod-product-compliance
Lightning Source LLC
Chambersburg PA
CBHW070304290326
41930CB00040B/2142